THE HOUSE BY THE DVINA

The House by the Dvina
— A·RUSSIAN·CHILDHOOD —

by

EUGENIE FRASER

To my father.

MAINSTREAM
PUBLISHING·EDINBURGH

First published in 1984 by
MAINSTREAM PUBLISHING COMPANY (EDINBURGH) LTD.
7 Albany Street
Edinburgh EH1 3UG

The publisher gratefully acknowledges the financial assistance of the
Scottish Arts Council in the publication of this volume.

The author wishes to express her thanks to Dr Ian Campbell for putting
her on the right road; to Philip and Marjorie Harper for their constant
encouragement; and to her husband Ronald, without whose constant
prodding this book would never have been written.

ISBN 0 906391 69 5

Typeset in 10 point Andover by Studioscope in conjunction with
Mainstream Publishing.
Printed by Forsyth Middleton & Co. Ltd., Kilsyth.

CONTENTS

THE SCHOLTS FAMILY

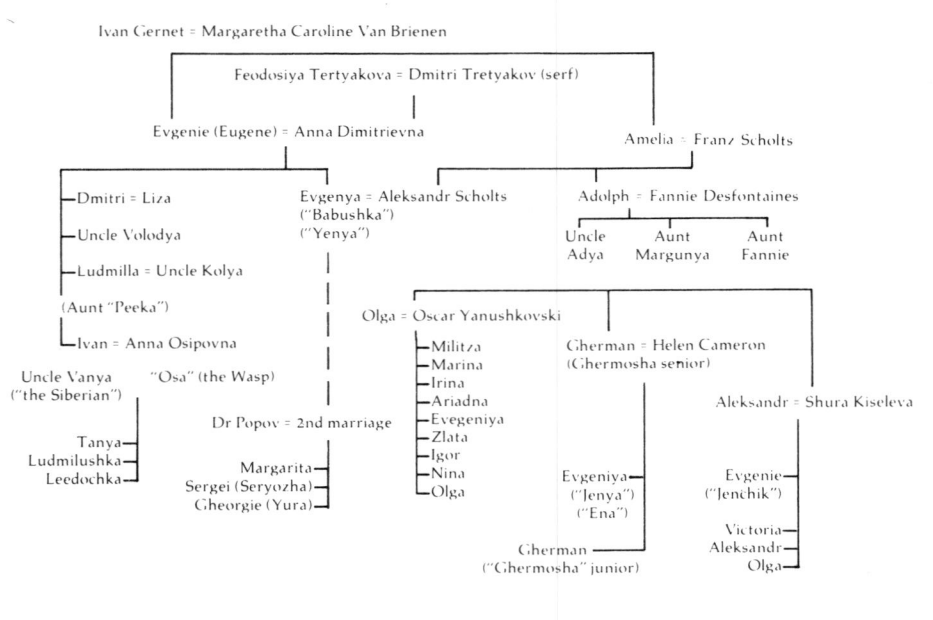

Ivan Gernet = Margaretha Caroline Van Brienen

Feodosiya Tertyakova = Dmitri Tretyakov (serf)

Evgenie (Eugene) = Anna Dimitrievna

Amelia = Franz Scholts

—Dmitri = Liza

—Uncle Volodya

—Ludmilla = Uncle Kolya

(Aunt "Peeka")

—Ivan = Anna Osipovna

Uncle Vanya   "Osa" (the Wasp)
("the Siberian")

Tanya—
Ludmilushka—
Leedochka—

Evgenya = Aleksandr Scholts
("Babushka")
("Yenya")

Dr Popov = 2nd marriage

Margarita—
Sergei (Seryozha)—
Gheorgie (Yura)—

Adolph = Fannie Desfontaines

Uncle   Aunt   Aunt
Adya   Margunya   Fannie

Olga = Oscar Yanushkovski

—Militza
—Marina
—Irina
—Ariadna
—Evegeniya
—Zlata
—Igor
—Nina
—Olga

Gherman = Helen Cameron
(Ghermosha senior)

Aleksandr = Shura Kiseleva

Evgeniya—
("Jenya")
("Ena")

Evgenie—
("Jenchik")

Victoria—
Aleksandr—
Olga—

Gherman
("Ghermosha" junior)

Members of the Household
Sashenka (tutor)
Kapochka (housekeeper)

Friends of the Family
Petya Emelyanov
Adelya and Verochka
Pavel Mikhailovich Kriloff

THE CAMERON FAMILY

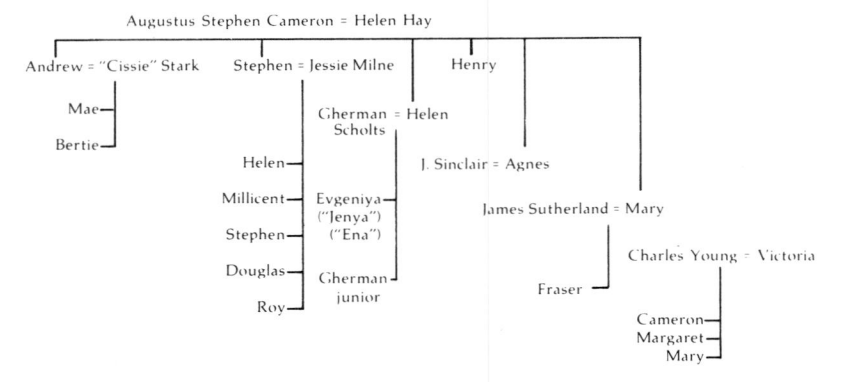

Augustus Stephen Cameron = Helen Hay

Andrew = "Cissie" Stark   Stephen = Jessie Milne   Henry

Mae—

Bertie—

Gherman = Helen
Scholts

J. Sinclair = Agnes

James Sutherland = Mary

Charles Young = Victoria

Helen—

Millicent—

Stephen—

Douglas—

Roy—

Evgeniya—
("Jenya")
("Ena")

Gherman—
junior

Fraser—

Cameron—
Margaret—
Mary—

PART I

When All Was Young

1

1912

I REMEMBER the station. Nikolayevsky Vokzal, it was called in those days. I remember the cold and darkness and my father standing beside me holding my hand. He has a small parcel in his other hand and keeps telling me over and over again that it is for me and that I am to open it after the train leaves the station. My mother, in a short sealskin jacket and small hat perched on her dark hair, is standing facing me. Beside her is Petya Emelyanoff, a young man and friend of the family. Petya is studying music at the Conservatoire in St Petersburg and is now going home for his Christmas vacation. He has been commissioned to take charge of me for the long journey to Archangel where he will hand me over to my grandmother.

I had been staying along with my mother and young brother for a short holiday in Scotland, in the house of my Scottish grandparents; and then in Hamburg where my father was involved in some business. There, before leaving for St Petersburg, I had developed pleurisy and became very ill. My parents, who were to remain in St Petersburg for some time, had decided that the clear, crisp air of the distant north might be better for my health than the prevailing damp and fog of St Petersburg. It was also necessary for me to be tutored for the entrance exam to the local gymnasium (grammar school) in Archangel where I was to begin my education the following autumn.

Other people had arrived to see me off, but their faces are long since forgotten. I remember a light flickering somewhere, the bright shafts lighting up the faces in our little group and then plunging us back into gloomy darkness. My parents kept talking and smiling anxiously as if trying to reassure me, but instead were unconsciously transferring their sadness and anxiety to me. This was my first separation. The first of many.

In front of us lay a journey of two nights and days. Endless forests and snows, flat fields broken by poor dark cottages sunk in snowdrifts and small grey stations flashing past. We shared a compartment with two young merchants travelling to Vologda. I was allotted the top bunk above Petya.

The train had departed and now I was eagerly unwrapping the parcel. Sitting there curled up on the top bunk in my cosy isolation I gazed with wonder at my present. I had never been showered with too many sweets or presents, but here was a box of chocolates all to myself. It was not an ordinary box. The day before, my parents, my brother and I had gone for a walk along the Nevsky Prospect. It was a lovely winter morning. The sun, the frost and the glistening snow. Nevsky Prospect, always beautiful, was now preparing for Christmas and wore a festive air. The shops, jewel bright, were spilling over with their rich and varied merchandise, catching the eyes of the passers-by. We sauntered slowly along from window to window until we came to the shop of a confectioner renowned for his chocolates. Here, against a background of black and crimson chocolate boxes were displayed. All were of the same strange design, fashioned in the shape of mice. Pale grey, complete with sparkling crimson collars, red bead eyes and silver tails that moved and trembled. All sizes. Repelling and yet fascinating, they attracted crowds of people. I could hardly bear to leave the window and longed to possess one of these boxes there and then, but no one had paid any attention to my demands. Now it lay on my lap. I opened the lid cautiously. There inside, wrapped in silver foil with tiny red collars round their necks, were chocolate mice laid out in compact neatness. I planned never to eat a single one of them. Never to spoil the smooth circle of these little creatures sitting in such orderly perfection, nose to tail. I played for a long time with that box, arranging and rearranging the chocolates but in the end, tiring, put it under my pillow.

Meanwhile, below me, Petya and the two young men were talking and laughing as if they had known each other all their lives. I sat, my legs dangling over the edge of the bunk, listening to the steady flow of conversation beyond my understanding. One of the young merchants was constantly laughing. He appeared to have an endless supply of jokes and droll remarks. At times, looking up at me, he would say something, or wink and smile, as if he and I were sharing some secret joke. "Nye tak li, Jenichka?" . . . "Is that not so, Jenichka?" he would ask me, and I, sensing his kindness, would eagerly nod my head and smile back, although I did not really know what it was all about.

It was all very strange. I was not quite seven and travelling alone in the company of grown-up men.

By now the northern evening was closing in. It was impossible to see anything outside through the dark windows, frosted over in white ferns and mysterious forests and mountains. The wheels turning round kept a steady rhythm as if they were repeating something over and over again, something sad, something lonely.

The attendant came in, balancing a tray laden with tumblers of tea. Hampers appeared. I watched with interest as they were opened, revealing the contents wrapped in white linen. These little hampers, usually packed with all kinds of home baking, played an important part on long journeys. There would be a variety of "pirozhkis", the pastries filled with chopped meat, mushrooms or eggs, the "vatrushkies", the small flat tarts with sweet cottage cheese, soft cookies and spiced biscuits, rich and delectable, so dear to the Russian heart and stomach.

I have a vague and distant picture of a young child sitting on that top bunk, contentedly swinging her legs and cheerfully accepting all that these young, good-natured men were passing up to her.

The whole of that journey is like a jigsaw puzzle with pieces missing. One of the young men produced a balalaika. He began to strum gently and sing in a soft tender voice some old, plaintive folksong. Petya joined in. This was the first time I had ever heard him sing. As I sat alone, apart from the others, listening to their voices falling and rising in deep sadness or suddenly changing into a song full of wild and gay abandon, it was as if something of Russia herself crept into my young heart.

Neither I nor the other passengers crowding round the door of our compartment knew they were listening to a voice already famous in the far north. "Severny Solovei", "The Northern Nightingale" he was affectionately named there. As a friend of the family he often visited our house. When asked to sing, he would sit down at the grand piano, strike a chord, and begin. I, no matter what I was doing, would leave everything and hurry so as to be able just to stand nearby and listen.

I don't remember how long I sat listening to the singing and watching the people gathered around our compartment. I must have been very tired and in the end I fell asleep.

I was awakened suddenly by a great urgency. Everything was in darkness, relieved only by a small glimmering light. My three companions were sound asleep. I had to find the toilet room immediately, but had no idea where it might be. It had never occurred to anyone to show me where to go or explain anything. To waken Petya or any of his companions was out of the question. From a tender age I had been completely independent over private matters. I had been fully dressed when I fell asleep but someone had removed my shoes and covered me with a blanket. I climbed slowly down, carefully gripping the edge of the lower bunk with my feet so as not to waken Petya. I succeeded in reaching the door, but Petya, even in his sleep, must have been attuned to his responsibilities. He sat up immediately. "Where are you going?" he called out irritably and then, not waiting for an answer, dragged open the door and pushed me in front of him to the toilet room at the end of the passage. "In you get," he said, impatiently stretching and yawning, his flaxen hair standing on end and his eyes heavy with sleep. I hurried in, too relieved and thankful to think about anything. It was then I found myself in a terrible predicament. In my time, a child wore a white cotton bodice buttoned down the centre of the back. The underpants fastened to the bodice. I mastered the side buttons with comparative ease and expediently ignored the centre back button.

The day of the journey, my mother had helped to dress me. She securely fastened all buttons. I now stood, frantic with anxiety, twisting and turning the centre back button with mounting desperation. The simple remedy of tearing the button off never entered my young head.

In the end, I was forced to come out and in great mortification explain my difficulty. "Turn round!" Petya ordered abruptly, and as I did so, he lifted my dress, undid the offending button, gave my bare bottom a playful slap and pushed me back into the lavatory. The intense relief was only equalled by my outraged dignity, and the shameful humiliation of that experience remained with me for a long time. When I came out I displayed no gratitude, but hurried past him, clambered back on to my bunk, and lay there with my face turned to the wall.

Gradually the pale winter daylight filtered through the frost-laden windows. The attendant arrived bringing tea and "kalachi", the round glossy rolls with a hole in the centre renowned all over Russia. People were awakening. There were sounds of laughing and talking. Another day had begun.

Little by little the sun rose, flooding the carriage with a warm glow. I stood in the corridor, my face close to the window. By peering through a small corner of the window untouched by frost, it was possible to watch the winter landscape swiftly rushing past and vanishing for ever more. The everlasting telegraph poles, the stations appearing for a fleeting moment, the neat square stacks of logs piled high on a siding, and always, always the forest. The endless rows of birches, their curly heads silvered by the frost, snow-laden pines standing close together deep in their winter sleep. The high banks dazzling white against a wall of green and black. There was little sign of life. Only a bird, startled by the incoming monster, would fly up suddenly and vanish somewhere into the woods beyond.

As I stood at the window, I became aware that the train was slowing down. A great activity began around me. The train was steaming into Vologda. Passengers were gathering their belongings, running up and down the corridor calling on each other, kissing and saying their final goodbyes. Some were leaving for their homes and others, like ourselves, were completing the first stage of their journey. Only one more night remained and tomorrow we would be in Archangel. Meanwhile we had to leave this train and take the line that went due north.

Our two friends in the compartment were leaving us in Vologda. In front of them was a long journey by horse into the depth of the country, but first it was agreed that we would adjourn to the restaurant in the station. Petya helped me into my shuba — the fur-lined coat — and felt boots, and tied a shawl over my fur hat. We stepped down on to the station. After the overheated compartment, the bitter cold was almost unbearable, yet the crowd bustling all around us did not appear to be aware of it.

Vologda is an important junction. From here passengers were leaving for Siberia, to Archangel, Moscow and St Petersburg. Everywhere were people, their breaths emitting clouds of steam, jostling and pushing. All hurrying somewhere.

They are all here. The poor and the rich with their unmistakeable stamp of class and society. The peasant in his nondescript bulky clothing, his face patient and weatherbeaten, struggling along with his bundles. He is travelling "hard", the cheapest possible way. The opulent "kupets", the well-to-do trader and his young wife in a neat-fitting jacket and flowered kerchief framing her round face; the proud lady with her children, and governess, moving toward the first-class compartment. Her husband, no doubt a wealthy landowner or some important civil servant, is following behind. He has a detached and faintly bored expression. A group of young officers, dashing and debonair, are hurrying along bound on some journey, oblivious in their haste of the milling crowd around them. Here one is also aware of a faint, undefinable yet all-pervading atmosphere. In his magnificent prologue to *Russlan and Ludmilla*, that magic fairytale, Pushkin called it "dookh". The word conveys a mingling of many things, expressing all at once the spirit, sense, smell and the very breath of Russia. One can recognise it all over Russia. In towns and villages, rivers and fields and on the boundless steppes.

Inside the restaurant there was a welcoming air, underlaid with the aroma of food, fresh linen, and burning wood. Against the far wall stood a high sideboard. On top were rows of coloured bottles, an assortment of items and a steaming samovar. We sat down at a table near the entrance. A waiter in a white apron brought a tray laden with a variety of "zakuska" — salted herring, caviar, dill cucumbers, mushrooms and of course the inevitable bottle of vodka. Other dishes followed. After the confinement in the train I was content just to sit and watch all that was going on around me. The men kept talking and laughing and heaping up my plate.

People were constantly coming and going. Every time the door opened there was a stream of cold air and the clean smell of snow.

Suddenly there was a shrill sound of a clanging bell. A voice, loud and urgent, was calling out, "All passengers for Archangel!" Petya stood up. "Time for us to go, Jenya," he said. He took my hand and we went out into the cold and frost.

We walked slowly towards the train. I was suddenly possessed by an anxiety and fear that we might miss the train and perhaps never see Archangel. I would have run ahead if it wasn't for the greater fear of being lost in the crowd. We reached our carriage door and Petya still kept talking to his friends. The second bell rang. I remember being lifted, kissed soundly, Russian-style, on each cheek, and pushed inside. "Proshchaitye" . . . "Goodbye" . . . "Prieszhaitye v Arhangelsk" . . . "Come to Archangel." The usual farewells and invitations, sincere for the moment, for of course we never saw them again. The third and final bell rang its warning. The wheels began once more their monotonous dirge. Tomorrow we would be in Archangel.

Our compartment was again shared by two young men. They played cards, talked a lot and ignored me most of the time. Back beside the window I watched the woods that seemed to get darker and more forbidding as we continued climbing north. At times the train halted at some wayside station. There would be a banging of doors, loud voices, some passengers leaving and others joining the train. The sun changed from a golden yellow to a deep vermilion and vanished somewhere behind the trees. Night came down. I peered into the darkness that seemed to come so early, but there was nothing to see beyond some pinpointed lights in the distance.

Petya had recognised a few friends and took me along to their compartment. They, in turn, kept coming and going and as usual had endless discussions. The hours went by so slowly. I climbed back to my bunk and played with my chocolate mice. They became a little soft and began to lose their shape. I cannot remember what happened to that precious box in the end. In the excitement of leaving the train I must have forgotten it and left it behind me.

I was awakened next morning by the sound of voices and the tinkling of glasses. Our two neighbours were up. They had pushed up the bunks against the wall, and sitting together with Petya were drinking their tea. "Nu vot, Jenya" . . . "Now then, Jenya," Petya called to me, handing up a glossy kalach. "We shall soon be in Archangel." How soon, I wondered? It was dark as night outside, although it was morning. We were travelling through the north where nature spreads her dark mantle over this land for the best part of the year and the sun comes out for just a little while. It had been snowing through the night. The giant snowflakes clung to the window like some fluffy moths.

The passengers were gathering their belongings and preparing to leave the train. We too began to put all our baggage in order. The night before, as I settled down for the night, Petya had advised me to take off my dress and fold it neatly at the foot of my bunk beside my shoes. Now he brought everything down and pushed my bunk against the wall. After I was dressed, he removed a towel and soap box from my travelling case and ordered me to go to the end of the corridor and wash my face. He offered no assistance for he was aware that I had devised a system of my own that did not need any help. When I came back, he combed my hair the best he could and helped me to slip on my "valyenki", the heavy felt boots that are the best protection against the intense cold and frost. Then we sat down to wait. How awful is the slow passing of time when one is very young and impatient. How often did I bombard this patient young man with the everlasting question of how long did we still have to wait for that glorious moment of our arrival. How irritating I must have been, yet he bore with me, took care of me to the best of his ability, never letting me out of his sight.

Gradually, almost imperceptibly, the steady rhythm of the wheels changed to a slower more drawn out tempo and stopped altogether. We were in Archangel!

Archangel, endlessly dear and lost for evermore. Faces that have vanished and voices forever silent.

2

1912

My paternal grandmother, Evgeniya Evgenievna Popova, the wife of Dr Aleksandr Egorovich Popov, my step-grandfather, was awaiting my arrival in the Issakagorka Station, as it was called in those days. I can still see the tall, full figure dressed in a blue, fur-trimmed shuba, with a round fur hat to match, worn over a white lace shawl, tucked into her collar. She carried a muff and another shawl hanging loosely over her arm.

I was only five years old when I had last seen her, yet I somehow instinctively knew that this tall, fine lady, with dark curly hair framing a round face and kind laughing eyes, could not belong to anyone else but me. She was my grandmother, my babushka. I ran towards her, stumbling in my clumsy boots. She hurried forward, spreading her arms wide and caught me up with muff, shawl and all, held me close and kissed me over and over again.

Petya's father, a thick-set elderly man, was also there, to meet his son. They embraced and kissed in the traditional manner. For a short while they all stood together discussing the journey while I burned with impatience. Babushka repeatedly thanked Petya for bringing her granddaughter safely home after what, she knew, must have been a burdensome journey. At last there were the final goodbyes and we walked over to our sledge.

Standing beside the horses, stamping his feet, was a young fair-haired man dressed in a heavy padded overlapping coat, reaching down to his felt boots.

"This is Mikhailo," Babushka said. "Don't you remember him?" Mikhailo laughed. "How would she remember me?" he asked in turn, in his lilting peasant accent. "She was only so high." He pointed with his knout to a few inches above the ground.

Two small dogs rushed forward, barking a shrill welcome. I remembered them, or perhaps I imagined I did. My parents used to tell me many stories about them — Scotka and Borseek. Scotka was a black Scotch Terrier originally named "Scottie" but rechristened "Scotka", a name which came easier to the Russian tongue. He was brought by my father from Scotland, along with a small flock of black-faced ewes. They arrived in a cargo ship when Scotka was only some ten weeks old. Everyone knew Scotka. After six arctic winters, his thick coat became much thicker and longer. He resembled a small ferocious bear. His appearance belied him. Below the overhanging eyebrows twinkled a pair of friendly brown eyes. He was intelligent, courageous and an expert rat catcher. No Russian rat was ever too big for this true representative of his small country! His constant companion Borseek was found one Christmas morning by my father inside our gates. He was a tiny puppy and almost frozen. My father revived him with hot milk laced with a little vodka. I was only a few weeks old at the time. We grew up together and from all accounts he suffered patiently all my antics. He developed into a sturdy small mongrel with a soft russet coat and a bushy tail that curled over his back. Tucked away somewhere in his head was a very crafty brain.

Favouring a chosen few, he looked at the rest of the human race through his amber eyes with lofty contempt.

The big woollen shawl Babushka carried was wrapped over my head, crossed in front and securely tied behind my back. I was completely enveloped, for Babushka had a real fear of frostbite. Through the whole of the journey she constantly kept pulling the shawl over my cheeks. We climbed into the sledge. Mikhailo tucked the bearskin rug over our knees and scrambled into his seat in front. "Nu . . . Poshawl," he called out in that gay ringing voice so special to drivers, jerking his reins and waving his knout. Off went the horses to the jingling of bells and wild excited barking of the dogs running behind us.

The station is on the left bank of the river Dvina. All communications between it and the town on the other side are maintained in the summer by a ferry. In the winter after the ice freezes to a great depth, the river bears all traffic.

We drove down a gradual incline on to the river itself. Wide and dazzling, it stretched before our eyes, disappearing into the distance beyond the island of Solombala on to the sea. To the right, sweeping away in a wide curve to the north, lay the ancient city of Archangel. The sun lit up the pastel buildings and played on the golden domes of the churches. High above, the crosses glinted against the blue porcelain of the cloudless sky.

How glad, how perfect was that morning. The sun, the crystal air, the clean smell of the snow. The horses breaking into a gallop skimmed the tight-packed surface of the river. "Gei, gei, gei, my darlings," Mikhailo kept calling out, and they ran faster and faster, their heads thrown back in wild abandon with flying manes and jingling bells. The little dogs raced at full stretch, sometimes keeping up with the sledge, sometimes falling behind. I sat close to my Babushka, muffled in my shawl, warm and secure, and laughed as only children can laugh when they are happy.

We reached the shores of Archangel and halted beside the road leading into the town. The dogs had fallen behind. They came running up, panting heavily, their breaths small clouds of steam. Babushka patted the bearskin and they leaped up joyfully into the sledge beside us.

The sledge drove slowly into a busy market place, past warehouses and stalls where peasants in heavy clothing were offering their produce. When we reached the crossroads, the sledge turned left into Troitsky Prospekt, the wide main street running through the whole length of Archangel. We drove on through the heart of the city, past the ancient cathedral with its painted frescoes on the white walls dominating the square in front.

In spite of the sub-zero temperature the town was busy. Pedestrians, muffled in shawls and furs, hurried along the footpaths between high snow-banks heaped up against the pavements. At times only their heads were visible. Sledges, small and big, of every style raced up and down.

Over all lay the deep snow and the great silence of an arctic winter. Only the sound of creaking runners and the bells or the sudden cry of a crow in flight broke the silence.

We turned into a street called Olonetskaya Ulitza and drove down towards the river. The horses suddenly quickened their pace. In the corner of the street close to the river stood the house. The double gates wide open. Leaning on his broom, Vassily the old gardener was standing there. Babushka laughed, waving her hand to him.

The horses raced through the gates. Straight ahead, I could see, sunk deep in the snow, the dark tips of a hedge separating the courtyard from the garden. Beyond in the garden on a small hill surrounded by pines and birches stood a white summer house fashioned in the style of a castle. From the turret a flag fluttered lazily. The trees, like silent sentinels, guarded the castle.

We swept past the two wings overlooking the courtyard, up to the front entrance. The sledge slowed down and stopped. Babushka helped me down and, taking my hand, led me through the double doors and up the crimson-carpeted staircase. Suddenly the inner doors on the top landing burst open. Looking down were the smiling faces of two young boys and a girl. Behind them in the hall stood a group of people.

I entered the house. It embraced me, holding me fast for the next eight years until the morning of my childhood was over.

It was a rambling house built on two levels. The long single storey overlooked the wide expanse of the Dvina. French windows led out into a balcony with wrought-iron railings. There during the long, clear summer nights, friends and members of the family sat talking or listening to the voices carried from the river as they watched the sun moving along the western horizon behind the dark line of the opposite shore.

To the north lay the island of Solombala. All ships coming in from the White Sea skirted the island, appearing suddenly into view.

The two double-storeyed wings of the house jutted into the court-yard, facing east. Round the corner of the north wing was the front entrance and a few yards along was the second set of double gates leading out on to the river front. The ground floor of this wing housed a self-contained flat of two rooms, a kitchen and private entrance.

Some years earlier, an old nanny, who had been in the family for several generations and who had had the unique experience of seeing the remnants of Napoleon's Grand Army retreating near the district of Smolensk, lived there. She was known as Nanny Shalovchikha. After she died, the flat stood empty for some time. When I arrived Uncle Sanya was living there. Uncle Sanya was my father's younger brother, a young man in his twenties at that time. The private entrance of the flat suited my uncle's bachelor activities. He led a gay life of parties with nocturnal visitors who came in shadowy drozhkis (hired cabs) gliding silently through the gates and out again after discharging their mysterious passengers.

At times when the revels reached their crescendo and the loud sudden burst of laughter, the raised voices or the strumming of a balalaika would penetrate the thick floor upstairs, someone would laugh tolerantly, but Babushka's face always darkened.

A large square balcony connected the two wings of the house. French doors from the dining room led on to it. I cannot remember it ever serving any useful purpose except when during the summer Babushka would suddenly decide to go into town. She would then go out to the balcony, lean over the railings, cup her hands over her mouth and in a clear resonant voice call over to the lodge, "Mikhail . . . lo, poda-a-a-avai." Mikhailo would appear on the steps, call back and hurry down, fastening his coat as he ran to the stables. In no time the horse and carriage would be cantering towards the entrance.

A favourite game after lunch was to feed the chickens. Holding a plate filled with all the leftover food and bread, Babushka would stand, throwing handfuls over the railing and at the same time call to the chickens in a very special, drawn out, caressing tone, "Tze-e-e-eep, Tze-e-e-eep meelenki-ya" . . . "Tzee-e-ep, tzee-eep, my darlings." The magic effect of this never failed to throw me into fits of laughter. I myself would then start calling in unison with Babushka. The "little darlings" rushed across from all directions — chickens, hens, all colours and sizes with trailing wings and piercing cries, geese, turkeys appearing from nowhere. Ducks, only seconds before diving peacefully in the depth of the pond for weeds and little fish, were suddenly galvanised into hurrying up the bank, madly rolling across the lawns, in a frenzy working their way through the hedge stumbling and falling over themselves, inevitably to arrive too late.

In the winter, when all the windows and French doors were sealed in double frames, the balcony became inaccessible. The snow lay thick up to the top of the railings and only the faint, lace-like tracks of the crows and sparrows marred the smooth white perfection.

At the far end of the yard was the lodge. It was divided by a narrow passage into two separate houses, each containing two rooms. In one lived Mikhailo with his young wife Masha. The other half housed Vassily the gardener and a young boy named Yashka employed to run messages, deliver notes and perform endless tasks.

During the winter the hens were transferred to Vassily's warm house from their summer quarters. Vassily cheerfully shared his two rooms with Yashka and the hens, periodically opening the cages. The hens ambled around his feet, clucking contentedly, as they pecked away at the wooden floor for some invisible insects.

Straight ahead at the far end of the yard, curving to the right in a crescent, were the stables, the coach house and an old cow shed where were housed the Scottish black-faced ewes imported by my father. In Scotland, my father was strongly advised against this whim. The sheep in Scotland, they argued, were used to wandering in the hills nibbling the sweet, rich grass. My father was adamant. He was convinced they would become adjusted. He was right. The sheep not only became adjusted but thrived, multiplied and grew magnificent thick coats.

At first they timidly nibbled the grass on the drying lawn in front of the stables, but later, little by little, they ventured outside the gates and trotted down to the river exploring the banks. The banks of the Dvina in our parts were high, built up by great boulders to keep the ice floes and spring floods at bay. Between these boulders grew all kinds of succulent grasses and herbs. It was here the sheep found what must have been the nearest resemblance to their own natural habitat in Scotland. Soon they became a familiar sight to all passers-by.

Every evening they trotted back to their shed. During the long clear nights of the arctic summer when there was no darkness and the sun still shone, these sheep were aware it was evening and some deep instinct drove them back to the only shelter they knew. Through the dark winter months, while the sun made a brief appearance, fodder was thrown on to the snow and the sheep came out of their dark quarters. After they were fed, they would enjoy short excursions down to the river while there was still a little daylight. One day when Vassily was sweeping away the snow from the path beside the gate his ears were suddenly assailed by the shrill sound of terrified bleating. He was horrified to see the whole flock rushing back from the river and past him through the gates, followed closely by a large dog.

Mikhailo and Vassily were peasants. They recognised at once that this animal was not a dog but a wolf driven by hunger from the woods across the river. For a short time the wolf was trapped in the yard, his retreat cut off by Mikhailo and Vassily, with Yashka joining in the hunt holding a long poker. The young servant girls ran out of the kitchen waving towels. They were accompanied by the hysterical barking of Scotka and Borseek running behind them at a safe distance. The whole cavalcade in wild excitement, stumbling and falling in the snow, advanced upon the wolf hoping to chase him into the woodshed through the wide-open doors. The wolf, by now, was as terrified as any sheep. Like all creatures cornered he suddenly lunged at his tormentors. Instinctively everyone leaped aside. The two little dogs, their tails between their legs, streaked back to the kitchen. The girls screamed in terror. In that split second the wolf darted through, out the gates, and away back to the safety of the river and the woods beyond.

The years are rushing past faster and faster as I grow older. I must hurry for perhaps there is not much time left. There is the consolation that like most old people I can remember with greater clarity the people I knew and the events that took place during my young impressionable years than what happened years later.

I can see the house quite clearly in all the seasons of the year. In the summer the rooms appearing flooded in sunlight. I can almost hear the sounds of the river coming through the open windows and smell again the pungent freshness of the great timber rafts slowly floating down to the sawmills. The voices of the women rinsing their washing at the edge of the pier, the shrill laughter of the children bathing or sitting naked on the boulders drying themselves in the sun, all echo back over the years.

In the winter, as soon as the second frames were placed in the windows, shutting out all sound and the terrible cold, the house became warm and intimate. Soft pools of light on the tables, the peaceful flickering of the lampadas lighting up the sacred faces on the ikons, the sweet humming of the samovar created an atmosphere drawing everyone into a closer circle. The fragrance of birch and pine pervaded all the rooms as the logs burned and crackled inside the great stoves.

Three main rooms ran the whole length of the house fronting the river. They were given an impression of even greater spaciousness by the wide open archways in each connecting wall. These rooms were rarely used, with the exception of the end room in the south-west corner of the house. In this pleasant room, where the comfortable chairs were upholstered in a soft shade of reseda green with matching curtains, my grandmother sometimes entertained her friends. It was essentially a woman's room with the feminine atmosphere of flowers, photographs and ornaments on small tables.

The ballroom at the other end was a long impressive room. Suspended from the centre of the ceiling was a bronze and crystal chandelier. Matching candelabras jutted out from the wall. Light gilt chairs lined the walls and a grand piano stood in the corner. Between the windows and the French doors leading out into the balcony were long mirrors in gilt frames stretching up to the ceiling. At the base of each mirror were wrought bronze baskets containing plants and flowers which were reflected in the mirror.

Between the ballroom and the end room was the "gosteennaya" — the guest-room or drawing-room. The crimson velvet upholstered chairs and sofa, polished mahogany tables displaying family albums, bronze ornamental clocks under glass covers, the porcelain and bric-a-brac in corner cabinets all reflected the heavy fashion of the Victorian period. There were paintings on the walls. One depicted Mary Queen of Scots walking down a flight of steps on her way to her execution.

Masses of flowers and plants grew on all window sills. My grandmother, whose great hobby and passion were her garden and flowers, grew rare, exotic plants never seen anywhere else in our parts. Oleanders and passion flowers, sweet-smelling lemon trees, fuchsias and pelargoniums, rare cacti and orchids all came in their seasons even in the dead of winter and nodded their lovely heads to the still white landscape outside.

The golden honey of parquet flooring covered the rooms of the entire house, but in these three rooms the workmanship was extremely fine. Hardwood in many shades formed a design that was unusual and beautiful. Two young men dressed in high-necked, black cotton shirts and trousers, came to polish these floors. After removing their boots, each slipped a thick sock over one foot. On the other was a special short boot fitted with a brush, firmly strapped round the ankle. Crossing one arm behind his back each man skated over the floor, the leg with the attached brush swinging back and fore in a wide sweep while the other dragged behind twisting and hopping. The free arm moved like a pendulum swinging up and down. Their damp shirts clung to their backs, but they continued skating up and down the room, only stopping to change the boot to the other foot or drink a glass of kvas — the cool beverage brewed from black bread and raisins, drunk all over Russia. This strange, rhythmic hopping and twisting continued from room to room until the floors shone with a golden brilliance.

The heart of the house was the dining-room, lying between the two wings. The dining-table ran the length of the room. Every night at six o'clock some ten or twelve people sat down to dinner. In the corner of the wall was a lifesize ikon of St Nicholas. A small table stood in front with an ancient bible on it. Close to the ikon was a row of small candles lighting up the face of the saint. This ikon, black and almost indiscernible, had been in the family for over two centuries. It had been found floating down a river during the religious persecution of the "Old Believers". My great-grandmother from Kaluga brought it to Archangel.

According to the old Russian custom everyone paused in front of the ikon to cross themselves before sitting down at the table. I followed the others hurriedly crossing myself, afraid to look directly into these dark unfathomable eyes. This ancient ikon of St Nicholas was alleged to have some strange miraculous power. Babushka was fond of recalling how her brother Dmitri, a giant of a man, had once blasphemed in the presence of the ikon, referring to it as a piece of black useless wood only fit to burn inside a stove. When he went back to his home he found his infant son stricken with dyphtheria. He had rushed back and, sweeping everyone aside, prostrated himself in front of the ikon, screaming his repentance and beseeching St Nicholas to save his child. The baby recovered. Uncle Mitya was a wild and reckless man, not very religious and not very likeable, but I can still see him when he called at the house, standing looking with reverend intentness at the ikon as he crossed himself with a wide sweeping gesture.

In the corner of the dining-room stood a round serving table. After dinner, when the tables were cleared, a plush cover was placed over this table. The centre hanging lamp was lowered, casting a pool of soft light. One by one everybody deviated to it. Babushka had a passion for nibbling pine kernels with the lightning speed of a squirrel. This was a practice usually of peasants and the lower strata of society, but Babushka also had some peasant blood flowing through her veins. She would place a big bowl of these nuts on the table and everyone gathered round, cracking the small brown kernels while they talked and had these endless discussions.

Best of all was when Seryozha read to us. Seryozha, my elder step-uncle, still at school, had the great gift of reading in a soft expressive voice. The Russian language, always infinitely rich and pliable, flowed straight from his heart, falling and rising in sorrow or joy. He held his listeners in rapt attention until the last word faded away. No one spoke. Babushka, her hands pressed into her cheeks, looked down intently at the table, and Marga, my young step-aunt, gazed straight ahead somewhere beyond.

It was at this table in the house where I was to spend my early impressionable years surrounded by all that was Russian, customs, religion, the people who came and went and talked in their own

inimitable Russian style, all that and more, that I, although of
Scottish-Russian parentage, began to absorb and develop that strange
elusive substance often referred to as the "Russkaya dusha" or
"Russian soul". It has stayed with me always, overshadowing the
Scottish side of my being.

Quietly flowed our provincial life these days in this backwater. No
one at all appeared to be aware of the distant rumble of the
approaching storm. If they were, they never said so.

3

In 1903, when my father, Gherman Aleksandrovich Scholts was 23, it
was decided that he should go abroad. After three years at the
University of Riga, he felt ready to take his late father's place in the
family timber business. His guardian — Uncle Adolf — and his mother
thought differently. He would get some experience abroad first.
Dundee was chosen because firms there traded with Archangel in flax
and timber, and there were relatives there whom my grandmother
imagined might keep an eye on her, at times, irresponsible son.

On his first day in Dundee, Gherman was standing at the window
of his hotel room — he used to recall that the clean streets, solid stone
buildings and tidy pedestrians gave him a lasting impression of order
and stability. People were strolling in the warm sun. Horse-drawn
vehicles of all kinds trundled up and down the cobbled street. As he
stood absorbed, he saw a young woman in a lilac suit and a white
flowered hat on the opposite side of the street, walking with her fox
terrier. The dog stopped, attracted by a lamp-post. Gherman found
himself willing the girl to look up at him. She did so, and he saw a look
of faint surprise on her face. For a moment their eyes met. Then,
turning her head abruptly and giving the lead an impatient tug, she
went on her way.

Gherman found lodgings in Broughty Ferry and was taken on for
two years by a firm of flax merchants. Having a natural flair for
languages, he was soon talking English quite fluently, and even
adopting local idioms. He travelled daily into Dundee by train and was
soon accepted in their own special circle by the group of young men
with whom he used to share a compartment.

One day, his cousin Bertram took him to a charity dance in

Broughty Ferry. It was the interval when they arrived. Young men were escorting their partners back to their places. Gherman appeared to be gazing at someone at the opposite end of the hall.

"Tell me," he asked, "who is that girl beside the one in blue?" "That," Bertram explained, "is Nelly Cameron, the local beauty. The one in blue is her sister Agnes, and the two young men are their brothers. I'm acquainted with the family. The parents are known to be extremely strict and the brothers can be difficult. I suspect," he concluded in a bantering tone, "you would like to meet Nelly — if so, I can introduce you."

They sauntered casually across the floor. Gherman was introduced to the two young women, their elder brother Stephen, and Henry, twin brother of Agnes.

Nelly did not belie Bertram's description. Slim, of medium height, a flawless complexion accompanied by the classical beauty of finely chiselled features, blue eyes and dark hair coiled high in smooth perfection, she appeared to stand out above all others. Agnes, a plainer version of her sister, kept up a cheerful flow of small talk until the interval was over and the strains of a Viennese waltz came floating over the room. Couples were taking to the floor. Gherman crossed over to Nelly and bowed.

A long time after, when my mother was quite old, hearing the melodies of these old-fashioned waltzes on the radio, she said to me, "No one could waltz like your father. He had a style of his own. He took long gliding steps and swung you round and round until you felt as if you were floating, your feet hardly touching the ground."

They danced in silence for some time. Then suddenly he asked her: "We have met before, have we not?" She laughed. "Yes, we have. You were the man in the window."

They danced all night after that, completely oblivious of others circling around them, and unaware of Stephen's silent disapproval of this foreigner monopolising his sister.

Sitting together at the supper table they talked of many things. In his broken English Gherman described his life in Russia, his home, his mother. He tried to convey a picture of his beloved country, of her immense vastness, the endless forests, great rivers, the snows and frosts of the winter and the lovely white nights of summer when the sun glided around the horizon and there were gay midnight parties down the river. Nelly listened intently. She had lived all her life in Broughty Ferry. She had never been out of Scotland and spoke about simple mundane things. He learned that she was the eldest of four girls, that two of her five brothers were abroad in Kenya and New Zealand and Henry was hoping to go to India. Her life consisted of helping her mother in the house and travelling every Saturday afternoon by train into town to do some shopping.

As they danced the last waltz he asked if he could take her home. She became confused. "You will have to ask Stephen," she said unhappily. Stephen was cold and distant. "I and I alone will escort my sister home," he answered shortly.

That night, walking home through the dark empty streets, Gherman remembered the conversation at the supper table. "I travel to town every Saturday afternoon", Nelly had said. The rest was simple. He knew the timetable of the trains departing in the afternoon from the small station at West Ferry. Passengers approached the platform either from the east or west entrance. Arriving early the following Saturday afternoon through the east entrance, Gherman watched the passengers coming in. Nelly, whose home was to the west of the station, was bound to come through that entrance. Soon after, a train steamed in. Passengers were opening doors and settling down in their compartments. He was already preparing to wait for the next one when he saw the familiar figure hurrying across the platform and disappearing into the front carriage. Running towards the same compartment he opened the door, sat down and leisurely scanned the passengers. In feigned surprise, he discovered Nelly sitting opposite.

At Dundee, he accompanied her along the streets, waited patiently outside all the shops and escorted her back to the station. They travelled together back to West Ferry.

This little game, as old as time itself, continued for several weeks. With a little ingenuity Gherman varied the pattern. At all times these meetings had to appear accidental. Boarding an earlier train to Dundee he would stand near some unobtrusive place and approach her casually as she mingled with the other passengers.

One Saturday, my father boldly suggested that if Nelly cared, they could go to the theatre the following Saturday afternoon. Poor Nelly, torn between fear and longing, eventually timidly agreed. She had never been anywhere with any young man and was excited and apprehensive as the day of their appointment drew near. She hurried to finish her shopping, met Gherman and slipped into the theatre as the curtain was rising.

From that day there were no more "surprised" meetings. They met every Saturday and attended the matinée. Her sister Aggie, who was very close to Nelly, and in whom Nelly confided, helped her in every possible way. She often did all the shopping and after meeting them, travelled back with them to West Ferry. Nelly never allowed Gherman to escort her to her house. They parted as they came out of the station.

Nelly blissfully continued meeting Gherman every Saturday. It was obvious that sooner or later someone, even innocently, might inform her parents. She tried not to think about it, living only for these few precious hours that passed all too quickly. In the end the inevitable happened, but not in the way she imagined.

It was also my grandfather's custom to travel every Saturday afternoon to Dundee to his office. He usually caught an earlier train than Nelly and came back on the 4.10. Being set in his ways, this arrangement never varied. Nelly travelled back on the 5.10 train, which was an hour later than her father's. It fitted in very nicely with her attendances at the theatre.

That certain Saturday, as she stood on the platform talking to Gherman while waiting for the train, she was horrified to see her father walking towards them. He did not appear to be aware of the young couple and stopped a short distance away.

My grandfather, Augustus Stephen Cameron, was then a man in his early fifties. Of stocky build, he had clearly defined features and deeply set blue eyes that contrasted sharply with his silver white hair and ruddy complexion. A handsome man, always immaculately dressed, usually in a navy blue suit complete with a grey stetson hat and flower in his buttonhole, he was a well-known autocrat, capable of great generosity or petty tyranny. He also had the disconcerting habit, when annoyed or contradicted, of staring long and hard right through his opponent.. Now he was standing still, gazing straight ahead.

Nelly already visualised the dire consequences at home. The end of all her happy meetings. To my father, this was an opportunity he did not intend to miss. He walked resolutely up to my grandfather, with Nelly a few paces behind him, raised his hat and asked if he would be allowed to introduce himself. He had been introduced to his daughter at a dance some time ago, he continued, and had since met her several times. He hoped Mr Cameron did not think he was too presumptuous to want to meet her father.

My grandfather glanced coldly at his daughter and back to the young man in front of him. My father felt himself being silently appraised and stood waiting. "Tell me," my grandfather enquired unexpectedly, "what is happening exactly between your country and Japan?" If my father was taken aback, he certainly did not show it. At that time the attention of the whole world was focused on the war between the small yellow men and the Russian colossus. My father, who like all Russians pasionately loved his country and kept abreast with all the events, expressed his opinion. The train came in and after a moment's hesitation they all got into the same compartment. The conversation continued until they arrived at West Ferry. Walking out of the station, Gherman raised his hat and prepared to take his leave. There was again some hestiation, as if my grandfather was trying to make up his mind. "Young man," he said suddenly, "I enjoyed our conversation. I should like to hear and know a little more about your country." Something warm and elusive like a shaft of sunlight lit up his proud countenance. "Perhaps," he continued, "you may care to come along and join us all for lunch tomorrow?"

Nelly, sitting beside her father, had travelled in silence, listening to the conversation. Now she was too relieved to say anything at all. My father bowed, expressing his thanks and acceptance. Raising his hat once again, he turned and walked away.

That night he sat down and wrote a long letter to his mother. He described Nelly in every detail. How he had met her and was now invited to meet her people. He was certain his mother would like her. He loved her and wanted to marry her. In the end, according to the old Russian custom, he begged his mother for her blessing.

The following day Gherman arrived at the house and rang the bell. Bay House, aptly named, stood on the sheltered banks of the bay in West Ferry. It was a typically solid Victorian house, built at a time when neither money nor materials were spared to create an air of elegance and prosperity.

A young maid opened the door and led Gherman into the drawing-room. He found my grandfather talking to a young man who, he learned, was Andrew, Nelly's elder married brother, paying his usual Sunday visit with his wife and children.

My grandmother entered, politely shook hands and sat down. She was not blessed with any outstanding good looks, but possessed fine taste, and in spite of her numerous children, had a neat, well-proportioned figure with the small waist so fashionable in her day.

Nelly appeared, flashed a quick shy smile, said a few words and vanished. The family had all been to church. The girls were busily engaged in setting the table and assisting with the preparations for the lunch, as was their custom every Sunday.

At this point my grandfather stood up and suggested that Gherman accompany him to the conservatory and inspect what my grandmother described with a fleeting sly smile as his latest toy. Curious, my father followed him into the garden and into the conservatory. Standing in the middle of the floor on a tripod was a powerful telescope. My grandfather invited Gherman to scan the opposite shore. Having no experience of telescopes, my father was amazed to see the line of vision brought so close. He was able to discern the smallest details, even down to the flowers decorating the

hat of a young woman. He watched her smiling face as she talked to a
man reclining beside her on the bank.

Their game was abruptly interrupted by the loud clanging from the
house of a gong announcing that the lunch was ready.

The whole family were assembled in the dining-room. It would
never have occurred to any of them to sit down before the head of the
house took his place at the top of the table. Gherman was introduced
to the two other sisters — Mary, a pretty round-faced girl with a
reticent manner, and Vicky, the youngest, a happy extrovert.

The maid brought in a steaming tureen and placed it on the table. At
the other end of the table, my grandfather, resting his head on the
palm of his hand, in a manner that never varied through his whole life,
said the grace. My grandmother began to ladle out the soup.

This was the first occasion the Cameron family entertained a young
man. The conversation, with the exception of the head of the house,
was a bit constrained, but as the meal progressed and the plates with
the carved Sunday joint were being passed round, all gradually
relaxed.

Grandfather was a man who could talk on many subjects. Well read,
with a keen, shrewd mind, he had at times almost an uncanny insight
into what was going on around him and in the outside world. The
question of the Russian-Japanese war was brought up again. At the
end of January 1904, the Japanese fleet had treacherously attacked the
Russians in Port Arthur. Russia was doing badly, and my grandfather
deplored her weakness. Then, suddenly turning to my father, he said,
"Just the same, mark my words, laddie. One day, not in my time, but
perhaps in yours, Russia will become a force the whole world will be
obliged to notice. Yes," he added grimly, "that will include us as well."
These strangely prophetic words, spoken at a time of Britain's
greatest power and prosperity, my mother was to recall many years
later.

Talking about himself, he told my father that he was the youngest
child of a big family and was brought up by his aunt, a Mrs Dick, who
was known as "Grandma Dick". His mother had died at the time of his
birth and this childless aunt had taken him to her home in Broughty
Ferry. He was completely cut off from his brothers and sisters during
his childhood. This aunt, who was quite well off, having no children of
her own, had lavished all her love and devotion on her nephew and
when she died left him all her estate. That set him off on the road as a
prosperous property owner and house factor.

Having spent all his life in Broughty Ferry, my grandfather had
witnessed the fast-changing scenes of that period. As a schoolboy, he
had travelled in an open carriage in the first train, to the Dundee

Grammar School, as the present High School was named in those days. As a young man he had watched the building of the famous Tay Bridge and had seen the triumphant journey of the first train to cross what was reputed to be the longest bridge in the world. A mere two years later he also witnessed the terrible diaster, although he was not actually aware of it at the time.

It so happened that my great-grandmother, a widow, who was known as Helen Hay and lived in Leuchars in the Kingdom of Fife, was spending Christmas with her daughter and son-in-law. On 28 December 1879, she was preparing to leave on the evening train back to her home in Leuchars. During the day the weather worsened. Angry white horses galloped across the Tay and thundered against the pebbles on the beach. My grandparents became alarmed. Great-grandmother, a determined old lady who disliked having her plans altered, was in the end persuaded to stay overnight. She was fated never to cross the bridge.

In the evening, when the force of the gale had reached the highest pitch, grandfather decided to inspect the garden for any damage. He donned his heavy coat and struggled down to the foot of the garden. The furious lashing of the waves against the shingle, the screaming of the wind like some demented soul, all fused into one horrifying roar. In the pitch darkness, he could see very little beyond a few lights from the opposite shore and the winking eyes of the lighthouse. Involuntarily he glanced to the west where a long ribbon of lights could be seen spanning the river. A small red light appeared to be moving from the opposite side towards the high girders of the bridge. As he watched, the lights vanished and everything plunged into darkness. He struggled back to the protective warmth of the house. The two ladies were sitting beside the glowing fire enjoying their cup of tea. "I've just seen the lights on the bridge go out," he told them. "I don't like the look of it," he added.

A few hours later the news of the Tay Bridge disaster reached the house. The train and passengers had all been swallowed by the angry waters of the Tay. In the cold grey light the following morning my grandfather rose and went down to the beach. The storm had abated, but the waves were still lashing against the shore and already throwing up the broken wreckage of the carriages.

In my father, grandfather found a good listener, one who asked many questions and was interested in everything that was said. Scotland was still comparatively new to my father. He wanted to know everything about her customs, traditions, her way of life, so that he in turn could feel, absorb and understand everything and in this way perhaps would be accepted.

Lunch over, all adjourned to the drawing-room. Gherman, not wishing to overstay his welcome, rose to take his leave, but was persuaded to remain for tea.

In a house where a strict Presbyterian rule never permitted any music other than psalms or hymns to be played on a Sunday, the family were amazed to hear their father asking Nelly to play some Scottish airs. She obediently sat down to accompany Mary, who had a fine contralto voice. One by one all gathered round the piano. My father, who possessed a good voice and was by now familiar with the well-known songs of Scotland, joined in the singing. Later Nelly played some of the favourite pieces she knew by heart. Gherman was surprised and delighted, for she had never mentioned that she had this accomplishment.

Back in the dining-room they all sat down to a Scottish tea. The table was laden with home-baked scones, cream cookies and cakes. A friendly relaxed atmosphere prevailed. Gherman began to feel as if he had known them all for a long time. After tea, the girls, along with Stephen and Henry, prepared to set off for the evening service in the church.

Father bowed and thanked my grandparents for their hospitality. They in turn invited him to come back again and to treat this house as his second home. "Haste ye back," my grandmother said, dropping her habitual aloofness and reverting to the homely vernacular.

Gherman walked with Nelly behind the others. They said goodbye at the church gate and my father continued on his way back to his lodgings. A fortnight later he approached my grandfather and asked to marry his daughter. Permission was granted. According to the Scottish custom he bought a diamond ring. He and Nelly became officially engaged.

There were several aspects of a Russian-Scottish marriage that had to be explained and eventually agreed upon. Letters were exchanged between the British Embassy in St Petersburg, the head Russian Consulate in London, and my grandfather's lawyer. According to the marriage laws of Russia my mother had to have the consent of her parents before any marriage could take place. By marrying my father she would automatically become a Russian subject. Any children of the marriage would likewise be Russian subjects and be baptised in the church of that country and of their father. My mother was a Presbyterian. My father belonged to the Russian Orthodox Church. In deference to his church he wrote to the Arch-Priest Father Evgeny Smirnoff, chaplain to the Russian Embassy in London. "My son," replied Father Evgeny, kindly explaining that while there was no objection to a Presbyterian service, the Orthodox Church would consider the marriage invalid unless it was solemnised in the Russian church as well. One of the important rituals in the ceremony is the crowning of the bride and bridegroom, when the two groomsmen, standing behind the couple with outstretched arms, hold the heavy golden crowns above the bridal pair and follow them as they are led by the priest three times round the lectern. The church also did not approve of any wedding taking place during the period of Lent, when the great fast of seven weeks begins around the end of February and lasts until Easter Sunday.

If my grandparents had any misgivings about their daughter becoming a subject of that vast, and to them unknown, country, they tried to brush them aside. After all, some members of the family were already scattered to the far corners of the Empire, others were soon to follow, so why not Russia? As for my mother, she did not mind any laws or rules and would have cheerfully followed my father into the very depths of China if need be. She remained throughout her whole sojourn in Russia a Presbyterian, but attended the most important services of the Russian church where she enjoyed the magnificent singing of the choir, and especially the deeply moving ritual of the Easter service.

Meanwhile a steady flow of letters was pouring in from Russia. My grandmother and my father's guardian asked many questions. In the end Gherman decided he would go to Russia during his vacation in the early summer, where he could discuss the various aspects of his future. He was now anxious to curtail his stay in Scotland, for he saw no reason for a prolonged engagement. He was possessed by an impatience to get married, take his bride to Russia, begin his new life and become established in his business.

Nelly had never been so happy. There was a new sense of freedom she had never known before. This was her spring. Life was new. Life was wonderful.

I have often heard my father say, echoing the sentiment expressed by other foreigners, that Sundays in Scotland could be dull as opposed to in his own part of the world. There was nowhere to go to except church or to pay calls on friends or relatives. Now it was different. As the days became longer and clearer he enjoyed walking with my mother, exploring for the first time the lovely outskirts of the town as yet unspoilt by the sprawling buildings of roads and houses. At other times they joined the throng of young people strolling on the promenade or listening to the band in the park.

One Sunday in the early summer they decided to have a small

expedition to the opposite side of the river. They took the train to Dundee and from there crossed on the ferry affectionately nicknamed the *Fifie* to Newport. From there it was possible to stroll back along the road on the Fife coast to a point directly opposite Broughty Ferry. From this small port, known as Tayport, they planned to cross on a second ferry, called the *Dolphin*, back to Broughty Ferry, thus completing the round trip.

The day was very warm. They strolled leisurely in easy stages, halting to admire the neat and tidy gardens, the flowers and trees in full blossom.

When they eventually reached the pier they found to their dismay that the *Dolphin* had left a few minutes earlier and was now in midstream. There was nothing they could do but wait until it returned. They walked back down to the beach and settled on a grassy bank. By now it was late afternoon. All was peaceful. From the opposite shore a small boat was crossing the river. They watched it idly. The rower appeared to be in a hurry. As the boat drew nearer they were astounded to recognise the stocky figure of my grandfather. They had forgotten that on an afternoon such as this, when there was neither mist nor rain to disturb his vision, Grandpa, glued to his telescope, was having a field day.

He had seen the *Dolphin* leave the pier in Tayport and watched my parents walking down to the shore, sitting on the grass and perhaps, who knows, exchanging a few kisses. That was enough. He had rushed to the beach to the boating shed, housing his yacht and dinghy, dragged the dinghy down the slipway and raced across the river. My parents hurried to the water's edge to meet the approaching dinghy. Grandpa leaped out and dragged the boat on to the shingle. His face was was crimson with rage and exertion. All efforts to help were brushed aside. "Get in that boat," was the short and curt reply when Nelly, for once defiant and indignant, had enquired what he thought they had done. Gherman was ordered to follow suit.

Later, perhaps realising that he had gone too far, my grandfather explained his action by pointing out that by bringing them back direct to the beach so near the house they were spared the long walk from Broughty Ferry. If so, why did he display such anger? It was difficult to understand the workings of such an eccentric mind. Much easier to accept his belated explanations and ignore the rest.

Soon after, my father left for Russia. He was accompanied by Stephen. My grandparents had approached Gherman, tentatively suggesting that if possible it would be a good idea if Stephen, who had never travelled before, went with him. Behind this request, of course, was an opportunity for a member of their family to observe everything and draw his own conclusions. My father understood this and readily agreed. By now the northern Dvina was free from ice. They sailed direct to Archangel in a cargo ship.

Six weeks later they returned to Scotland. On Stephen these few weeks in Russia left a lasting impression. He liked the people. He was overwhelmed by the hospitality he received everywhere he went. There were endless dinner parties lasting into the early hours of the morning; midnight picnics down the river to the islands; an excursion up river of a few days' duration on one of the paddle steamers that sail up and down the Dvina during the summer months.

The Dvina meanders for hundreds of miles until, eventually spreading herself around all the islands at the mouth of the river, she flows down to the sea. Churning up the sparkling spray the steamer paddles along for days on end, nosing her way through the oncoming timber islands that float down to the mills. Skirting around the ever-changing coast through deep or shallow waters, it sails past sandy shores where splashing children wave their hands.

The town itself, Stephen thought, had a certain charm. The cobbled streets were wide, flanked by raised wooden pavements. There were many fine old churches and buildings dating back to the days of Peter the Great. Most of the privately owned houses were built from timber and varied considerably from the solid handsome buildings of the prosperous citizens to the grey, shabby cottages of the poor. There were leafy parks and tree-lined avenues on the river front. He saw no high tenements darkening the streets. Yet in many aspects, he continued, there were moments when he had the impression he was transported to a bygone age. There were no tramcars. People either walked or travelled by horse. In the best houses, in spite of parquet flooring, rich furnishings and electricity, every drop of water had to be brought in from the river.

Every morning he watched the horse cantering down to the pier with the empty barrel jolting in the cart and later dragging the heavy load uphill back to the kitchen door. From there it was emptied into a second barrel standing in the passage adjoining the kitchen. The water was then carried into a boiler in the kitchen and distributed round the house. All refuse in turn had to be dumped into a pit, discreetly hidden behind the stables.

Upstairs in the house were two adjoining small rooms. In the first one there was a marble-topped table with ewer, basin, mirror, soap and other requisites. In the second room were two lidded seats of different sizes built over a chute some twenty feet deep, partially buried in the ground. In the early spring men came along, cleaned and removed all refuse to a certain part of the river. Later, when the river moved, the ice floes carried everything out to sea.

Overall Stephen believed his sister would be happy. It was a close community, friendly and hospitable. Life in this small but busy port could be very gay. There were clubs, gatherings, dances, plays and operas, all in their seasons. Above all, he knew all the relatives were prepared to welcome her into their circle and do their utmost to make her happy.

I will never know what talks transpired between my father, his mother and guardian. Many years later I was given a small hint by one of his cousins, by now a very old lady. "I will have her and no other!" my father was reputed to have said at the end of a lengthy discussion. Perhaps they had questioned the advisability of bringing a young bride to a country where she had no relatives or friends of her own. The language was difficult, the customs, the harsh winters and the whole way of life so vastly different to what she was accustomed. They did not of course know my mother and were not aware that she, like most Scots, had the inherent quality of being able to adapt herself to any conditions. In any case, it did not matter what each side of the family thought or said. The wedding was fixed for 18 January 1905.

4

From the moment the date was finalised the house became a hive of great activity. Grandfather, determined his daughter should have a wedding worthy of himself, gave my grandmother a free hand to order all that she considered was necessary for her daughter's trousseau. My delighted granny, who had come from a humble home and whose mother had been a widow, embarked on a great shopping spree.

Bundles of blankets, embroidered sheets, linen of every description from the damask tablecloths down to the humble kitchen towels were delivered in a steady stream to the house. A sewing maid was engaged to make the special square pillow-slips used in Russia. Nelly and her sisters spent hours embroidering and marking every article with her initials.

There were constant excursions to shops and dressmakers. One well-known furrier was commissioned to make a fur-lined shuba with fur hat and muff to match. This was necessary, but in spite of my father's assurance that the houses were warm and that Nelly was not embarking on an expedition to the North Pole, Granny, undaunted, ordered two old ladies, who kept a wool shop in the town, to knit endless pairs of thick woollen stockings, shawls, scarves and other garments. The two ladies sat knitting feverishly all day long right up to the day before the wedding.

From Archangel came the glad news that my Russian grandmother would come to the wedding. She was happy, she wrote, to be able to attend her son's wedding and looked forward to meeting her future daughter-in-law and her family, and to seeing Scotland for the first time.

To the festive atmosphere of Christmas was added the exciting anticipation of the wedding now a mere three weeks away. A few days later a telegram arrived. Gherman's grandmother had suddenly taken a stroke and was not expected to recover. His mother, who had been happily preparing for her departure, had to cancel all arrangements. It was impossible to leave her mother and in the end she never saw Scotland. Gherman was very attached to his old grandmother. When he saw her last during his summer vacation there was no trace of any illness. She talked to him for a long time, asking many questions about his Scottish bride and in the end blessed him as he was leaving again for Scotland. She died early in January, adding to the bitter dis-appointment that his nearest and dearest relative would not be present at the wedding.

The following day, Henry, who was leaving for India a few weeks after the wedding, received instructions from Calcutta informing him that his sailing date had been brought forward. He left for India on the eve of the wedding. He was my mother's youngest and favourite brother. Eight years and more were to pass before she saw him again.

As the wedding date drew nearer, there was great interest in Broughty Ferry in this Scottish-Russian union. Of special attraction was the wedding cake displayed in the window of the bakers in Broughty Ferry renowned for their artistry and quality. Instead of the usual floral decorations on the top tier, the cake had two silver and gold-fringed flags. Against the royal blue brocade, embroidered in silver, was the double-headed eagle of Russia and beside it the gold and scarlet of the Lion Rampant.

The marriage service took place in the parish church of St Stephen's in Broughty Ferry. There was even a faint touch of spring in the clear sky. Serene, completely composed and lovely, Nelly, her long train and veil trailing behind her, walked down the aisle, her hand resting lightly on her father's arm. Her three sisters walked behind her. To her surprise she noticed her father was strangely agitated. His arm trembled visibly as he handed his daughter to her bridegroom. The church was packed and there was a big crowd of onlookers outside. Among them there stood a lady who by some strange quirk of fate was to become my mother-in-law.

The reception was held in the house and the numerous guests spilled over all the rooms downstairs. A glimmer of pale sunlight allowed a family photograph to be taken on the porch outside. The reception had to be curtailed as in the late afternoon the bridal party, some relatives and friends had to embark on a train journey for the second church ceremony.

Years later my aunts and mother used to recall this journey. From all accounts it was hilarious. Bertram Luhrs, my father's groomsman, had brought aboard a case of champagne. While the older members of the party sat quietly resting in their compartment the young people crowded in beside the newly-weds and continued the celebration until they arrived in Newcastle. There the whole party put up in the Station Hotel. The following morning after breakfast the party continued their journey to London. Tired and weary, and some more weary than others, they were all glad when the train steamed into London. They all stayed in the Langham Hotel in Portland Place. There they were joined by another cousin, who had just arrived from Russia. Adya Scholts, who was to be one of the crown bearers, was a handsome, debonair young man. He joined in wholeheartedly in all the activities of the next few days. There were luncheon parties, dinners and theatres, shopping and sightseeing and on the last evening a big party in the Hungarian Restaurant where the orchestra played gipsy music and Russian folksongs.

On 23 January, Nelly, by now having been married for five days, donned once again her bridal dress and veil and set off for the second marriage service to be held in the Russian church in Welbeck Street. She carried no flowers, for in the Russian Orthodox Church the bride and bridegroom stand together holding lighted candles entwined in orange blossom.

The marriage rites of the Russian Church are impressive. The singing of the unseen choir deeply moving. The ritual of exchanging rings moves on to the circling round the lectern led by the priest and followed by the groomsmen holding the crowns over the heads of the bridal pair and adroitly side-stepping the train and veil. The chanting of the priests, the singing, the flickering lights of the candles and the saintly faces of the ikons had a strange dreamlike effect on my mother. As they slowly moved behind the priest, the inner tension, the unaccustomed odour of the incense wafting all around her, proved too much. She was overcome and had to be taken to the vestry. Shortly after, Father Evgeny sent the deacon to enquire if "Miss Cameron" was able to proceed with the service. "Miss Cameron" pulled herself together and went back to complete the ceremony which in the eyes of the Russian Church gave her the right to be recognised as a married woman.

In the afternoon, after tearful partings from the family, they embarked on another journey by train to Hull. There they had to join a ship which would carry them across the North Sea and through the Baltic to Finland.

In Helsinki they were met by my father's sister, Olga Aleksandrovna, and her husband, Oscar Semyonovich Yanushkovski. Aunt Olga embraced and kissed Mother on each cheek. From that moment they became great friends. Throughout her life my mother held a deep affection for her kind and slightly eccentric sister-in-law. Oscar bowed and lifting my mother's hand pressed it to his lips. To Nelly that was a novel experience.

Two sledges awaited them. Oscar helped Nelly into the first sledge and tucked the apron around her knees. They travelled together. The language barrier was overcome by Oscar's knowledge of a few English words and a charming manner. He succeeded in putting Nelly at ease by pointing out various landmarks as they raced along the clean white streets of Helsinki. She never forgot that first drive in a sledge. All was so new, strange and exciting.

Behind them in the second sledge sat my father beside his beloved sister. After a long absence they were happy to meet again and were eagerly exchanging all their news. Three years his senior, my aunt had a protective attitude towards her brother. At a tender age they had tragically lost their father and perhaps on this account developed a strong mutual affection which never weakened even when they were apart.

During that period and up to the time of the revolution Finland belonged to Russia. Uncle Oscar held an important position as Councillor of State in the Russian Civil Service in Helsinki. They lived in a pleasant house in one of the main streets in Helsinki.

When they arrived and entered the house Nelly was mildly astonished to find the walls of the hall and all the main rooms lined with display cabinets. Each shelf was packed with a great variety of fine old porcelain and other antiques. His sister, my father explained, was a renowned collector of antiques and especially porcelain. Aunt Olga was a loving but at the same time a careless mother. She displayed no interest in any form of housekeeping, her only concession being the dusting of her precious ornaments, a task no one else was allowed to perform. She knew nothing of cooking and there were sad instances when, after a cook suddenly giving notice, the whole ménage would depart for the nearest restaurant.

Yet at the same time she desperately longed for a son and regularly year after year with undaunted optimism set off on another pregnancy. Still only in her twenties, she already had six daughters. One more was due to arrive in a few months. Each child, with the lightheartedness of a cuckoo, was passed on to the care of a wet nurse, a nanny and later a governess. At last, years later, she was delivered of a longed-for son, followed by another two daughters. The son, cherished and adored, turned out to be a source of sorrow and anxiety. The daughters, energetic and resourceful, made their way in the world.

Shortly after their arrival my parents were taken to the nursery to meet the children. It was a large room with many windows, light and warm, but rather austere. Cots and cradles stood against the whole length of the wall. There were also, it seemed to my mother, as many women as children milling around the nursery. An old nanny who had once suckled my aunt reigned supreme over this female kingdom. Aunt Olga was attached to her old "mamka" who, unable to bear the separation from the child she had nursed, followed her to Finland.

It was a noisy and cheerful company but as soon as they became aware that they were observed, everything stopped. The women stood up and bowed. The children ran to their mother, glancing curiously at their new visitors. They were all dressed alike and very pretty. All in turn were introduced to their new aunt and curtsied politely. The eldest child, Militza, was a fair-haired little girl, eight years of age, who in time was to develop into a very attractive young woman and acquire no less than three husbands. Marina, Aunt Olga's second daughter, with large expressive eyes, came over and took my father's hand. Marina, Father explained sadly as he picked her up in his arms, was totally deaf. When barely two years old she contracted scarlet fever. Complications followed and when she recovered it was discovered that her hearing was destroyed. She had entered a silent world where she was to remain for the rest of her life.

My parents did not stay long in Finland. They had planned to go to St Petersburg. Oscar suggested that he and Aunt Olga should join them. Oscar was brought up in St Petersburg and had many friends and connections there.

St Petersburg. No one but Peter the Great, whose genius and imagination equalled his stature, could have conceived the gigantic scheme of building his second capital five hundred miles to the west of Moscow. With a determination that brooked no opposition, unspeakable cruelty and the bones of all the countless thousands who laboured, he laid upon a treacherous swamp the foundation of one of the most beautiful cities in the world.

St Petersburg, during my parents' honeymoon, was at the height of its season, or so it appeared to them. A mere fortnight earlier there was the tragedy of "Bloody Sunday", when hundreds of citizens were trampled and mown down during a harmless procession to the Winter Palace. The Japanese had also inflicted terrible reverses in the East. There were distinct rumblings of the approaching storm, but on the surface these events did not seem to cause much concern or apprehension.

My mother fell in love with St Petersburg. The graceful spires glinting in the winter sunlight, the great domes of the cathedrals, the palaces, pastel-coloured mansions, canals and bridges and the silver ribbon of the frozen Neva all combined to present a scene of unsurpassed elegance.

Oscar's friends opened their doors with true Russian hospitality. There were invitations to dinner parties. They attended the ballet and opera. Shortly before they left St Petersburg, their hosts booked a box for Glinka's opera "Zhizn za Tsarya" . . . "Life for the Tsar" nowadays renamed "Ivan Suzanin". From their box they had a clear view of the Royal Box occupied by one of the Grand Dukes and his entourage. Every seat was occupied and the whole theatre was ablaze with light and colour. The cream of St Petersburg's society was present. The silver and gold of the uniforms, the sparkling jewellery on the bare shoulders of the women, the rich gowns and furs all fused into one glittering scene never to be forgotten. In the front stalls, occupying a whole row, was a group of handsome men dressed in black and silver uniforms — the famous Death Hussars, often referred to as the Black Hussars, most of whom were bachelors, men completely dedicated to the service of the Tsar.

There came a stirring moment when the orchestra struck the first chord of the national anthem. The actors on the stage, the Black Hussars and every member of the audience stood up and, turning towards the Royal Box, sang in magnificent unison that most moving anthem, "Bozhe Tsarya Khrani" — "God save our Tsar".

Outside in the bitter cold and snow the coachmen waiting for their masters stamped their feet and waved their arms in an attempt to keep warm. Groups of onlookers watched the wealthy patrons setting off in their carriages and sledges to their homes and palaces, to the islands, to some private, gay, intimate parties. This was the zenith of high living for the favoured few. In the short space of twelve years all would vanish, never to return.

They did some sightseeing of famous and historical places, but my aunt, who had seen it all before, preferred to indulge in her favourite pastime of haunting the streets in search of her beloved antiques. In her new shuba and fur hat perched on top of her pretty head, Nelly trotted happily beside her sister-in-law. Aunt Olga, well known in the world of collectors, was welcomed in many fine establishments. Long years after, my mother used to describe one in particular. A high-class place where it was possible to acquire objects that were unique and of great artistic beauty. It was there that her sister-in-law, after a long scrutiny, bought a small ornament. She had it carefully wrapped up in a small box. Somehow mother could never remember the name of that unusual establishment.

The following day my parents left for Moscow. Aunt Olga and Oscar came to the station to see my parents off. As they embraced just seconds before the train left, Aunt Olga handed to my mother the small box she bought the day before. This ornament was a small tumbler carved out of rock crystal and gave the impression it was half filled with water. In the centre was a small twig of willow catkins. It was perfect and very simple. Mother kept it for many years and wherever she went she took it with her. Some thirty years later she passed it on to me as I was leaving for India. After my mother's death I discovered that the "fine establishment" mother described, long since vanished, was that of the legendary Carl Fabergé. The little tumbler and the catkins are still in my possession.

In Moscow there was a constant coming and going of friends and relatives, all eager to meet the young "Anglichanka". The cheerful humming of the samovar never ceased except when it was removed from the table to make room for lunch and dinner. The meals were endless and no sooner was the last course finished and the table cleared than the samovar appeared again — a signal to begin another discussion.

Moscow to St Petersburg is like an older cousin, simpler in her approach and bigger hearted than her younger and more sophisticated cousin in the West. At that time it was the manufacturing centre of Russia. My parents spent many hours shopping. They ordered furniture, carpets and a piano. As a very special gift for Nelly, Gherman ordered a dinner service for the "Easter Table". It was a beautiful set in gold and crimson with my mother's initials marking each plate. There were wine and liqueur glasses to match. Who knows, perhaps it is still gracing some table in a house or cottage! I do not regret Mother being unable to bring it out. It helped my father to survive when he had to exchange it for food.

Their stay in Moscow was now drawing to a close. The distant north was beckoning. . . .

I have sometimes wondered what were the thoughts of this young woman so far removed from her own homely scenes, sitting trustingly beside her husband, travelling through a vast alien landscape of drab little villages, snowdrifts that grew higher and the forests darker with every hour, as the train rumbled on further and further to the north.

A short distance before their final destination the train halted at a small wayside station. A young woman came aboard and joined my parents. She was my father's cousin, Tanya, whose husband held a position connected with the railway. Tanya had been commissioned by my grandmother to assist my parents with their luggage and make certain it was delivered safely to the house. Tanya embraced and kissed my mother and her cousin. Of a bright and friendly disposition, she presented an extraordinary spectacle, being completely enveloped in black diaphanous material stitched round her fur hat and falling in folds down to her ankles. Nelly was astonished and overawed. "Is she some kind of nun?" she enquired. "No," my father explained shortly. "She is in deep mourning for our dear grandmother." Nelly felt chastened. For the next few minutes they kept up a friendly conversation interpreted by my father and accompanied by smiles, gestures and nodding of heads. The train steamed into Issakagorka Station. On the opposite side of the river lay Archangel.

Two sledges awaited them. Tanya immediately took charge of the luggage. She briskly commandeered all the porters and in no time had all the boxes placed on her sledge. My parents walked over to their sledge. Gherman embraced the old coachman fondly and introduced him to his young wife. The old man glanced at Nelly, smiled broadly and said something that appeared to please my father. Tucking the bearskin round them while addressing my father by the familiar "thou" and first name, he fussed for a little and clambered onto his seat. He raised the knout and off went the horses. Behind them on her sledge, perched high on top of all the luggage, sat Tanya, her black draperies flapping behind like the wings of a gigantic bird.

Faster and faster flew the horses. They had now turned into Olonetskaya Street. As they ran through the gates the high turret of the summer house dominating the garden caught Nelly's eyes. "Look," she suddenly said to my father and pointed to the sky. There, fluttering high against the arctic sky, welcoming the Scottish bride, was the gold and scarlet of the Lion Rampant. She always told me that as she gazed up at this proud symbol of Scotland she knew that this was something that was her very own, something that was part of her being, and it seemed to be saying, "You must never be afraid, for I shall always be with you."

The horses drew up sharply at the front entrance. My father helped Nelly down and they walked together up the crimson-carpeted staircase. Through the open inner doors could be seen standing in the hall a tall woman dressed in black who bore a strong resemblance to the photograph Nelly had of her mother-in-law. For a moment she thought that it might be her, but my father, introducing her, explained this was his Aunt Ludmilla, his mother's sister. "You must hurry," Ludmilla told them anxiously, "they are all standing waiting for you in the ballroom."

As a young servant girl hurriedly removed her heavy shuba and fur hat, Nelly had wondered if she could be allowed to tidy herself a little and comb her hair, but that, it seemed, was not possible. Gherman took her hand and led her into the ballroom just as she was, her hair untidy and her dress all crumpled after the long journey. In the middle of the room stood her mother-in-law, a tall, resplendent figure in a golden brocade dress with a long train. In her hands was a large ikon of the Virgin and Child. She made no sign of welcome or movement towards them. Beside her stood her husband, my father's stepfather. He was holding on a silver tray a large round loaf of black bread topped by a salt cellar — the traditional Russian symbol of welcome. In the background grouped around them were all the friends and members of the family.

Still holding Nelly's hand, Gherman walked up to his mother and knelt in front of her. Standing beside him, bewildered, not knowing what was expected of her, Nelly hesitated. "Down, Nelly, down on your knees," her husband urgently whispered as he pulled her down beside him. My grandmother stepped forward. Holding the ikon, she slowly and reverently made the sign of the cross over their bowed heads and then stepped back. My step-grandfather took her place and gave his blessing with the bread and salt. That was all. The brief traditional ceremony was over. My grandmother laid down the ikon, opened wide her arms and holding Nelly close to herself, smiled and kissed her on both cheeks. She tried to tell her in her broken English that she now had another daughter. All the other relatives gathered round kissing them both in turn. All except old Nanny Shalovchikha, now in her hundred and fifth year, a small shrivelled old woman, who stood aloof and glanced coldly at my mother. When my father called to see her during his short leave from Scotland, she had asked him if he did not think there were enough good-looking girls of his own kind to choose from. "Do you have to marry a foreigner?" she had demanded bitterly, "and an 'Anglichanka' at that?" A subject of a country where had reigned that other "Anglichanka", the detested Queen responsible for the Crimean war and the death of her only son.

In the drawing-room were the gifts from the Russian side of the family. With the expansive generosity of the merchant class they had presented gifts of pure silver that overwhelmed my mother. There, on a separate table, were the pieces of jewellery long since laid aside by my grandmother for the wife of the eldest son. There was no time to ponder and admire. Babushka, who had missed her son's wedding, was now determined that she also would have a wedding reception worthy of her son and daughter-in-law. Already the table was set and the hungry guests were eagerly waiting to sit down.

They had to hurry and join the party. Nelly, remembering that her mother-in-law was wearing a gold brocade gown, changed into what she thought was suitable for the party, but when she entered the dining-room she discovered to her dismay that Babushka had changed into mourning dress. The gold brocade gown was only worn for the ceremony of the blessing. Glancing round, Nelly found that with a few exceptions, everyone was dressed in black. Even the two little boys, aged four and six, were wearing mourning bands on their sleeves. For a fleeting moment she felt a strange, almost uncanny sensation. It was a time when mournings were taken seriously and by none more so than the Russians, especially in the depths of the north. It may not have looked like a wedding reception, but that did not deter all the guests from enjoying what was now to Nelly and Gherman the third wedding celebration and proved to be the gayest gathering of them all.

Some eighty guests had gathered round the table which stretched from the dining-room into the hall. There were again the endless courses, vodka, champagne, toasts and the traditional Russian wedding customs. A custom that seemed strange to Nelly was one that was usually followed at the table of newly-weds, and although my parents had been married for more than three weeks it did not stop the guests from following it now.

One of the guests remarks casually to another that the food or drink has a slightly bitter taste. The other guest immediately agrees. "Decidedly it is bitter," he says and the message is passed on to the next one who in turn repeats the same word until the chanting of "Gor'ko, gor'ko" . . . "Bitter, bitter"—forms a chorus from all parts of the table. At this point the only way to sweeten everything is for the young couple to turn and kiss each other. This was repeated several times. Odd as it must have been to Nelly, she obediently complied each time.

One by one the guests dispersed in their sledges to their own homes. It was a gay and exhaustive party, but along with all the drinking and eating, the toasts, the jokes and the old customs was the realisation that they had all done their best to make this young, foreign bride happy and were accepting her into what was a close community. Perhaps I should now say something about the background of the Russian family. All that I was told during my impressionable years when I listened, enthralled, to the tales of a bygone age.

5

When Tsar Peter the Great, that mighty and pitiless reformer, arrived in Archangel in 1693, he began to build a shipyard on the island of Solombala. To assist him in this enterprise, Peter imported from Holland designers, craftsmen and shipbuilders. Among them was a Dutchman named Rutger Van Brienen. In spite of the harsh climate and the backward conditions of the town, Van Brienen settled down in Archangel and never went back to his native land. A little more than a century later his descendant, Margaretha Caroline, was born and in 1818, at the tender age of seventeen, married a merchant, Ivan Gernet. They were my great-great-grandparents.

Margaretha Van Brienen was a proud woman. Proud of her name and distant associations with Peter the Great. As in St Petersburg, so in Archangel, Peter was fond of holding his famous "assemblies". On one occasion he was supposed to have asked the wife of Van Brienen to dance with him, but she being large with child was forced to refuse this great honour and begged to be excused. Having read a great deal about Peter and his habits, I find it difficult to believe that a mere pregnancy would have deterred him from having a canter around the ballroom had he wished to do so. This story, however, has persisted throughout the generations.

Ivan and his wife Margaretha had several children, but I am only concerned with two of them. Their son Evgeny, or Eugene, and their daughter Amelia.

Like many mothers, Margaretha was ambitious for her family and especially for her son Eugene. Some time during the summer of 1842, Eugene was commissioned by his father to go to the district of Kaluga, a thousand miles away, to buy merchandise required for their business. Every year an important fair took place and merchants from many parts of Russia gathered to buy or sell the produce of that rich and prosperous county. When he arrived in Kaluga, he put up in the house of the local landowner who was a business associate and friend of the family.

The landowner was a widower. The whole running of the house lay in the hands of an able housekeeper named Feodosiya who was assisted by her young daughter Anna.

Somehow from the very first day Eugene became aware of this girl. He saw her busily engaged in her various tasks, bringing the steaming samovar and the food to the table or hurrying across the courtyard on her way to the village. He heard her talking and laughing or singing to herself like some happy bird on a spring morning. There was no contact of any kind. She remained in the background, for she was only the servant and he the guest.

One evening in the village there was a "goolyanie", meaning a stroll or a "walkabout". Joining the younger members of the family, Eugene went along to the village. It was a warm summer evening. The girls in their fresh cotton dresses and bright sarafans were strolling arm in arm up and down the street. The youths in their clean embroidered shirts and hair plastered close to their heads, strutted like cockerels in groups meeting and passing the girls. Someone produce an accordion, another strummed on a balalaika. There was dancing and singing to be followed by the Khorovod — the great circle when everyone joined hands and chanted as they circled faster and faster round a figure in the centre. Eugene and his friends were drawn into the ring and joined hands. In the centre, dancing with great style and abandon, was Anna. She was gliding around in that inimitable manner in which the flick of the hand, the shrug of the shoulder, the tilt of the head conveyed something that was elusive, truly Russian, and is second nature to every peasant girl. She was following the various commands of the chanting, "Bow to us all — Ai Lullie, Ai Lullie. Bow to us all — Ai Lullie." She stopped and bowed, touching the ground with the tips of her fingers and danced on to the next bidding and finally on to the last command when the circling halts and she is told, "Kiss the one that you love best — Ai Lullie, Ai Lullie." For a moment she hesitated, then danced across to Eugene, kissed him lightly, pushed him inside the circle, and, taking his place, joined hands with the others.

The circling and chanting commenced again, this time around Eugene. That is what the Khorovod is all about and that was how the romance began between a simple peasant girl and a cultured young man from a privileged background.

Anna was not only attractive, but also highly intelligent. Brought up in the big house where there were books and having been taught to read and write by the local priest, she avidly read everything she could possibly find. Likewise she was influenced by a deeply religious mother whose moral standards were high. Eugene had known many girls, had many flirtations, if not affairs, in far off Archangel, but now this was something different. They fell sincerely in love, yet both knew that between them there lay a great gulf, impossible to be bridged. She was a peasant and a serf as well. Both she and her mother belonged to the landowner. The days when Aleksandr II would free all serfs were still in the future. Anna was resigned to saying goodbye when the time came for Eugene to go back to the north. Eugene, a determined young man, had other ideas. He had decided to marry Anna. Knowing that the only way was to buy her, he approached his host, who was horrified and adamant in his refusal to sell the girl. He warned Eugene of the wrath to come if he agreed to his proposition, and that he himself as a friend of the family would be placed in a position where Eugene's parents, with every justification, would accuse him of betraying their trust in him. Yet in the end, after prolonged arguments and discussion, perhaps because of some spark of humanity, or a romantic streak in his nature, or even possibly a profitable offer, he agreed to sell Anna.

Now there came a second formidable barrier, this time from Anna herself. Her mother was a widow. There were no other brothers or sisters to take her place if she left her. She and her mother, having only each other, were very close, and, as much as this golden future beckoned, she utterly refused to leave her mother. The bargaining and cajoling began all over again. In the end the landowner, by now resigned to the inevitable, sold both, the mother and the daughter.

What was the price? I have at times wondered idly. It is a matter of interesting conjecture, but I shall never know the answer.

They were married by the local priest in the little church in the village. The young sons of the landowner acted as sponsors and Anna's mother, Feodosiya, gave her blessing. From the church, accompanied by the villagers singing and chanting, they returned to the house where a table had been spread by their kind host for a few friends.

In the courtyard, beside the steps of the house, a troika was waiting. A group of children and villagers had gathered to say farewells to the bridal couple and Feodosiya. Nothing like this romance had ever happened before in their village. That Anna was not only free but was married to a "Barin" — a gentleman, and was now a "Barynya" herself, a lady who would have her own house and servants, own carriages and horses — was nothing short of a miracle. That would be something to talk about for years and pass on to their children. They left as the sun was rolling to the west. The horses ran briskly through the village then turned and took the road to the north.

Many romantic songs and tales have been written about troikas, their drivers and their journeys across the length and breadth of mother Russia. Romantic they may have been, but on long journeys they were devoid of all comfort. Yet throughout their hazardous journey, cramped in their carriage, tormented by dust and the merciless rays of the sun, or drenched in torrential rain, our travellers seem to have remained cheerfully happy, bearing all discomforts with inherent patience.

Deeply hidden, however, was the anxiety about their future. It increased as they drew nearer to the north. How would Eugene's parents treat their peasant daughter-in-law so suddenly thrust upon them? Being deeply religious, their faith sustained them. "God did not mean us to travel so far for nothing," Feodosiya reasoned, sensing her daughter's anxiety. Eugene also had misgivings. He feared his proud mother and pinned all hopes on his more tolerant father.

Eugene's parents knew nothing until the day when the cook, hurrying from the market, brought the news that Eugene had been seen in the outskirts of Archangel and should be arriving at any moment. They ran out on to the porch and stood eagerly awaiting the arrival of their beloved son. The troika with great style flew through the gates, turned and drew up beside the porch. Eugene got out and ran up the steps to his welcoming parents. Anna and her mother remained standing beside the horses, confused and timid, not daring to go any further.

In the first few seconds of their happy reunion Margaretha did not appear to notice the two women, or perhaps did not consider them worthy of any attention beyond enquiring casually who these peasants were. The moment Eugene dreaded had arrived. "Mamushka," he said, using the endearing ending, "this is my wife and her mother. I beg you," he continued humbly, "to give us your blessing." Margaretha's face turned scarlet, then deathly pale. She staggered and would have fallen if Eugene had not caught her. He and his father helped her to reach her bedroom where she collapsed on the bed.

When she recovered she forgot her habitual dignity and could not contain her hysterical rage. She could never accept, she told Eugene bitterly, a primitive peasant as a daughter-in-law. He, her son, had betrayed not only her and his father but everything that they stood for. She would never be able to face her friends and relatives again.

This terrible condemnation was far worse than Eugene had imagined. It poured like a torrent of angry waters upon his defenceless head. In the end, collecting herself, in a voice that was cold and distant and more wounding than her towering rage, she told him to take his peasant wife and her mother anywhere he liked. They were never to cross the threshold of her house. That went for him as well. She completely disowned him.

Eugene ran out of the house and down the steps. The troika was still standing. Anna and Feodosiya were also waiting. Their heads bowed, dejected and utterly humiliated, they had stood throughout this terrible scene bitterly regretting they had ever left their beloved Kaluga.

At this point Eugene's faith in his father was justified. Ivan hurried after his son. It was Ivan who found a temporary place where they could stay until such time as they could find a permanent home, and it was Ivan who shortly after bought a house for them in a place called Maimaksa, not far from the mouth of the river and near their place of business, where all the timber industry was concentrated.

There they spent their married life and raised their family. Their youngest child, a daughter, was born in 1857, and she proved to be more gifted than all the others. They named her Evgeniya, after her father. She was my grandmother.

"Strange are the ways of God." How often I heard this old saying quoted in Russia! Gradually Margaretha drew closer to Anna. Slowly also came the realisation that there was more to her daughter-in-law than met the eye. In the years that followed a close friendship developed between the two women.

What Margaretha never realised, nor for that matter Eugene nor anyone else, was that from Kaluga there came an influx of fresh blood from a young, healthy peasant girl, which was essential for the health of future generations in a close-knit society, especially amongst those of foreign origin where a great deal of intermarriage took place between close relatives, who, like Royalty, preferred to marry within their own tight circle.

It was as if someone had flung open a window and allowed a cool fresh wind to clear away the stale air from a room that had been closed for too long.

Not long after Eugene and his young wife settled down in their house, Eugene's sister, Amelia Louise, married a young timber merchant, Franz Scholts. The name, of course, is of German origin. The family may have come from Riga, a port which had many connections in the timber trade with Archangel. This union must have pleased the great matriarch Margaretha. She may now have consoled herself with the thought that what she had lost in her son she regained in her daughter. Although there was not even the faintest trace of blue blood coursing through the veins of her son-in-law, he had something of far greater importance, namely money.

The Scholts family had been in the timber trade for generations and had gradually acquired considerable wealth. They belonged to that group of merchants who had the necessary qualities to achieve this affluence. They were shrewd, hard-headed and industrious.

Archangel and the vast surrounding district had always been a land which offered opportunities to everyone, including the peasant, in trading and many branches of business. In this great expanse of forests, rivers and marshes, there had never been any serfs, or souls as they were named, who could be sold, bartered and gambled away over a gaming table. The dreaded words of "to the stable", the place where the peasant was sent by the landowner to be whipped by the knout for some real or imagined misdemeanour, were never heard in this part of Russia. Poor or rich, the peasant was free. The north, in spite of many hardships, was unique in this respect. The woods abounded in game and animals, the skins of which were in great demand. The peasant fished in the river and the rich White Sea and sold his produce in the market.

The people in our parts were referred to as the "Bielomori", meaning those of the White Sea, or, in a more derogative term, the "Treskoyedi" — the "Cod-eaters". Certainly this was the land of the famous fish pies. In this great province too could be found the true Russian Slavs, with all their ancient customs and manner of speech, for there had never been any contact with the Tartars who, in the 13th century, like an evil black cloud of locusts, overran the holy land of Russia but never advanced as far as the distant north.

Amelia and Franz also settled in the Maimaksa region near all the sawmills. Amelia, a tall, well-built young woman like the other members of the family, was very devoted to her brother. They had always been a united family, and now, living within reach of each other, there was a constant coming and going between the two houses. Their numerous children grew up side by side. Eugene and Anna had four sons and three daughters. Amelia and Franz were likewise blessed by a large family of sons and daughters.

Every christening, every birthday, every name-day, not only of all the children, but of parents, grannies, great-grannies, aunts and uncles, was an excuse for a party and a gathering of all the relations.

Anna became completely accepted by the family. She was especially popular with all the children. I remember an old great-aunt recalling the times when they were children; how they loved nothing better than when Tyotya Annushka—Aunty Annushka, as they called her, would dance and sing to them and join in all the games that she herself played as a child in her distant village. "She was always so gay and young," I recall the old lady saying, "just as if she was one of us children and loved being with us. Her mother, Babushka Feodosiya, was also a great magnet to us all. She was a gifted story-teller and would gather us close around her knees and in her Kaluga accent and lilting voice, full of mystery and suspense, would begin her tale how in a certain kingdom, on a hill high above a fast-flowing river, there lived a wise Tsar who had a beautiful daughter. Gradually the story would unfold and we children listened spellbound, afraid to miss a word, as she carried us far, far away on her magic carpet over forests and rivers, seas and mountains, to all these wonderful magic places of strange happenings, good and bad, but where at all times there were happy endings.

One decade followed the other and the children were now young men and women. "The old grow older and the young blossom out" — so goes the old Russian saying. The noisy fancy dress parties became sophisticated masque balls. The little sledges on which the children used to slide down the ice chute in the back yard to the accompaniment of shrill laughter and screaming, were now replaced by the large sledge and horses galloping along the moonlit river during the Shrove carnival to some distant friends in the town.

Evgeniya, or Yenya, as the family called her, had reached her seventeenth birthday. She was tall and slender. Escaping tendrils of dark chestnut hair framed her round face with the high cheekbones inherited from her mother. From her mother also came the sweet expression radiating warmth and the joy of living.

It was noticed that Aleksandr, Amelia's son, was very friendly with Yenya and appeared to single her out from all his friends and cousins. At parties and dances it was with Yenya that Aleksandr danced most of the night. During the great festivities of the Shrove carnival it was found that somehow Yenya and Aleksandr always contrived to sit side by side in the same sledge. Aleksandr often called at the house on the slightest pretext and stayed on for the evening.

There used to be in those days a special fancy dress ball held annually in aid of some charity. One year it was decided that all the guests would go to the ball as characters from Pushkin's works. Yenya, who had a fine artistic sense and a pair of clever hands, with great ingenuity created the dresses for her sister Ludmilla and herself. Ludmilla chose to go as the sinister "Peekovaya Dama" or "The Queen of Spades". From then on she was nicknamed "Peekovaya Dama", later shortened to "Peeka" and as she grew older to Tyotya Peeka or Aunty Peeka. As a child I never knew her as anything else and was surprised to discover one day that her name was not Peeka, but Ludmilla.

Yenya had gone to the ball as the "Water Nymph" from the opera of the same title. I remember Tyotya Peeka describing the event. "My dress was very beautiful," she said. "So many people admired me and hinted that I might be the one to win the prize. You can imagine my disappointment when the judges called out Yenya's name instead of mine. Yet," she continued without any rancour, "I had to admit she looked lovely. It was such a simple dress — green and blue chiffon intermingling together just like the waters of a river and her long hair hanging loose and unadorned. Our mamushka," she went on, "was rather angry as Yenya had insisted on dancing around on her bare feet, explaining that no water nymph ever wore shoes. That was a very daring thing to do in our days. They carried her shoulder-high round the ballroom at the end of the dance," she concluded a little wistfully.

Shortly after the ball, Yenya and Aleksandr approached their parents to ask for their consent to be married. The Russian Orthodox Church does not approve of marriages between cousins but somehow this obstacle was overcome. Yenya, eighteen, and Aleksandr, a few years her senior, were married. They were my grandparents.

During the first two years of their married life, Yenya and Aleksandr lived close to their parents. Later, after the birth of their daughter, Olga, Aleksandr bought the house in Olonetskaya Street. It was thought at the time by all the relatives that Yenya was too young and lacking in experience to take charge of a house which required so many alterations and where the surrounding ground was nothing more than a wilderness. They were mistaken.

Yenya was a visionary who had the gift of knowing exactly how any project she undertook should look when it was finished. Blessed with an artistic sense and boundless energy, she also had the tenacity to overcome what at times seemed an impossible obstacle. Yet, when confronted with what she believed to be the decree of fate she accepted it with the spiritual endurance of her people.

One day in the early summer, when the house and courtyard were completed, she and Aleksandr explored what was described as a garden, separated from the courtyard by a broken wooden fence. Inside there were no signs of any paths or of anything remotely resembling a garden. Cattle from the adjacent neighbourhood ambled around in perfect freedom and peaceful contentment. A few stunted saplings struggled for existence. A small pond was choked by green slime and weeds. Against the boundary wall was a row of lime trees masking the gaping holes which allowed free access to all animals and to those who on occasions used the pond for the disposal of unwanted kittens and suchlike unpleasant activities. Beside the pond was a mound of excavated earth and rubble.

It was a dismal scene, brightened only on the east side of the grounds by a long avenue of slender young birches leading to a banya, or bath-house, almost hidden by nettles and wild elderberry bushes in the north-east corner of the wall. The avenue also served to screen the vegetable garden running from the north to the south.

"What can we do with this place?" Aleksandr had asked Yenya, looking helplessly around him. She did not answer at first. Then, "We shall have a garden," she said with quiet determination. "A garden the like of which Archangel has never had before. We shall enlarge the pond and raise this mound. It will be a small hill and on top we shall build a fine summer house. "There," she added, "on this field will be lawns and flower beds, rare trees and bushes. I promise you," she went on earnestly, "if you will allow me, we and our future children shall have a beautiful garden. A rare garden that will be a great heritage which they will also pass on to their children."

She kept her promise. At least part of it. It was not within her power to see too far into the future.

Helped by books, workmen, clever joiners and painters, there gradually appeared out of a wilderness a unique garden which was the true realisation of her dream.

All walls were rebuilt. A leafy hedge, spangled with golden flowers, separated the courtyard from the garden. The pond was enlarged and stocked with carp which bred and multiplied. Irises, daffodils, bullrushes grouped themselves around the grassy edge. Two white piers complete with railings jutted out over the water. On the west bank behind one of them, was built a rustic summer house nestling against a clump of birches.

Dominating the whole garden, on top of what was now a small hill, stood a miniature replica of a fairy castle. Steps between flowering bushes led to a room furnished with table and chairs. The diamond-shaped multi-coloured panes of the Gothic-style windows were a great source of delight to us children when we gazed through them and saw the garden immediately transformed into a strange, mysterious place, dark and haunting, or in turn golden and bright.

From this room was a door to an outside stair leading to a flat roof, enclosed by low crenellated walls. In the corner was a tower, through which a steep stair came out on to a small platform with a flagpole. From this high point one had a fine view of the surrounding district and the river.

Looking down on to the garden below were lawns, flower beds, unusual trees and bushes. They came from many parts. The blue spruce and stately dark-green pines from our own district, the balsam poplar with the crimson, scented catkins from Siberia. Plants and bulbs from the steppes. The surrounding shores of the great Lake Baikal provided a source of many rare and beautiful flowers. Lilac bushes in all shades grew in great profusion, for they could stand up against the destructive frosts.

Throughout my childhood bundles wrapped in straw and sacking kept arriving to the house. From the north of Scotland came roses and, on one exciting day, an apple tree.

Perhaps nowadays apple trees can flourish in the distant north, but seventy years ago our apple tree was the only one in the whole of Archangel, if not in the district. In the early summer, groups of schoolchildren were often brought round to see this great rarity blossoming in our garden.

The garden was a living monument to a great achievement. She who created it could have stood alongside many of the greatest gardeners, for it has to be remembered that everything had to be coaxed out of earth frozen for eight months in the year.

Many years later, after everything was destroyed, they came to her, to the small room where she and Dedushka were living some distance away from the plundered house and garden. In beguiling tones of flattery they asked her to rebuild the garden all over again. They would assist her in every way, they added grandly. My grandmother looked at them coldly. She was now an old woman whose life was drawing to a close. She walked over to a corner of the room where were kept her few remaining precious books. Placing them in their hand she said with fine irony: "You have destroyed. You can rebuild." The garden remained untouched.

Aleksandr, infected by his young wife's fervour, assisted her in every way, sparing no expenses to carry out all her ideas. The vegetable garden flourished. The fruit bushes growing in orderly rows promised a rich crop of berries in the early autumn. The tender green of the young grass pushed through in the lawns. Their little daughter, Olga, was growing and running along the newly gravelled paths or playing in the little spinney where her father had erected a swing between the trees.

They were now expecting their second child. Both hoped that it might be a son. They had so much to look forward to.

6

One long, hot summer day in late June 1880, my grandparents were invited to attend a christening in the northern outskirts of the city. The young father had chosen Aleksandr to be godfather. There was no doubt that this was going to be a lively gathering with a plentiful supply of food and drink.

In the morning, Yenya, having spent a restless night and suffering more than usual from the symptoms of an early pregnancy, reluctantly decided to remain at home. She was afraid that the long drive over rough and cobbled roads combined with the heat would only aggravate her condition. Aleksandr, who always preferred to drive himself when travelling alone, set off with his horse and trap promising to return early in the evening.

After the ceremony, they gathered round the laden table. There were the usual repetitive toasts for the health of the new young citizen, the happy parents, all the babushkas, dedushkas, the god-father and godmother, the priest, the deacon and all the other important guests.

The white nights can be deceptive. By the time Aleksandr decided to take to the road it was much later than he thought. He had raised and emptied too many glasses and was now highly elevated. The night was cool and fresh. He felt cheerful and happy at the prospect of soon being back in his own house and bed. The horse, sensing it was going back to its stable, playfully trotted along the road between the wooden houses and grey, weathered walls enclosing leafy gardens.

For the past two years, Aleksandr had used the road through the barracks as a short-cut to his house. The men and officers knew him. Now, as he turned to go in, he was astonished to find the sentry barring his way.

Aleksandr drew up. He had never seen this soldier before. It was obvious the soldier had never seen him and was unaware that Aleksandr had permission to use the road through the barracks. The sentry merely said, "It is forbidden."

Had Aleksandr been sober, common sense would have prevailed, or if Yenya had been with him, she would have persuaded him to take the longer road to avoid all arguments. But there was no Yenya and Aleksandr wasn't sober. Frustration and anger welled up inside him. The sentry's manner of insolent self-importance was offensive. Throwing down the reins, he walked across to him.

No one ever knew the full details of the altercation. The fact remains that the sentry raised his gun and aimed at Aleksandr. Aleksandr, casting aside all sense and caution, threw himself at the soldier and snatched the gun. There was short struggle, culminating in a shattering report that echoed all over the barracks. The soldier slumped to the ground.

The sudden realisation of what he had done shocked Aleksandr into sobriety. He stood unable to move, not knowing if the soldier lying at his feet was dead or alive. The boy's young face was deathly white. A small crimson pool was slowly spreading over the ground.

From all ends of the barracks men were running towards the gate.

In the cool of the late evening, Yenya went out into the garden. The sun, gliding slowly to the west, was shedding a soft and tender light. The white light was spreading her mystery over a sleepy garden. Not a leaf stirred and the birds were long since silent.

Time moved slowly. She strolled along the paths between the sweet-scented flower beds, through the silver avenue of the birch trees and on to the pond where she circled around until, tiring, she stood leaning against the white railings of the small jetty, gazing down into the dark, mysterious depth.

A nagging resentment was building up. Aleksandr had promised to return in the early evening. It was now almost midnight. She turned away and began to walk slowly back. It was then she heard coming from the courtyard the sound of voices and the crunching of wheels over the gravel.

In the centre of the courtyard stood Aleksandr's horse and trap. Men in uniforms were beside it. Nanny Shalovchikha, in her night cap and with her shawl thrown over her shoulders, was talking to them. Yenya saw no sign of Aleksandr. Fear, ice cold, began to churn inside her.

At first, stunned and horrified as she was, Yenya did not realise the full implications of what had occurred. It was a blessed relief to learn the soldier was not killed and not even seriously wounded. Also, she reasoned naively, Aleksandr after all did not mean to hurt the sentry, but only intended to remove his gun. The terrible impact of the truth came later. The barracks and soldiers represented the defence of the realm. The young sentry defending the gates of the barracks was the Tsar's soldier. To attack him in any way was tantamount to treason. Treason demanded a heavy price.

The news spread quickly. All through the night relatives kept arriving at the house. The first to arrive were Yenya's parents Anna and Eugene. Franz and Amelia followed. Through the day brothers, sisters and friends continued to call. Like small birds, huddled together, weathering a storm, Yenya's parents and all who were close to her rallied round her. All wheels were set in motion to engage the best legal aid. Those who held important positions were approached and others who had friends in high places, even in distant towns, were assigned to use their influence. No money was spared. The best known advocate in St Petersburg was commissioned to defend Aleksandr.

Throughout that summer of anxiety, when the days alternated between hope and despair, Yenya still travelled every week to the market to buy all the provisions, bought berries and made jam. Salted cucumbers and cabbage. Dried mushrooms and herbs. Planned for the winter and supervised the house and garden. She kept herself occupied, but anxiety never left her. It was her constant grim companion throughout her waking hours. Sleep brought forgetfulness, awakening the anguish of reality.

The trial took place in the late autumn. Aleksandr was sentenced to Siberia.

The sentence plunged the family into despair. Amelia wept incessantly. Although the conditions in Siberia for political prisoners were almost benign when compared to the horrors that were to come four decades later, Amelia was convinced her son would never come back. Yenya, for the sake of her unborn child, hid her grief and remained calm.

No one expected the verdict to be so harsh. Yet it had to be recognised that during the reign of Aleksandr II, there had been a constant succession of revolutionary plots and so many attempts by the Nihilists to assassinate the Tsar who had freed the serfs, that it caused him to ask in despairing tones, "What have I done that they should hate me so?" It was not surprising therefore, that all laws and regulations were tightened and those who broke them were severely punished.

Once more all wheels were set in motion, this time to organise an appeal for clemency. They might have spared themselves the time and effort. The sentence stood.

The advocate who had worked untiringly on Aleksandr's behalf travelled from St Petersburg to Archangel. He still held one small trump, but found it was necessary to see the family before he could show it.

In those days there was no railway connecting Archangel to St Petersburg. People still used the horse as a means of conveyance just as they did in the time of Peter the Great. By now the whole of the north was in the grip of winter. After a cold and hazardous journey he arrived in Archangel and was welcomed to the house of Yenya.

Shortly after his arrival, on a dark November evening, there was a gathering round the dining-room table. All the nearest relatives were there. Margaretha, by now a widow of many years, came also. Her contemporaries, Feodosiya and the faithful retainer Nanny Shalovchikha sat together. Yenya sat between her parents.

The man who had done all he could briefly went over everything they knew already. He then quietly told them that there was still one avenue left.

There were certain days, he explained, during the sacred holidays of Christmas and Epiphany, when the Tsar exercised clemency to petitioners who made personal appeals to him. This could only be done by someone who was a close relative of the convicted person. Already enquiries had been made and the opportunity of presenting the appeal to the Tsar was possible. He turned to Yenya. "I am convinced," he said, "that you are the only one who could do this and the only one who would perhaps arouse the Tsar's compassion. Yet, I have to remind you that this journey may prove to be very dangerous. There would be the terrible cold and frost. A snowstorm could cut you off from all habitation. There are also wolves. A journey such as this in the dead of winter is not a pleasant prospect for any traveller, and in your condition, I fear it would be well-nigh impossible. However," he added, "I have no other solution to offer."

"I will go," Yenya said quietly. "There is no other way."

"Yes, she will go," echoed Anna. She took her daughter's hand between her own and held it firmly. "We shall travel together," she added.

One day, in early December, when a faint light was breaking through the darkness, a troika harnessed to a kibitka — the hooded carriage placed on runners — stood waiting at the front entrance. In the half-light shadowy figures could be seen hurrying from the house to the kibitka, carrying valises, pillows and packages.

From the time the advocate had left there had been endless preparations for the journey. The best driver was engaged — Stepan, as he was called, was renowned for his expert knowledge of the highway to St Petersburg. The manager of the mill, Pavel Mikhailovich, a man of great integrity, was assigned to accompany the ladies. All provisions had to be carried. The cook was kept working for days on end roasting partridges, baking pirozohkis and cookies. For a journey such as this the traveller had to be prepared for any eventuality. Yenya was now almost eight months pregnant. Anna hid her fears and prepared for the worst.

Now all the bustling was over. In the hall, relatives had gathered to see Yenya and her mother setting off on their memorable journey.

Yenya and her mother emerged, dressed in heavy shubas, fur hats and shawls. The moment of departure had arrived. Old Feodosiya moved over to her daughter. "Bogh Milostiv" — "God is merciful," she said and blessed her. Eugene kissed and blessed his wife and daughter; the others followed. "We must sit down now," he said. According to the old tradition, everyone sat down and for a moment remained silent. They then stood up and moved towards the door. Yenya and Anna were helped into the depth of the kibitka and sat huddled under shawls and bearskins. In front were Pavel Mikhailovich and Stepan.

Stepan, gathering the reins, made a clicking sound. The horses, accompanied by jingling bells, began to run towards the gates. There the servants had gathered to watch the kibitka drive through and turn down to the river. There had been a lot of talking amongst themselves. "God is too high and the Tsar too far away" goes the Russian saying, but here was their barynya setting off to see His Great Majesty to plead for her husband, and her so young and heavy with child. They wished her well and prayed for her.

From the windows, the troika was seen emerging on to the river. Running lightly in a wide arc, it turned to the left and halted. And then as if sensing the freedom of this boundless highway, the three horses fanned out in great style and, galloping at top speed, flashed away to the south.

Many years later, in 1920, during the troubled aftermath of the revolution, one autumn evening my grandmother asked me to spend the night with her in her room.

I remember that dark night. The wind beating against the trembling window panes, the stormy river. Babushka drew the curtains and, sitting down beside me, began to brush her hair. She talked of many things. I lay curled up on the edge of the big empty bed and listened. A crimson light from the bedside lamp cast a warm glow in our corner and lit up my grandmother's face. She had aged during that terrible year. Grief and anxiety had left their mark, but she still possessed the capacity to ignore the unhappy present and travel back to happier distant scenes of her childhood — youth, marriage, and on to the momentous journey to St Petersburg.

"Tomorrow," she said, "I have to leave you all and go to Dedushka, who needs me. It is strange, but forty years ago almost to a day, your own grandfather was also sent away and later, in the depth of the winter, I had to travel to St Petersburg and beg the Tsar himself to allow him to return. It was a difficult and at times a frightening journey, especially as I was expecting your father. My mamushka travelled with me and in front beside the driver sat Pavel

Mikhailovich. As for Stepan, the driver, there was just no one like him. We raced up the river and through the woods. No one was allowed to overtake us and to those who were in front he would call out, 'Doloi — Doloi' — 'Out of my road'. They would wave us on and laugh as we rushed by. Stepan was a bit of a devil, a joker, and known to be a great singer as well as the best driver in our parts. He joked and he sang and my mamushka, who knew all the songs, joined in. I could never sing like her. As for the baby, he just lay quietly inside his own special travelling case and never bothered me at all." She laughed a little at her own description. "He was always a patient child even then," she added quietly and fell silent for a moment. "You can't imagine," she went on again, "how beautiful were our woods when there were only the horses running along the roads and nothing was spoiled. The snowdrifts sparkled in the sun, slowly turning to a pale rose as the short day closed in. How enchanting were the encrusted trees, and the branches of the birches like fine silver lace, shimmering in the pale sunlight! In those days there were no thundering trains in our parts to frighten the wild animals. We saw so many of them — foxes, mink, the black-tailed little ermine scampering across the road. The blue-grey squirrels came out of their hiding places when the sun shone brightly and danced on the heavy laden branches of the pines, scattering the powdery snow around them."

These were the bright patches that sustained them as they journeyed on in their kibitka across the frozen marshes, rivers, woods and bare plains in conditions that would have tried the most hardened traveller, let alone a young, pregnant woman. Only those who have experienced such a journey by sledge can possibly conceive the discomfort of the restricted space inside the kibitka, to be endured for hours on end between the stations scattered far and wide, the lack of sanitation, the primitive conditions in the stations and above all the bitter onslaught of the elements. Anna Dimitrievna, who had seen the ravages caused by frostbite, was constantly scanning her daughter's face for the white tell-tale spots and rubbing her cheeks. The food in the baskets became frozen and between each station they had to take out the roasted partridges which they had brought with them, and hold them under their arms to thaw them out. Once they reached a station, the partridges were cut up and heated in the stove. There was always a boiling samovar, tea and bread provided. They would rest for a short time while the horses were being changed and then take to the road again. Time was precious and could not be wasted, for they never knew what might be in front of them.

The Russian is born to snow and frost. It is part of his being, especially in the north, but even to him there is a limit of endurance.

One day the troika set off in brilliant sunshine for a station a long way off. As they travelled, the temperature began to drop until it fell to such a level that a crow, frozen in mid-flight, dropped like a stone from the sky. That kind of frost was rare even in our parts. Everything became very still. The two hooded figures in front barely moved. No one spoke. It was difficult to breathe. Nostrils and eyelids kept sticking and breath turned to ice on the shawls pulled over their faces. The two women clung to each other for warmth. A thick rime like a shroud came down enveloping them all and obscuring the signposts. Only Stepan's intuition kept them on the road. The horses also were suffering. Snorting and throwing up their heads, they were fighting for breath. Stepan was forced to climb down and clear their nostrils of ice. The intense cold can dull the mind and just as they were reaching the dangerous stage when a somnolent indifference to their fate was setting in, the dark mass of the station came out of the mist.

It was impossible to thaw out quickly the food frozen into a solid mass, but the woman in the cottage brought out of the stove a big earthenware pot of baked buckwheat and warm milk. She placed a boiling samovar and a newly baked loaf of black bread on the table.

The cottage boasted a "gornitza" — a bedroom-cum-sitting room, reserved only for special guests and rarely used by the family. It was clean and humbly furnished. There was an ikon hanging in a corner and a lampada — the small perpetual light, in front of it. On the painted floor was a hand-made rug, but pride of place was given to a large bed piled high with feather mattresses and a pyramid of pillows.

Exhausted by their ordeal, Yenya and her mother dragged off their heavy shubas and felt boots and scrambling up the small steps beside the bed fell into the depth of warm softness and sweet oblivion. In the same room, on a mattress on the floor, slept Pavel Mikhailovich, but to Stepan was allotted the warmest corner in the cottage. He slept beside the children on top of the stove.

During the early hours of the morning, a wild blizzard followed the frost. It was impossible to go on. For three days, tormented by anxiety, they remained stranded in the cottage, but on the fourth day the weather cleared. The kibitka went off again, the horses struggling through deep snowdrifts on to the next post house.

The weather continued to improve. There were clear nights and the frost was bearable. One evening the troika set off for a village that was nearby and boasted better conditions than most stations. It was a peaceful starry night. The fresh, sturdy horses ran cheerfully along the moonlit path when suddenly for no apparent reason they bolted at great speed.

"Derzhityes — Volki — Hold on. There are wolves," Stepan called out. The horses had sensed before the passengers that there were wolves nearby. None were seen at first but as they peered into the darkness they saw the small green lights of eyes weaving through the trees and moving in the same direction as the sledge.

Anna Dimitrievna, who had a superstitious fear of wolves and firmly believed they were possessed by some evil power, crossed herself. "The power of the Cross protect us," she said, using the prayer that wards off all evil.

The horses, maddened by fear, now out of control, raced on. The kibitka bumped and swayed over the frozen ruts. Any moment it could turn over and they would be thrown out and perhaps killed. There was the added fear that the wolves would run to where the road and the wood met and cut them off from the village. Then in the dip of the road, there came into view the row of orange lights from the cottages. There, the villagers had heard the urgent ringing of the bells. A loud chorus of dogs, barking and howling, shattered the stillness of the night. The troika rushed through the open gates of the station and stopped inside the safety of its walls. The horses stood trembling in clouds of steam, foam dripping from their muzzles.

On the eleventh day after leaving Archangel, the troika entered the streets of St Petersburg. There were only three days to Christmas.

They drove slowly along the Nevsky Prospect, watching in silence the activity around them. The lit-up shops, small booths selling brightly coloured toys, sledges and carriages rushing by, people carrying parcels, the bustling on the streets, all told them that they had arrived in the midst of Christmas preparations.

All were too tired to absorb the beauty of the palaces, fine buildings and streets, and were thankful when the troika drew up beside the entrance of their hotel, where everything had been arranged, near the Winter Palace. There they stayed and waited.

A week went by. Pavel Mikhailovich was preparing for the return journey. It was imperative that they should leave as soon as the interview with the Tsar was over. Yenya was determined that her child would be born in Archangel and refused to contemplate any other place.

The old year passed away and the fateful year of 1881 took over.

A few days later, Yenya crossed the great square on her way to the Winter Palace. Her mother and Pavel Mikhailovich accompanied her as far as the heavily guarded entrance. From there she was escorted into the Palace and led into a waiting room. Other people were sitting there. All were silent, lost in their own thoughts. One by one, as their names were called, they left the room. Yenya never saw them again.

Then, at last she heard her own name. A fluttering, like the wings of some bird caught in a net, began inside her. She fought hard to appear calm as she was led to a room where on each side of the double doors stood the Tsar's own personal guards in resplendent uniforms. The doors opened and closed behind her. She was standing in the Tsar's study.

"As I entered the room," Babushka said, "I saw at the far end two uniformed men sitting behind a large desk. Of course, in the past I had seen portraits of the Tsar, but now I suddenly panicked. Both men were handsome, both appeared to be alike, but as I stood rooted to the floor asking myself which was the Tsar, one of them rose and walked towards me. I knew at once he was the Tsar. He was tall and possessed great majesty, yet that wasn't what overwhelmed me.... Never, never in all my life have I seen kinder or more compassionate eyes.... I forgot all the instructions and advice, all that I had to do and not to do.... I simply went down on my knees and wept." She paused for a moment then continued. "He helped me to my feet. 'Nye-nado, nye-nado'...'this isn't necessary,' he chided me gently. 'I know of your case,' he went on. 'I understand that you have come all the way from Archangel?' I nodded dumbly. He began to ask me all about the journey, Archangel, my family, and as he spoke simply, kindly — it came to me that after all the Tsar was just another human being like all his subjects with the same griefs, joys and frailties.

"At first I answered timidly, but gradually with more confidence. I sensed his genuine interest in our town, where once his illustrious ancestor Peter the Great built his first sea-going ship and sailed it across the White Sea. He mentioned our ancient Solovetsky Monastery on the islands in the White Sea. Had I ever been there? 'Oh yes, your Majesty,' I said. 'We go there almost every summer. It is beautiful. Your Majesty should see it.' The Tsar smiled. 'Perhaps one day I shall visit these places.' He fell silent for a moment. Then, looking down from his great height, he placed his hand on my shoulder and said the words which were to remain in my mind and heart for all time. 'Your husband is very fortunate to have you for his wife. Go back to Archangel. I give you my word that your child will have his father and you can tell his mother that her son will return. Go with God.' He said no more. The interview was over."

The following morning, after despatching a telegram to Archangel proclaiming the good news, they left St Petersburg.

Fate, always capricious, now favoured them. There was no fog, and the clear crisp frost, although intensely cold, was not followed by blinding blizzards. The troika kept up speed on the highways and

skimmed over lakes and rivers. Villages, churches, woods and fields
flashed by. Fresh horses available in all the post houses avoided any
delay. They halted only for the barest necessities, refreshed themselves, drank some hot tea and drove on. A sense of achievement and
of great exaltation spurred them on. Yenya herself, now in the last
stages of pregnancy, and suffering acute discomfort in the confined
space of the kibitka, was sustained by the Tsar's promise. "The Tsar
has promised — the Tsar will keep his word," she kept repeating to
herself like the words of some happy song. On the other hand, Anna,
always calm and an inspiration to them all, now became worried and
agitated. Her experienced eye had told her that the position of the
child had changed and that the birth could be imminent.

Stepan, who drove with his usual skill and sang happily at the
prospect of being well rewarded for his achievement and of returning
to his own young wife and his children, had to bear the brunt of
Anna's impatience. "Faster, faster," she would command him and
when he complied and the kibitka rolled and leaped over ruts, she
would call out in anger, "Do you wish to kill my daughter?" It was
impossible to please her. She worried when in the heat of the post
houses Yenya's face became flushed and she worried when Yenya was
cold. Exasperated, Yenya turned on her mother. "What is all this fuss
about, Mamushka? We could always reach a village and a midwife if
need be, and if the worst came to the worst you would know what to
do." Anna was horrified. Before leaving Archangel she had listened to
some instructions on what to do in case of an emergency. It all
sounded very simple. Now her confidence had vanished and the
thought of risking her daughter's life terrified her.

After seven days of hard driving, the troika approached the last
station before Archangel on the morning of 12 January. They were
met by a strange sight. Moving towards them was a long train of
sledges, pulled by single or double horses or the inevitable troikas.
There was the sound of laughing, singing and someone playing a
concertina. As they drew nearer, each sledge moved to the side of the
road and waited. When the kibitka approached and passed the row of
sledges, loud cheering rent the air. Passengers and drivers were
waving and throwing up their hats. Then all the sledges turned round
and escorted the kibitka.

In this manner the whole cavalcade, accompanied by the jingling of
bells, music and singing, arrived at the station. A great reception
awaited them in a hall booked by Yenya's father-in-law. In his
expansive way, he had ordered food and drink to be brought from
Archangel. A lavish table was spread for all the guests. Midst laughter
and cheering, Stepan and Pavel Mikhailovich were regaled with the

old time-honoured custom of being tossed several times up in the air and carried shoulder high inside the hall.

The success of the mission was celebrated in the traditional manner by eating and drinking, singing and dancing, until finally the kibitka — still followed by her lively retinue — set off on her last lap of some eight miles to Archangel.

The short day was drawing to a close when the horses approached the river. The winter sun was vanishing fast behind the dark line in the west, but the slanting rays still splashed the sky in crimson and gold. From the east could be seen the sombre kibitka and her troika in the midst of the picturesque entourage racing across the river bathed in the rosy glow of the sunset.

In gathering darkness the wearied horses and passengers were nearing their journey's end. A few sledges still followed the kibitka as it glided slowly through the gates and halted beside the front entrance.

Not waiting to be assisted, ignoring her condition, the pain in her cramped limbs, Yenya scrambled out and struggling up the staircase the best way she could, entered the hall. They were all there waiting for her. In their midst stood Amelia holding her little granddaughter. Yenya took her child and held her close to herself. She carried her through to the dining-room and sat down at the table.

A second reception was being prepared. Friends and relatives kept arriving and more places had to be found. Chairs were carried from other rooms, extra food from the kitchen. Stepan and Pavel Mikhailovich were given the honour of sitting at the top of the table. It was a happy but a more contained gathering. Those who had traversed the long distance were exhausted. The hollowed eyes, the white, drawn faces told their own story. The impetus which drove them on regardless of their own well-being was no longer there. The men had suffered most. They had slept in short snatches, at times exchanging the reins and dozing fitfully in their seats, while exposed to the bitter elements. They had achieved what they set out to do, but now reaction was setting in leaving no desire for any further celebrations.

Gradually the house emptied. Only those staying overnight remained.

Earlier in the day orders had been given to clear the path to the banya, or bath-house, lying in the far corner of the garden. The banya was heated, brass basins polished, small wooden tubs scrubbed white and bundles of birch twigs laid out beside the folded sheets on the benches.

Yenya, her mother and Babushka Feodosiya, accompanied by a

young servant girl, crossed into the garden and walked along the avenue between the sleeping snow-clad birches. After undressing in the small ante-room of the banya, they entered the adjoining chamber where they were immediately enveloped in steam and heat. No bathing in Russia is complete without the ritual of beating the body with the birch twigs, to promote the circulation and a sense of well-being. This was followed by scrubbing, sluicing and massaging until all weariness was shed and they lay relaxed on the benches. Back in the house there was the welcome purring of the samovar, tea and cloud-berry jam, soft lamplight and all-pervading peace.

For a whole week Yenya and her mother had been denied the comfort of a bed. Now, in her own bedroom, lying between fine sheets, sleep eluded Yenya. She still heard the monotonous jingling of the bells and felt the swaying of the kibitka. On the other side of the wide double-bed Anna slept soundly. Finally Yenya also drifted into a dreamless sleep. She was awakened in the early hours of the morning by a painful stabbing in her back. "Mamushka," she called softly to her mother. Anna immediately sat up. "Thank God we are back in time," were her first words. The whole house became alive. Lamps were lit, footsteps hurried across the hall and down to the kitchen. Someone ran out into the courtyard to arouse the coachman. His sledge rushed out through the gates and soon returned, bringing the midwife. The doctor followed.

Yenya's labour continued throughout the whole of the day and into the late evening of 13 January, when my father was born.

He was a small baby. Smaller than usual with finely chiselled features. His arrival was earlier than Yenya expected. The clothing prepared for him was too large and smaller garments had to be made in a hurry. Many years later Babushka gave them to me and I was able to dress my doll in them.

Yenya named her son Gherman after St Gherman of the Solovetsky Monastery. He was the first saintly man to inhabit the holy island of Solovets on the White Sea. Throughout his childhood and even later my father was known to his relatives and friends as Ghermosha, the diminutive of his name. At the last minute, for some reason, the pleasant and healthy young woman engaged as a wet mother was not available. Another nurse had to be urgently found, for although Yenya was only too willing to nurse her own child, she was unable to do so. The new nurse was known as Seraphima.

I remember Seraphima. A tall, gaunt woman with harsh features, deep-set dark eyes and iron-grey hair. She was deeply attached to my father, but had no time for my mother nor yet us children. My great-aunt Tyotya Peeka once, in a burst of confidence, informed my mother that Seraphima tippled, but by the time this unfortunate trait had been discovered it was too late. Seraphima had the quaint habit of hiding somewhere inside her numerous petticoats a bottle of vodka. Often while suckling little Ghermosha, and possibly feeling bored with life, she would take a swig from the bottle.

As her own child was left in the village, she became deeply attached to her small charge, was untiring in her devotion and fiercely jealous of any interference. In spite of her many strange ways, the loud harsh voice resounding through the house when she sung her lullabies, she was accepted by Yenya. Seraphima loved much — therefore much was forgiven.

The baby thrived. His thin little legs and arms filled out and he became an attractive child.

One day in late February, when already there was a faint promise of spring, a hired sledge drove up to the back entrance. A tall, thin man, shabby and pale-faced, stepped out and after paying off the driver and collecting a few belongings walked through the passage into the kitchen. Aleksandr had returned.

Nanny Shalovchikha, assisting in some task in the kitchen, threw up her hands and hurried to embrace him. "At last God has answered my prayers," she exclaimed, overcome by emotion. The homely faces he knew so well encircled him with their affection. Everything was just as it was. The scrubbed deal table, the kitchen chairs, the copper pots, the food cooking on the range and the warm smell of the bread baking in the great stove. A young servant, eager to be the bearer of glad tidings to the barynya, ran towards the door leading upstairs, but Aleksandr stopped her.

He climbed the back stairs and opened the door of the nursery. In this sunlit room, Yenya, engrossed in her embroidery, was sitting beside the children. She raised her head and saw Aleksandr framed in the doorway. Bursting into tears, she rushed across the room and threw herself into his arms.

Olga, recognising her father, was overjoyed and yet bewildered. Her papa, the loving man whom she associated with toys and sweets and many happy times, had one day suddenly vanished and now just as suddenly had appeared again and to her delight was throwing her up and kissing her just as he did before.

The baby, wide awake, was lying peacefully in his cot. Aleksandr lifted him gently and held the small bundle against his breast. To Yenya it seemed as if from a long distance away the words, never to be forgotten, were echoing back. "I give you my word your child will have his father."

7

The christening of the baby took place a few days after Aleksandr's return. The font was brought from the church and placed in the drawing room.

The following day the horrifying news of the Tsar's assassination reached Archangel. The whole of Russia was shaken.

Every Sunday it was the Tsar's custom to attend a cavalry parade in the grounds of the Mikhailovo Palace and occasionally pay a call on his cousin the Grand Duchess Catherina. For weeks the assassins had watched the Tsar's movements and were now stationed on the street where the Tsar and his retinue were due to pass. Soon the carriage, flanked on either side by cossacks in scarlet Circassian coats, mounted on black horses, came into view, followed closely by sledges carrying the Chief of Police and uniformed functionaries.

The first bomb exploded under the back axle of the carriage, killing two guards, horses and an innocent young baker's boy delivering bread. The Tsar was unharmed. Disregarding the advice that he should hurry back to the Palace, he stepped out of the carriage and walked over to see what assistance could be given to those lying on the snow. Seeing they were beyond help he turned back to his carriage and was heard to say, "God has spared me again, but what of the wounded?" At this moment another of the assassins cried, "You are mistaken, Aleksandr," and threw the second bomb. It landed at the Tsar's feet. When the smoke cleared the Tsar was seen lying with one of his legs torn off and his body terribly injured. He was alive and still had enough strength to say, "Take me home." Then he lapsed into unconsciousness. He was rushed to the Palace and carried into his study. Princess Yurievskaya, his former mistress and since the death of the Empress his morganatic wife, threw herself in utter despair over the blood-soaked body calling out his name, but the Tsar was now beyond all hearing. He died soon after.

Such was the reward of the "Tsar Liberator", the man who lived by his resolve to do good for his people, who freed the serfs and planned to further their lot, who abolished corporal punishment, instituted the jury system and established equality for all before the law. On the very morning of his death he was working on a charter which would have set Russia on the road to a Parliamentary Government.

No one of all the sorrowing subjects grieved more than my grandmother. A mere few weeks earlier she had seen him alive and well. In the packed cathedral where the Requiem was held, she knelt beside the weeping congregation and prayed with all her heart for the soul of the martyred Tsar. In the years to come, on each anniversary of his death, she would light a candle to his memory.

A public hanging of the murderers took place in St Petersburg. During the course of his reign Aleksandr II was subjected to many attempts on his life and each time miraculously escaped the fate which in the end overtook him. Had the assassins succeeded earlier than they did in killing the Tsar, the journey my grandmother undertook to St Petersburg would never have taken place. Aleksandr III, in his bitter anger over the death of his father, would have been most unlikely to consider any amnesty. As it happened, during that short period before the fatal Sunday, 13 March 1881, luck favoured Yenya.

Aleksandr III was a man totally opposite in character to that of his murdered father. Renowned for his size and physical strength, who with perfect ease could bend a fork or a coin, tear a pack of cards in two halves with his bare hands, he was also a man who refused to tolerate anything that might remotely endanger the security and order of the state. One of his first decrees was to cancel many of the reforms granted by his father. The universities were especially affected and all those who spread revolutionary ideas were promptly expelled or banished to Siberia. Those who were caught plotting further assassinations were summarily executed. Among them was Aleksandr Ulyanoff, the brother of Lenin.

A second son was born to Yenya and Aleksandr. They named him Aleksandr, but he was known as Sanya, one of the several diminutives of his full name. Blue-eyed, fair-haired, he was a sturdier child than his elder brother.

Not long after Sanya's birth, died Margaretha Caroline, the proud matriarch of the family. She was followed by her contemporary, Babushka Feodosiya, the teller of fine tales from Kaluga. Only Nanny Shalovchikha, their other contemporary, lived on. Like a small but sturdy old tree she weathered all storms.

One day when Ghermosha was five years old, and she in her eighties, he asked her if should would take him for a walk in the garden. It was a beautiful spring day. Not a trace of snow remained on the lawns and paths, but the pond shimmered like a white saucer under a thin layer of snow and ice. They were walking slowly along the winding paths when, unexpectedly, in the manner of all children, Ghermosha darted ahead and leaped on to the pond. There was an ominous crack as the child vanished below the ice. Never hesitating, the old woman threw herself after him. Breaking the ice all round her she succeeded in grasping Ghermosha and dragging him back to the safety of the bank. From there, holding the half-conscious child to her breast, she ran stumbling and weeping to the house where, refusing all assistance to herself, she did not rest until she saw her charge revived, warm and safe in bed. Then and only then did she retreat downstairs to her own small room where she proceeded to doctor herself with her various herbal cures. She slept soundly all night in her feathered bed. The following morning neither she nor little Ghermosha were any the worse for their experience.

The winter of 1889-90 was remembered for a long time for its severity. It abounded with terrible frosts and blizzards. Many a man, setting off for the opposite shore of the river, would suddenly find himself in the grip of a blizzard. It would engulf and blind him, until, walking in circles and losing all sense of direction, he would lie down to die, overcome by exhaustion.

That winter, in the beginning of the new year, Ghermosha was approaching his ninth birthday. The past year had been especially exciting and happy. In the early autumn he had been accepted to the boys' gymnasium named after Mikhail Lomonosov — the great genius of the north. Ghermosha loved the school, the black uniform and silver buttons, the long trousers, the strong leather belt and silver buckle engraved with the initials of the school. Above all he loved the companionship of his school friends, all the fun and noise that went with it.

On 13 January it would be Ghermosha's birthday. He was allowed to have a party. A few of his cousins and favourite school-friends were coming. Already his mamushka had made a very special cake and only the final decorations remained to be added later. The Christmas tree was still standing. The candles would be lit to celebrate his birthday, as was the custom every year, and on the following day it would be removed.

Some days before his son's birthday, Aleksandr was driving home from Maimaksa in the early evening. The frost was unusually severe, but the night was clear and peaceful. The sky, a deep sapphire, was lit up by a luminous assembly of stars stretching across the heavens. Aleksandr was well muffled and warmly clad in his sheepskin shuba. A bearskin rug protected his knees.

Behind some cottages to the east, a crimson glow appeared in the sky and fanned out. Fires were common in these timber regions, but too often the distant fire brigade arrived only to find a heap of smouldering ashes. At the onset of a fire, the people themselves had learned to help each other the best way they could. Knowing this custom, Aleksandr turned and, driving fast, arrived at the scene of the outbreak.

A church was burning. Already the flames like giant tongues were greedily licking the walls, threatening to devour them. Men and women had formed a long chain down to the water-hole in the river, and were hurriedly passing buckets to each other. Others were running with ladders, ropes and hatchets. Ikons salvaged from the church lay piled on the snow.

A man standing high on a ladder, defying the smoke and flames, was endeavouring to quench the flames which were engulfing a vital part of the wall. Aleksandr joined the chain which was struggling to pass the buckets. The water spilling on the ground was turning to ice. People slid, stumbled, fell and carried on. Those fighting close to the walls suffered more, for they had to bear the scorching heat, the acrid smoke which stung their eyes and throats and, worst of all, the ice-cold water pouring down their heads and drenching their clothes. Yet, in spite of primitive methods and the appalling sub-zero temperature, in the end the fire was extinguished and the church saved. The people, too exhausted to express any jubilation, quietly began to disperse. Aleksandr climbed into his sledge. He unwisely refused to avail himself of the kindly offer of a hot meal and a change of clothing. He was already late and in any case, he explained, the journey was short. His patient horse once more set off along the familiar road, but soon the intense frost turned his clothing into solid ice and he was attacked by an uncontrollable fit of shivering, followed by a strange lethargy. The reins fell from his hands. The horse, with the reins trailing on the snow, instinctively carried on and ran into the courtyard.

Aleksandr was carried into the house and his frozen clothing removed. The restorative treatment, which is common knowledge to those brought up in these regions, was applied to revive him, until he gradually came round and was taken to his bed. All night Yenya anxiously watched over him. In the morning, although still tired, Aleksandr was almost his usual self. The doctor came and after a thorough examination assured them. Through the day Aleksandr remained cheerful. The sun shone through the frosted windows and the children came in with their toys and played in the bedroom. Amelia came and, after hearing her son laughing and joking, went away reassured. Yenya still anxiously watched him. During the night Aleksandr was restless and talked a lot in his sleep, and in the morning Yenya noticed that his face was flushed and the eyes appeared to be heavy. The doctor called again and repeated his examination, but this time said very little. Later to Yenya he admitted privately that he suspected pneumonia was setting in.

The house became very quiet. Everyone, even the children, spoke in whispers. It was as if some unseen presence had entered the house.

In the early morning of 13 January, Aleksandr asked Yenya if she would send for the priest. Swallowing her tears, she obeyed. The old father, who was the priest in the Church of the Assumption and who had christened all her children, came at once. He administered the Last Rites. After the priest left, the children came into the bedroom and stood beside their father. He was unable to say anything. His breathing became more laboured and he lapsed into unconsciousness.

In the afternoon of the day of his son's birthday Aleksandr died.

In the ballroom where only recently there had been a happy gathering, the Christmas tree was stripped of all decorations and removed to the woodshed.

In its place now stood the coffin. At a small table, an old man dressed in a cassock sat reading the prayers for the dead. His whispering, like the rustling of dry leaves in the autumn, was to be heard in the room for the next two days.

People called and spoke in muted tones. Olga, alone in her room, saw no one. The boys, their young faces bewildered, remained in the nursery with their babushka, Anna. Their paternal babushka arrived with her daughters and son.

Amelia, who in the course of three years had lost her husband, her brother Eugene, a son and daughter in the bloom of their youth, now, on seeing her dead son, became distraught with grief. She clung to him, kissing him, stroking his hair and calling him by all the endearing names of his childhood, until Nanny Shalovchikha gently led her away to the nursery.

In the evening the first of the funeral services took place. With her children beside her, amidst relatives and friends holding lighted candles, Yenya stood listening to the solemn intonations of the priest, the mournful singing of the responses. Her eyes kept turning to the coffin lit up by the candles in the candelabra. The still face held a serenity and somehow looked young again, recalling the distant scenes of their youth. Their years together had flashed by like the flight of a bird leaving a sense of desolation, the awesome finality of death.

According to the laws of the Russian Orthodox Church, on the third and last night after his death, Aleksandr's body was removed from his home and taken to the Church of the Assumption. There he was left alone to spend the last night within the consecrated walls of the church until the following morning, when the final funeral service took place.

The church was packed by relatives, friends, acquaintances and the usual assemblage of curious onlookers. At the end of the lengthy Requiem there was the last homage, the last farewell. One by one each member of the congregation came up to the coffin to kiss the hand which held a small ikon. The coffin was closed and carried to the hearse.

Outside in front of the porch in the bitter frost a procession was forming. The mourners walked behind the hearse drawn by horses in their funereal trappings.

The old priest led the procession. Behind him, long mourning veils hiding their faces, walked young Olga, clutching her mother' hand, and Amelia. In their wake, trudging along the frostbound road strewn with conifer branches, contrasting vividly against the snow, was the long dark line of mourners.

To reach the cemetery, about an hour's walk away, they had to endure the sub-zero temperature, the sudden gusts of bitter wind. Yet faithful to the old tradition they bore their ordeal to the end. Only the very old and weak took to the sledges driving slowly in the rear.

In the cemetery, the frozen earth had been broken for the grave. Aleksandr's coffin was gently lowered into his resting place close to his father. The priest read a short service and threw a handful of frozen clay on to the coffin and the others followed suit. The choir took up the chanting of "Vechnaya Pamyat" — "Eternal Memory". Their plaintive voices, rising and falling, drifted over the snow-covered mounds and faded into the distance.

Outside the cemetery, sledges had gathered to take the mourners back. One final ritual remained. In the house the table was being prepared for the traditional "Pomeenki", or wake. Special food was served and a bowl of "kootya" was passed round; each person took a spoonful of the preparation of boiled rice and raisins and made the sign of the cross in memory of the deceased.

The "Pomeenki", like the wake in Ireland and the comforting cup of tea in Scotland, have one thing in common. This is when relatives and friends, some after a long lapse of time, meet with each other. For a few hours the bereaved will not think on what may await them tomorrow and lay aside their burden of grief and anxiety. They talk about mundane matters, reminisce, laugh and recall incidents long forgotten.

In the early evening the house gradually emptied. The last of the sledges glided through the gates and was swallowed in the darkness.

The dreary winter months went by. An unusual resilience and moral courage, combined with a religious fatalism, maintained Yenya. There was a certain comfort in the knowledge that at least she was spared all the financial difficulties and humiliations that befall less fortunate women. Aleksandr had made sure that she would be well endowed and have no difficulties in running the household in the way she was accustomed to. She was in fact quite wealthy. Each child likewise was well provided for and according to his will and the law of the country, the eldest son would eventually inherit the house and the grounds.

Such then was the position. At the same time the previous shared responsibilities of bringing up the children, the running of the house and garden now fell solely on Yenya's shoulders. With an energy that allowed no time to sit and weep, she threw herself into all she was committed to do.

8

Two years went by. Then my grandmother, an attractive woman with a lively personality and in the prime of her life, met and married a well-known surgeon in the town.

My memories of my step-grandfather, Aleksandr Egorovich Popov, are of an unusually tall, broad-shouldered man whose serious face reflected his fine intelligence. The dark eyes were sometimes humorous and sometimes strict. I have no recollection of ever hearing him laughing although at times a broad smile would unexpectedly light up his grave countenance like a flash of bright sunlight. His integrity and entire devotion to his work always commanded respect from all who came in contact with him.

As a child I was given to singing cheerfully to myself when absorbed in some ploy. At times, completely overcome by my own exuberance, I would sing at the top of my voice until suddenly I would hear the familiar authoritative voice: "Jenka, stop your roaring." Dedushka stood no nonsense.

Aleksandr Egorovich was a man of independent means who might have preferred to begin his married life in a home of his own, but because of all the complexities connected with the house and the garden for which Yenya was responsible and, no doubt, after many discussions, he moved into the house of his predecessor.

The three children were sent abroad to boarding school — Ghermosha, aged eleven, and Sanya, two years younger, to Riga on the Baltic: Olga, now fourteen, to Germany and later to a finishing school in France. They could only get home in the summer and Christmas vacations. I have often asked myself why this uprooting was necessary. A mere two years earlier, they had lost their father.

Now, they were leaving the security and affection of their home, and above all their mother. Perhaps the all-knowing Tyotya Peeka gave the answer when she said to my mother once: "Yenya did not want to burden Aleksandr Egorovich with the children and just packed them off to boarding school."

A daughter, Margarita, was born of the second marriage: and then two sons, Seryozha and Gheorgie (known as Yura). The young faces of the new "mamkas" could be seen coming and going between the villages and the house.

Of the three former "mamkas", only one made a regular appearance. Seraphima would sit in the kitchen, waiting patiently for the moment when the child she had suckled would be back again, her dark eyes flashing defiance at anyone who might have the temerity to question her presence.

Four years later, having completed her education abroad, Olga returned to her old home. She was now eighteen. Tall, slender with laughing hazel eyes, fine features and dark hair, she had blossomed into an attractive young woman. She was fond of her stepfather, but unlike her two young brothers, who now referred to him as Papa, she always addressed him as Aleksandr Egorovich — to her there had only been one father and no one could ever replace him.

One day, in the house of a friend, she was introduced to Oscar Semyonovich Yanooshkovsky, a young man attached to the Civil Service. The following year they were married and later when Oscar was moved to a more important post in Finland, they settled in Helsinki.

When Sanya finished his education, he came back from Riga. He did not join the family business; after a period of indolence he bought an interest in a gold mining company in Siberia and travelled there. Later he sold his share and returned to Archangel. I have no recollections of him being concerned in any other business.

To Gherman, the University of Riga presented a lively contrast to school. Like many another student living away from home, receiving a regular allowance and being spared the irksome interference by relatives, Ghermosha was a law unto himself. He followed the path where life was gay and free from care. Although intelligent and with a remarkable gift for languages, he was not particularly studious.

Olga once paid him an unexpected visit and found him in bed. "Are you ill?" she asked anxiously. "Yes, ill," came the whispered reply. Olga placed her cool hand on what appeared to be an equally cool forehead. "Tell me," she said, settling down on the edge of the bed, "just what, exactly, are you up to?"

Olga had a way with her brother. It transpired that Kostya, one of his best friends, was in dire financial difficulties which had culminated in demands and threats. In despair, he went to Ghermosha who, having spent all his allowance for the moment, had nothing to give him. Undaunted, he took off his student's uniform and told Kostya to take it to the pawnshop. Of course, he admitted to Olga, it was not very convenient to be left with only one's underwear, but it would only be for another week! Then his next allowance would arrive and all would be well. Needless to say, it was Olga who redeemed his clothes.

When Gherman finally returned from Riga, he imagined it would be for good. Then he found himself embarking on another journey, to Scotland. Now he was back, with his Scottish bride.

While Gherman was searching for a house to suit their requirements, Nelly and he lived with the family. In this way Nelly was gradually drawn into it and got to know all the members intimately. Babushka took her everywhere she went. A close bond of affection developed between them. Nelly's parents, although no doubt loving their children, were not given to displaying their feelings. Babushka's warmth and open-hearted nature surprised and gladdened Nelly so that she in turn responded in the same way.

To all friends and relatives Nelly became "Nellynka", but those outside the family circle referred to her by the more formal patronymic of Elena Avgustovna — meaning Helen, daughter of Augustus. She was fond of the two little boys who followed their pretty sister-in-law all over the house. Yura, now five, was a lively, precocious child whose tawny colouring earned him the nickname "Pyzhik"—the baby reindeer. Seryozha, his elder brother, was a quiet, sensitive child. Their sister Marga, aged ten, attended the girls' gymnasium and every morning set off to school in a sledge and returned after lunch. Nelly found her attractive in her brown school uniform, with healthy colouring, large expressive dark eyes and wavy hair braided into a long plait down to her waist. At times warm and affectionate, and then in turn withdrawn and silent, she puzzled Nelly. She was a nervous child, terrified of the dark and unable to sleep alone. This fear resulted in the governess, Fraulein Valle, having to share her bedroom with Marga.

Fraulein Valle, a young German girl, and Nelly were drawn to each other and became quite friendly perhaps because both were foreigners and far from their own homes. Fraulein Valle was an inveterate smoker, but as Babushka did not approve of a governess smoking in front of the children, she was often forced to find a place where they could not follow her. With Nelly's arrival there were more opportunities to indulge, and when she had a little time to herself she would go to Nelly's room and produce her cigarettes. Soon Nelly also became addicted to the Russian cigarettes. Both young women liked to sit and chatter together in English and German while they smoked these cigarettes with their long cardboard holders.

What at first surprised Nelly but was later accepted by her as the way of life was the constant procession of friends, relatives, mamkas, old believers and pilgrims who frequented the house. There were also those who could only be described as hangers-on. There was, for instance, Sashenka. Sashenka, brought up in an orphanage, was a very odd child but endowed with a fine brain. Rejected by the other children, she aroused the compassion of my grandfather, who removed her from the orphanage and saw that she received a higher education. She eventually qualified as a teacher and became the headmistress of a small school endowed by the merchants in the town.

This new and fresh school had a separate small wing where Sashenka was provided with a bedroom, living-room, kitchen and the usual back premises. Two old women were likewise given their living quarters and employed to keep the school clean and attend to Sashenka's wants. This arrangement would have pleased most teachers, but Sashenka had other ideas. She decided instead to adopt the family. Every day at the end of school hours Sashenka could be seen winding her way down Olonetskaya Street. On entering the house, she took over all the duties she considered were her sole right.

She never sat with the family at the dinner table, but removed the plates to the adjoining round table for the maid to carry them away, while she humbly sat all on her own and ate what was passed over to her.

At night, she presided over the samovar at the table where everyone gathered. She poured out the tea and passed the cups. Late in the evening, she vanished. Not to her own little schoolhouse, but to the small landing beside the door leading to the garrett where stood an old wooden chest. There, on a thin mattress and covered by an old quilt, Sashenka slept. In the early morning she rose and walked back to her school to teach the children.

Sashenka was odd. I see quite clearly the short dark hair brushed severely back from her plain face, the black, mannish jacket, the dangling pince-nez, dowdy skirt and buttoned boots. The children teased her, those who were older insulted her. It was all as nothing. As long as Babushka didn't reject her, and Babushka never would, she would continue coming to the house.

With the arrival of the young Scottish bride, something crept into Sashenka's breast. She was overcome by a strange obsession. It expressed itself by an obsequious devotion in every possible way. When Nelly was sitting down to dinner, Sashenka was there pushing in her chair. She was there holding out the shuba when Nelly was preparing to go out, and kneeling on the floor pulling the felt boots over Nelly's feet with loving care.

At first amused and later irritated, Nelly was at a loss as to what to do.

And then there was the incident with the bath. One evening after returning with Babushka and young Marga from the banya, her damp hair streaming down her back, Nelly casually, and perhaps with faint nostalgia, remarked that although the city banya was an excellent institution, she still missed the convenience of the bath in her home in Scotland. This remark wasn't lost on Sashenka. A few days later a monstrous-looking zinc bath was dragged from the garrett and carried down to the maids' bedroom adjoining the kitchen.

This bath was obviously created by the possessor of an original mind who, in a flight of fancy, designed a bath unusually large and high and with a unique action similar to that of a rocking chair or seesaw. Once inside, the bather could enjoy the simulated waves of the sea as the foaming water rushed up to his neck or down to his feet. Unfortunately, any pleasure derived from this contraption was cancelled out by the necessity of possessing great agility and steady feet to avoid falling on the floor when attempting to get out of it.

Nelly was to have her bath. The family displayed a lively interest, but none more ardent and enthusiastic than the chief organiser of the whole project — Sashenka. And when the great moment came for Nelly who, like Aphrodite, was to rise out of the foam, Sashenka would be there, holding the bath-sheet, all set to catch and envelop Nelly.

Nelly, by no means anxious to have this bath, duly appeared in the kitchen in her dressing-gown. An eager crowd had collected there. The Russians have very few inhibitions regarding the naked body. The cook and the maids all were willing and anxious to assist the young barynya in her unusual ablutions. Standing at the door was Sashenka holding a bath-sheet. The door, unfortunately, had no lock. Sashenka's intentions were immediately obvious. Nelly sent for Gherman and when he arrived ordered him to guard the door and allow no one under any circumstances to enter the room. That, she added, stood for him as well. With these words she vanished behind the door, but emerged shortly, red in the face and with an angry glint in her eyes. She passed no comment and hurried up to her bedroom. The experience of floundering up and down in her rocking bath and, in her vain attempts to get out, tumbling out of it, was never to be repeated.

In a street known as the Technical Street, close to his old home, Gherman rented a single-storeyed house of some six rooms. The rooms were spacious and light. The windows in the west wall over-looked the shady garden of the adjoining Technical School. From the french doors of what eventually was to become the nursery, steps went down to a small garden where Nelly enthusiastically planted many colourful annuals. In the courtyard were stables and outhouses. Mikhailo, was the "kazachok" in the other house, the boy engaged to deliver messages and at the beck and call of everyone, was now promoted to coachman. The two handsome horses Gherman bought were the pride and joy of Mikhailo's life and he spent many happy hours grooming and taking care of them. A young kazachok was engaged to assist him as well as all the others in the house. His name was Pavel Tarasoff. A cook named Annushka, her assistant Manya, and a general servant, Irisha, completed the household.

With amazing adaptability and cheerfulness Nelly accepted the way of life so far removed from what she was accustomed to. She was not dismayed by the long dark days, the terrible frosts and blizzards such as she had never believed to be possible. She could not sit beside the comforting glow of a fireplace, for no such thing existed, but the Russian stoves reaching up to the ceiling kept the house much warmer than her home in Scotland. She sat beside a lamplit table doing her embroidery or reading the novels of her favourite author, Marie Corelli, banned by her parents and often snatched from her hands as unsuitable reading for young ladies.

There was this lack of sanitation, but everything was arranged very nicely. The pride of place in the "little room" was the fine porcelain bath imported from abroad. That it had neither taps nor any outlet did not unduly trouble Nelly. Willing hands filled and emptied it and Nelly had her bath in cosy comfort. Nevertheless, in the end she found it more convenient to follow the custom of the others and regularly attended the banya in the town.

Gradually the house took shape. Furniture, carpets, dishes and the fine glass ordered in Moscow duly arrived. The boxes from Scotland were opened and the contents arranged as Nelly wished. She was now the mistress of her own home and did not ask for more.

Life was gay in Archangel during the first decade of this century and up to the time of the First World War. It was also considered to be the most cosmopolitan town in Russia.

I remember my mother recalling her first party. Madame Surkova, the wife of a wealthy brewer, was celebrating her name-day. The invitation was for tea at 9 p.m. That meant, Gherman explained, full evening dress. "Full evening dress for a cup of tea?" was my mother's comment. "How odd!"

When they arrived at the party, their hostess was in the drawing-room, presiding over a silver samovar. "Come here, my dear," she said to Nelly. "Perhaps you speak to me about your interesting England — yes?" My mother was by now accustomed to hearing her beloved country referred to as England.

Young maids with trays of cups and tiny cakes mingled with the guests. Then the samovar was whisked away and tables were wheeled in, loaded with three shades of caviar — grey, black and deep orange, marinated herring, smoked salmon, ham pâté, lobsters and cheeses. This was accompanied by an assortment of vodka and a liqueur much favoured by ladies — ribinovka, distilled from rowan berries.

The night wore on. When everyone appeared satiated, the tables were removed. Nelly took this to be a sign that the party was drawing to a close. She signalled to Gherman, who was in conversation with a group of men. He merely shook his head and continued talking. Exactly on the stroke of midnight, the butler announced dinner. Nelly was escorted in by her host and placed beside him. There followed a gargantuan feast — consommé with mushroom pirozhkies, sturgeon in wine, partridge breasts in cream, pancakes stuffed with caviar, a meat course, and then ice-cream of various flavours and fruit.

Back in the drawing-room coffee was served. In the ballroom young people were taking to the floor. The married ladies sat gossiping for a while, but in the end left in their sledges. Their husbands retreated to the study where they played cards long after their wives were home and sleeping. At six o'clock breakfast was served after which the last of the "Tea Party" returned to their homes, changed and departed for business as usual.

9

During her sojourn in Russia, my mother corresponded regularly with her family, but especially with her brother Henry. Much of her correspondence with him was written on picture postcards of the town and of aspects of life there. She wrote mainly about domestic matters — the purchase of two new horses, a trip in a troika, Shrove week and pancakes, colouring Easter eggs, the Easter service, the weather, holidays, mosquitos in the garden. And then one of momentous significance: "Dear Henry — I have received such glad news. Papa and mama are coming for a short visit. They are sailing from Leith on a cargo ship and returning on the same ship. Papa has suddenly decided to visit Russia, but perhaps you already know this? It will be lovely to see them again if even for a short time. I am so excited. Love, Nelly." Soon after this postcard was sent off to India, my grandparents arrived in Archangel. Later it transpired that grandfather, true to himself, had one day surprised the family during his lunch hour by casually announcing that he had booked two berths on a cargo ship sailing from Leith to Archangel. Granny, who had never been out of the British Isles and harboured a secret longing to see something of the world outside them was overjoyed. This was also a heaven-sent opportunity to go on a special shopping spree, as only a few days earlier Nelly had written saying that she and Gherman were expecting their first child in early December.

A great welcome awaited them. A trip was arranged on a paddle steamer, of a few days' duration, along with Nelly and Gherman. My grandparents admired the rugged scenery and were duly impressed by the wealth of the timber regions. Their visit coincided with the arrival from Finland of my Aunt Olga and Uncle Oscar, accompanied by the entourage — six little daughters, a governess, a nanny, a wet nurse and Aunt Olga's own old mamka.

To mark this unique occasion, Babushka invited friends and relatives to meet my Scottish grandparents and threw a luncheon party. Tea was served later in the garden and a photographer invited to take a photo of the gathering. "It will be a memento of this happy day to be passed down to the children," Babushka had remarked. A memento it is, of a hot summer's day in early June so many years ago. The children sitting on the grass, their elders behind them and the pride of place given to the two old peasant women, my Aunt Olga's old mamka, and old Nanny Shalovchikha — she who had witnessed the retreat of Napoleon's army through Smolensk.

My grandparents enjoyed their stay in Russia, and the warmheartedness of all whom they met. They admired the garden and the house, they liked the broad streets and leafy gardens and the general peaceful atmosphere of a town where as yet life was close to nature. What left a strong impression on my grandfather was the singing of the workmen toiling to rebuild the pier. They laboured hard, dragging the beams with their bare hands down to the edge of the water. Their natural ability to sing in perfect harmony, to sustain them in their work, surprised my grandfather. He kept giving them money and gesturing for more songs, and they, to please this well-dressed "Angliski Barin", went on singing.

My grandparents were presented with gifts as tokens of their visit.

Years later I was to recognise them in their home, from the simple wood carvings and containers made from the bark of the birch by the peasants to the beautiful teaset where each cup was hand painted in black delicate lines against the shell pink of the porcelain depicting scenes of the famous Solovetski Monastery.

From the Scottish side there also came a variety of presents. The fine blankets woven from the best of Scottish wool were much appreciated by Babushka and replaced the usual quilted bedspreads. The Cameron tartan rugs were to be seen on all future travels. Nelly received many gifts, but the best present that came out of the ship's hold, which aroused delighted astonishment, was the handsome navy-blue English perambulator — an article of great rarity in these parts, which was to draw many admiring and envious glances when in the future, Nelly pushing her beautiful perambulator, would stroll leisurely with a nonchalant air along the leafy avenues of the Summer Garden.

After watching the ship carrying her parents skirting the island of Solombala and vanishing out of sight, Nelly became despondent. It was not that she ever complained, for it was not in her nature to do so, but she talked a lot about her home in Scotland, her family, and dear "Old Broughty" and for the first time Gherman became aware that she was homesick.

Back in Scotland life resumed its placid course. Granny was a creature of habit. For each day of the week, for each month of the year there were tasks laid down with the precision of a clock. It was now July — the month of ripening fruit and jam-making. There was also a backlog of letters waiting to be answered. Granny was a faithful and descriptive writer and, through her, all events and news were circulated between the members of the family abroad. Out of nine children only three remained in the end in Scotland. The letters were her only contact, but she was rewarded in turn by pen pictures of the life and customs in India, New Zealand, Uganda and Russia, and later Australia and Kenya. They were a source of great pleasure in a rather prosaic existence, and whenever the mail arrived she would retreat upstairs to a room adjoining her bedroom, where she found peace and no interruptions.

This room was known as "Grandpa's Boudoir". It was a long narrow room divided by a heavy velvet curtain. Behind the curtain stood a large bath fashioned out of real or imitation marble. Against the wall was a painted glass panel depicting reclining damsels whose voluptuous forms, partially hidden by crimson draperies, exposed magnificent plump breasts and arms. At their feet were flasks of wine and bowls of luscious fruit. White doves fluttered here and there. The same exotic scenes were repeated in the windows of this bathroom.

In the front half, where the tall windows formed a circle flooding the room with sunshine, stood a small table and a basket chair. On the table were invariably a dish of bananas and a decanter of whisky. It was grandpa's custom whenever he arrived from the office to retreat to this room and sit beside the table reading his newspaper or admiring the view while sipping his whisky and eating bananas.

Below his window was a rose bed. On to this bed from the window were thrown all the banana skins. Under no condition was the gardener or anyone else ever allowed to remove them. It was Grandpa's firm belief that nothing was as good for his roses as banana skins and the roses upheld his view by rewarding him with unusually large blooms.

The most intriguing part of "Grandpa's Boudoir" was the row of pictures running the whole length of the west wall. All represented the female form in various degrees of partial nudity — perhaps more titillating than stark nakedness.

There was one exception in the midst of this luscious gallery. It was an enlargement of my grandfather. He is taken standing alone surrounded by a great expanse of moorland. Below his proud countenance gazing sternly ahead, can be read the quotation: "I am Monarch of all I survey". This somehow never failed to arouse unseemly mirth in my cousin and me when we were so bold as to venture into the sacred precincts if no one was about. We were not encouraged to enter. Grandma preferred to be alone with her letters and Grandpa with his whisky and bananas.

In August a letter arrived from Russia addressed to Grandma in Gherman's writing. This was unusual, as all letters were normally written by Nelly and one had been delivered only a few days earlier. Hurriedly retreating to her little chair upstairs, she settled down and began to read. She was relieved to note that nothing untoward had happened, but at the same time became agitated as she continued reading — her son-in-law was inviting her to come to Russia.

Nelly, he explained, was not aware that he was writing this letter, as he did not wish to raise her hopes unduly, not knowing if his mother-in-law would accept his invitation. Nelly, he continued, had adapted herself to the Russian way of life in a manner that surprised and delighted not only himself but all the relatives as well. She had never been known to utter a single word of complaint, but recently he had noticed a certain despondency. Nothing, he felt, would gladden her heart more than to have her mother beside her during this critical stage of her life when their child was expected to be born. As for himself, he added, no one would be more welcome and wished for than his mother-in-law.

If it were possible for her to leave Scotland, Gherman went on, he would arrange everything. It would be comparatively simple for Mrs Cameron to board a ship in Hull which would take her across to Finland. There she would be met by his mother who was planning to spend a holiday with her daughter Olga in Helsinki. After spending a few days in Helsinki the two ladies would go on to St Petersburg and Moscow where his mother's friends would show them the sights of the two capitals. They would then board the train for the north.

But it was important that she should arrive in Archangel before the middle of October, as by that time the river begins to freeze and the ferry carrying passengers from the station to Archangel ceases to operate, so those wishing to cross have to wait until the river freezes completely or risk crossing between the forming ice floes in a simple rowing boat.

There was one more request. The child was expected in December and therefore the christening ceremony would take place in January. His own mother had consented to be the child's godmother and he hoped that his mother-in-law would agree to be the other. In conclusion, he wrote, he would be only too glad to pay for all the expenses incurred.

When she finished reading Grandma sat for some time gazing out the window.

Across the dancing waters of the Tay, sweeping round the bay and hurrying on to the sea, were the hills of Fife and behind lay the little village of Leuchars where Grandma was born and spent her youth. Her life had been simple, revolving around the few activities in the village. The family had always lived there.

The highlight of her existence came once a year when the Lammas Fair took place in the university town of St Andrews. She, her sister and brothers would all set off in the early hours of the morning and cheerfully walk the ten miles to the fair and return in the evening. It was there that she and my grandfather met and they were later married in the ancient Norman church in Leuchars. Grandma did well for herself when she married and went to live across the water. How small her world had been in her youth! Now her mind boggled at the thought of seeing these strange foreign cities and the prospects of travelling alone as free as a bird and not at the beck and call of her master, the way it had always been, no matter where they went. But of course it was futile to indulge in any flights of wishful fancy. The whole running of the house revolved around grandfather, who was set in his ways, and would not suffer any disruption even for a few days, far less months. It was Grandma herself who was responsible for Grandpa's dictatorial attitude. She had always firmly believed that the head of the house had to be obeyed implicitly. This belief she not only instilled in her children but in Grandpa himself.

However, it was not for nothing that Granny was born in the Kingdom of Fife. It has been said that the people there are endowed with just that little bit more of cunning than their fellow creatures across the water. What she had to do was to treat the letter casually and to create an impression that it did not really matter whether she went or not to Russia. To ask or to beg was to court a direct refusal. She had learned to her cost this strange contrariness in his nature. Downstairs she could hear her daughters setting the table. The midday train had already passed the house and soon all the business gentlemen would be wending their way home to lunch.

Grandma decided she would mention the contents of the letter to her daughters, but at the same time warn them to remain silent until the matter was resolved one way or the other. By her heightened colour the girls could see that their mother was more agitated than usual and in turn they also became excited. "You know Mama," said Vicky, throwing down the forks and knives on the table, "if Papa will not allow you to go — then perhaps I could take your place?" "Haud your wheest," Granny impatiently rejoined, reverting to the vernacular of her village. She had no intention of allowing anyone else to go to Russia if she couldn't.

The sound of Grandpa's footsteps on the gravel could be heard approaching the front entrance. "Ship Ahoy," screamed the parrot in welcome. He had been taught by Grandpa to say many seafaring expressions, as Grandpa had always nursed a secret longing for the sea and liked to imagine himself in the role of a sturdy skipper.

It was my grandfather's custom, when lunch was finished, to sip a glass of cold, rich milk. During that time he read the letters that had arrived during the morning. At this point, Granny casually passed over her letter. The girls began to clear the table while covertly watching their father. Granny remained seated silently studying the pattern on the tablecloth. Only the restless movements of her hands, brushing away invisible crumbs, betrayed her inner turmoil. "Don't you think," she suddenly said, hoping to further her cause, "it is kind of Gherman to offer to pay all my expenses?" Grandpa raised his head — and all the frosts of Siberia were in his eyes. "Have you no shame in your soul?" he enquired with all the scorn he could muster, "to imagine that I would be beholden to a son-in-law, and a foreigner at that?" Granny did not answer. Any hope she cherished was gone.

Grandpa rose and, laying down the letter, walked over to the window. Rocking on his heels while sipping his milk, he appeared to be deep in thought. The girls, saddened by their mother's mute resignation, hovered around finishing the clearing of the table.

When he had finished his milk, Grandpa turned and placed the tumbler on the table. "If you are to go to Russia," he announced, glancing across at the dejected figure of his wife, "you had better take yourself to town and buy some warm clothes. You will need them all in that outlandish place. And don't be buying anything that's cheap and shoddy and making a fool of me in front of all these Russians. There is one thing more," he added. "When you are gallivanting around all the shops, you can order a silver cup for the wee crathur and see that my name is engraved on it."

I have it still — a fine silver cup as a gentle reminder that many a time my grandfather' stern demeanour covered a generous heart.

The effect of Grandfather's magnanimity requires no comment. Grandma waited just long enough for his train to pass the house, and hurried off to the station to catch the next one. For the next few weeks there was joy unconfined as she rushed around shops and dressmakers. The accent had to be on elegance. She planned to make her debut in Finland in a fashionable sealskin jacket over a well-cut woollen dress. A hat to match, with a jaunty curling feather, was to complete the ensemble. During the final fitting she was so delighted with her image in the mirror that she there and then decided to have her photograph taken. Poor Granny. The monstrous fashion of high padded shoulders, the small hat, comical by present days' standards, did not enhance her looks.

Grandma was kept busy up to the last day of her departure. So much had to be done. Enough jam, pickles and bottled fruit to last the winter. Full instructions for each daughter were carefully planned, written and pinned on the kitchen wall — all of which were blissfully ignored.

It was decided in the end that Grandma should leave at the beginning of October and arrive in Archangel at the end of the month, when normally the frozen river could bear the traffic. This plan allowed for more time to be spent in Finland and the two capitals.

Grandma enjoyed every minute of her crossing to Finland. She had never before felt so free and, not troubled by any inhibitions, chattered in a pleasant and easy manner with all the passengers. The Scandinavian cold buffet was a special delight. Blessed by a healthy appetite and free from seasickness she tasted everything, refused nothing and downed the schnapps and vodka to the manner born.

When the ship docked in Helsinki, Babushka, accompanied by Oscar, was waiting. In her usual expansive way she warmly embraced and kissed Grandma. Oscar bowed and kissed her hand and, although un-accustomed to such gestures in Scotland, Granny accepted this with perfect sang-froid.

Sitting side by side in the carriage the two ladies chatted amiably. Since Nelly's arrival, Babushka's knowledge of English had vastly improved. A contingent of Russian soldiers, marching along the road, came towards them. "Ah zee soldiers," Babushka sighed. Her worried eyes followed the men. "Zere is much trouble in Russia just now — zey vant a revolutzia and zee Finns perhaps like to kill us Russians and be free. But zee good God will save us," she added cheerfully and crossed herself. "And here is zee house now." The horses were drawing up beside a tall building.

Grandma had met the Yanushkovsky ménage during her brief stay in Archangel. My aunt was fond of giving her daughters unusual names and had named her latest daughter Zlata. Her fourth daughter, by some strange gift from nature, possessed unusually flexible muscles and joints. Only six years of age, she was with great intrepidity and style able to perform the most difficult feats, such as turning a succession of cartwheels, walking on her hands and gener-ally dancing and bouncing like a rubber ball. She was named Ariadna but Granny preferred to refer to her as "Acrobat".

The whole ménage with cradle and cots, nannies and mamkas, tiny exotic birds that flew out and in their cages, the house itself, a veritable museum of fine porcelain and objets d'art, astonished Granny as it had Nelly — but over all there was this carefree, cheerful ambience that somehow fascinated and attracted her.

During lunch the conversation, translated by Babushka the best way she could, centred on the serious reports from St Petersburg of riots and strikes. The Finns, long under Russian domination, were taking advantage of the rising. Already there had been a few incidents against the Russians. Oscar was worried and preoccupied and immediately after lunch hurried away to attend a meeting.

The ladies moved into the drawing-room. Grandma settled down beside the tiled stove and produced her knitting. Outside, against the darkening windows, downy snowflakes began to drift. In the distance voices were heard singing some rousing refrain which grew louder as it approached the house. The ladies hurried to the windows and stood watching in silence the shadowy procession of men and women marching along the street carrying flags.

Babushka drew the curtains and went back to her seat. "Please not to worry," she said to Grandma. "People have now many processions but zee police come and stop zee nonsense. You have come to visit your daughter and see our Russia — you will see Russia." Even as she was talking, outlining their plans and trying to assuage Grandma's anxiety, a strange drama was unfolding in the kitchen.

The cook, returning from her shopping, brought the rumour that the Finns were planning to attack the Russians and were marking the doors where they lived. The old nanny, on hearing this, hurried down to the front door and, sure enough, found a white cross chalked on the door. Immediately all suspicion, right or wrong, was directed against the young maid, the only Finnish servant in the house. Pandemonium broke out. The furious Russian servants surrounded the girl and accused her of treachery. Hearing their angry voices, Babushka hurried to the kitchen, followed by Aunt Olga. Grandma, alarmed and curious, timidly approached the hall. At that moment, the kitchen door flew open, the accused girl rushed out and, running down the stairs, made for the door. Pursuing her like a swarm of angry bees were all the Russian servants and Babushka. The girl reached the door and vanished. She was not seen again.

Babushka took Grandma's hand and led her down the stairs to the street. "You see zee cross," she said, pointing to the door. "Zee Finns know zat here live zee Russians. Tonight perhaps zey make a revolutzia and some bad men come to zee house and cut our throats." Grandma was bewildered, frightened and also very cold, standing in the street with the bitter wind cutting through her. "I'm thinking," she said irritably, "that if we stand here much longer, we shall all catch our death o' cold and the Finns won't need to cut our throats." She hurried upstairs back to her warm corner and her knitting. Then suddenly the words spoken by Grandpa when they were travelling in the train to Hull came back to her. "Listen, Mother," he had told her, "if there is any trouble at all in that country, you will go and seek out the British Consul, you will ask his advice and do exactly what he tells you." Grandma had paid scant attention at that time to all he was saying, but now the words she remembered brought some relief. Yes, tomorrow, she promised herself, she would go and find the British Consul and follow his advice.

Comforted by this decision, she settled down to her knitting, but not for long. The door opened and Babushka entered, dressed in her travelling cloak and hat. Behind her was Aunt Olga, weeping helplessly. "Madame Cameron," Babushka addressed Grandma, "please to come with me. You and I must not stay in zees house and be killed like zee rats in zee trap. We will go out and die under zee heaven." "I shall do no such thing," Grandma rejoined. She saw no virtue in dying outside in the cold. If she had to die it was just as well to die in comfort. "Mamushka, dearest, please let us all stay togther," entreated Olga tearfully. Babushka was adamant. "I will not allow zee Finns to trap me, I go and die alone. It is better so."

There ensued a scene described by Grandma as the like of which she had never seen before. "Your Babushka," she recalled, "blessed your aunt and myself and made the sign of the cross in the direction of the nursery. She then sat down and bowed her head in silence and I thought that perhaps she was going to change her mind. But no, she got up, went down the stairs and out the door."

Aunt Olga and Grandma ran to the window. For a long time they stood with their faces pressed against the panes. They could see nothing. Somehow, the house became very silent. Only the distant voices of the children could be heard coming from the nursery. Grandma returned to her knitting. Aunt Olga produced a small feather duster and began, with loving care, to inspect her ornaments. From the dining-room could now be heard the homely tinkling of china — the setting of the table. Again the door of the drawing-room opened and there on the threshold, bedraggled, wet and dejected, stood Babushka. "I have come back," she said a little shamefacedly, "to die with my daughter. I have been much foolish and weak — please to forgive me." Relieved, but perhaps not very surprised, Aunt Olga rushed to embrace her mother. Old Nanny Marfushka popped her head round the door. "Tea is ready," she announced, a happy smile spreading over her homely face.

The samovar was singing a welcome little song as every one gathered round the table. The elder children and their governess came down from the nursery. Aunt Olga began to pour out the tea, but no sooner were the first few cups passed round than the shrill ringing of the front door bell filled the house. It was followed by an imperative knocking on the door. Marfushka stepped forward. "I will go down," she said. "I'm an old woman and have lived my life." Quietly, with great dignity, she went down the wide staircase and laboriously opened the bolted door. There on the doorstep, angry and impatient, stood Uncle Oscar and, behind him, a smiling young officer at the head of a small contingent of cossacks. Jostling and laughing, the men ran up the stairs and suddenly the house seemed to be full of soldiers. "An order has been issued," announced Uncle Oscar dramatically. "All Russian women and children, for reasons of safety, are to be taken to the Fort of Sviborg and these lads," he added pointing to the cossacks, "are here to protect and escort you. We have one hour to get ready — only the barest necessities can be taken."

And now a happy carefree change began. Relieved of all anxiety, delighting in this unexpected masculine invasion, the women bustled about laughing and joking with the men. "Never did I see the like," my granny was to recall later. "You would have thought they were all getting ready for a jaunt to the country." The rules of hospitality, of course, had to be observed. The young captain was invited to join the family at the table. More food was brought. He ate all he could and flirted outrageously with the young governess. Uncle Oscar, anxious and impatient, was urging everybody to hurry and arguing with Aunt Olga who, running out and in the drawing-room, was surreptitiously pushing some mysterious objects into her travelling case.

In the end, everyone had packed and was ready to go. My cousin Jenya, three years old at the time, was to remember quite vividly being held in the arms of a smiling cossack, who stood in the crowded hall on that night when all the Russian women and children, along with the only British lady, were evacuated to the Fort of Sviborg. "It is now time for us to go," announced Oscar, "but first, we must all sit down." All moved into the drawing-room. Those who could find seats sat down and others stood in groups around the room. It was a sombre moment. The soldiers removed their fur hats and for a short time no one spoke. "Now let us go," again announced Oscar. Quietly, all wound their way down the staircase and out into the darkness. A procession was formed in the middle of the road with the women and children in the centre, the cossacks protecting them on either side. Only old Marfushka remained behind and stood watching the exodus of the family. She had refused to go, saying that someone had to remain to take care of the empty house, all the treasures and feed the little birds of which my aunt was so fond. She also did not believe that the Finns would harm an old woman like herself.

The captain called out an order in a clear, loud voice and the group moved off. Immediately behind the captain, arm-in-arm with Uncle Oscar, walked Aunt Olga. She was carrying her small case and refused to let anyone touch it. Behind them trailed the two mamkas carrying the babies, the nannies holding the hands of their young charges and the governess with the older children. In the rear, her shoulders braced back, the feather in her hat waving defiantly in the wind and her steps firm, walked Grandma. Beside her, protectively holding Grandma's arm, was Babushka, the folds of her cloak flapping around her.

Some twenty minutes later, the family approached the waterfront. Not surprisingly, they were the last to arrive. The boat ferrying the women and children was packed and the barge to be towed behind it was rapidly filling up. Officers and sailors were shepherding the passengers over the shaky gangway into the barge. Granny found herself being lifted from the gangway and lowered gently into the depths of the barge. A young sailor smiled and said something. He pointed to the place where, rising out of the sea, grey and forbidding against the dark curtain of the night, was the Fort of Sviborg.

Now the boat was gently easing out of the harbour. The barge, a large clumsy duck, followed behind. To Grandma the whole scene was grey, forbidding. The dark, starless sky sent no comforting light. She was surrounded by strange waters where she herself was a stranger in the midst of people whose language she could neither understand nor guess. Somewhere far back was a warm fireside and comfort. It was best not to think about it.

The crossing to the fort was short. They found themselves being helped ashore and led inside the protective walls. They were directed to a spacious hall where mattresses were being spread on the floor and where groups of women and children were already settling down. The family took over a large corner of the room and the nannies began to busy themselves arranging the mattresses and bedding. Granny sat down on the mattress she was to share with Babushka and looked around. Here she saw no anxiety or fear but rather a cheerful philosophy with patient resignation that is peculiar to the Russian temperament. It had sustained them in the past and would sustain them again in the future dark years.

In this room many friends were congregating or calling across to each other, but to Grandma, listening to their voices, it had been a long day and intense weariness was setting in. Shadows danced on the walls as the women prepared themselves and the children for the night. Babushka removed her blouse and skirt and slipped on a short white jacket. She then went down on her knees and began to pray. She prayed long and earnestly, oblivious of her surroundings, crossing herself with a wide sweeping gesture and bowing to touch the floor with her forehead. Finally she took the small gold cross hanging on a chain around her neck, pressed it to her lips and, wishing Grandma a peaceful night, laid down beside her.

The lack of privacy disturbed Grandma. Yet she had no intention of sleeping in her clothes and in the end, after carefully removing her dress, she slipped on her dressing-gown and curled down for the night. There, in the darkness, she folded her hands and whispered the Lord's Prayer and, thinking that perhaps she ought to say something more, she repeated the twenty-third psalm. After that, feeling comforted, she tucked the quilt around herself and closed her eyes.

The following morning, after rumours and speculations, came the news that the situation in the town was contained. The threatened danger was over and the women and children were taken back to the mainland. Soon after the family returned to the house they were surprised by the arrival of my father. The serious situation in the two capitals and the general unrest spreading over Russia had alarmed Gherman. He had decided to go to Finland to escort the two ladies back to Archangel. Boarding the first available train, he had arrived two days later on the doorstep of his sister's house.

That same afternoon, Grandma, accompanied by my father, called on the British Consul. She was prepared to follow his advice, even if it meant her having to abandon all her plans and return to Scotland. The consul held a more optimistic view and advised her to go on to Archangel, where everything was comparatively quiet. At the same time he cautioned her to avoid spending any time in St Petersburg or Moscow and to travel north as quickly as possible.

The next morning, Babushka, Grandma and Gherman caught an early train for St Petersburg and arrived there after an eight-hour journey. With great difficulty, and only after offering an exorbitant fare, Gherman succeeded in finding two cabs. The little group set off for the station lying at the other end of Nevsky Prospect. A deathly silence, like the stillness before a storm, lay over the city. Not a shop or restaurant was open. The streets were empty. As the two solitary cabs approached the station, galloping horses came up behind them. The frightened drivers drew to the side of the road. The stern-faced riders thundered past without a glance and vanished.

After many disruptions and delays, they arrived at the terminal for Archangel. Tanya met them and confirmed what they already suspected — the river was half frozen and could only be crossed with difficulty by rowing boat. That abortive revolution of 1905 was the first crack of a chasm which would eventually engulf the whole of Imperial Russia. Had their previous plans not miscarried because of it, my family would have arrived a fortnight later and crossed the frozen river in comfort. Now they were faced with the dilemma of having either to cross through ice-floes and dangerous waters or accept Tanya's willing hospitality in her small house until the river froze completely. Both Babushka and Gherman were anxious to get back to their homes. In the end they decided to leave their luggage with Tanya and attempt the crossing.

Two rowing boats were hired. Grandma and Babushka stepped gingerly into one, accompanied by three boatmen. Gherman followed in the second and the two boats pulled away from the shore. A bitter wind cut into their faces — more bitter than Grandma had ever known. She had long since discarded her little hat with the jaunty feather and, like Babushka, had tied a thick woollen shawl over her head.

The going was hazardous. To keep moving, the men were forced to break the ice and push it aside. On the opposite bank, standing close to the edge, were Nelly, Dedushka, Uncle Sanya and others, all watching anxiously the slow progress of the boats. A critical part of the journey arrived. A wide sheet of ice, preventing all further movement, lay in front of them. On the other side of this floe, a short distance from the shore, was a clear strip of water. A boat from the shore moved up to the edge of the ice and waited.

To reach this point, the passengers had to leave their boats and run across the ice. Inching close to the floe, the boatmen stopped rowing. Babushka and Grandma stood up, bracing themselves to jump on to the ice. In that moment Babushka panicked. In her own words to me years later, she recalled their harrowing experience. "You see, Jenya," she explained, "I did not know how strong was the ice, nor did anyone else for that matter. Terrible accidents had happened in the past and the thought of being trapped under the broken ice terrified me. But even as I stood, unable to move, what did I see but your Scottish granny jump out of the boat and dash over the ice? I still remember her little feet, in black boots, skimming across and the way she leaped into the other boat and just sat there laughing. As for me — I had to be dragged along with my feet trailing on the ice. Then came your father running to join us. The men rowed us safely ashore and we were all reunited, kissing and hugging each other."

All this was a long way off from the ballet, the opera and all the wonderful sights my Granny had been promised, but at the same time all these adventures became a highlight of her life, which she was fond of describing in detail to her grandchildren.

10

Having eventually reached her destination, Grandma thankfully settled down in her daughter's home. Everything had turned out to be different from what had been planned, but she philosophically reasoned she was never meant to see the bright lights of St Petersburg and Moscow — she was here to be with her daughter.

By now the winter was closing in. The frost increased and the days shortened. The river was giving up her unequal struggle against the frost. For a few days the dark line of the swift current in midstream continued to defy the encroaching ice, but in the end surrendered. The Dvina became a mighty highway that stretched for hundreds of miles back to the south.

The first to appear on the river were the small northern horses hurrying from the opposite shore pulling the flat sledges of the peasants laden with fresh provisions for the market. They were followed by different types of sledges travelling in all directions.

To Granny's great relief all her baggage arrived safely. Christmas was approaching and she had brought gifts to all she could remember.

There was such entertaining and a constant coming and going between the two houses. Although having totally different natures the two grandmothers became very friendly and remained so throughout the years. Babushka was an extrovert who liked to confide in Grandma and give an uninhibited expression of her thoughts and feelings. Grandma was a sympathetic listener, but kept her counsel and divulged very little about herself or her family. Secretiveness and reticence in any form were alien to Babushka as they were to most Russians, the exception being if they were afraid, or guilty of some ulterior motive. Babushka openly discussed money matters from the price of food to the dress she had ordered for the christening of her future grandchild. She likewise frankly admired Grandma's clothes and with the same childlike frankness enquired what they cost. Grandma sidestepped such questions. She also admired Babushka's furs and jewellery, but passed no comment, and as for asking what Babushka might have paid for some article — that was simply not done and completely outwith her Scottish character.

On 26 November in the old Gregorian calendar, which was thirteen days behind Europe in those days, Nelly decided to throw a party in return for all the hospitality extended to her mother. As the child was not expected for another fortnight, she reasoned it would be more convenient to hold the party before the event rather than later. In all some fifteen people came. The dinner, consisting of Scottish and Russian dishes, was a great success and later all adjourned to the drawing-room.

Among the guests was my father's cousin Adya who had been one of the sponsors at my parents' wedding in London. He was a gay and popular young man, reputed to be one of the best dancers in the town. In those days there was a fashionable exhibition dance known as the "Cakewalk" and as the party continued swinging along with the usual gay abandon, Adya was asked to give an exhibition of the dance. After a little persuasion he donned a top-hat, took a walking stick and prepared to dance. Nelly sat down to play the accompaniment. This exhibition, presented with fine expertise, lightness and style, delighted the guests and in the end received prolonged applause and demands for an encore. Nelly went back to the piano and Adya resumed his dancing.

At this inopportune moment my mother was unexpectedly overtaken by the first pangs of childbirth. The party came to an abrupt end, the guests scattered and Nelly retreated to her bedroom.

The following afternoon of Sunday 27 November, old style, I saw the light of day, in a world fated to be torn asunder by wars and revolutions. I was Babushka's eighth granddaughter, but any twinges of disappointment that may have been felt at the arrival of yet another girl were brushed aside.

The Russians and the Scots have one trait in common — both are given to similar superstitions. It is considered unlucky by some people to prepare too lavishly for the unborn child, for fear of tempting Providence. The perambulator from Scotland was already there, but the cot once used by my father did not arrive at the house until the day after my birth. A bath and other articles still had to be purchased.

The following day, in spite of the cold, more intense than usual, the two grannies, sitting side by side in the sledge under piles of rugs, set off along the snowy road to buy the baby a bath. While they were happily engaged in choosing a bath and other articles, the priest called at the house to carry out the traditional ceremony of prayer and blessings and the sprinkling of holy water in all the corners of the room, and over the baby and the young mother.

Some time before I was born, Babushka had suggested that she herself should go across to one of the villages and fix up a healthy young mother to nurse the baby. She pointed out all the advantages of having a wet mother. Mother refused even to entertain such an idea. No strange woman was to suckle her child. So I was the first child in the family to be nursed by her own mother. Later Babushka was heard enthusiastically telling her friends that "Our Nellinka looked very beautiful nursing the child — so like the Madonna and the child in a holy painting."

When I was a month old, my parents bundled me up in numerous shawls and took me over to the house in Olonetskaya Street. The Christmas celebrations always took place on Christmas Eve as it was Babushka's name-day, soon to become mine as well. This double event invariably brought a happy gathering of close friends and relatives, but for the first time for many years Nanny Shalovchikha was not present as she was now too frail to leave her room. Knowing how eager she was to see me, my parents took me down to her quarters.

In the early summer when she learned that there was going to be another baby in the family, her attitude to my mother changed from cold indifference to warm friendliness. She knitted little boots for the child, brought dried raspberries, strawberry leaves and herbs to my mother, assuring her that there was a beneficial virtue in them for pregnant women. Mother accepted the boots and quietly discarded the rest. As summer turned to autumn the old nanny became obsessed with the approaching birth. "I must live to see this child," she kept repeating to my father.

Nanny Shalovchikha was now approaching the end of her long life. She had outlived all her contemporaries and many of those whom she had nursed. Although still in possession of her faculties there was the feeling that she had outlived her usefulness. She was wearied and spent long hours in bed, never leaving her peaceful room with its white walls, the ikon hanging in the corner, the comforting light of the lampada in front of it, and where she was surrounded by all her humble but reassuring reminders of distant times.

When my parents entered the room, they found her up and fully dressed, sitting in her chair. She was obviously expecting them. "Please give her to me," she asked my mother. Mother complied and the old woman, who had seen the remnants of Napoleon's Grand Army stumbling along the roads of Smolensk and who had known the bitterness of losing her only son in the Crimean war, now, in contemplative silence, sat cradling me in her arms. More than a century was bridged between us. "Take her," she said at last. "I am content. You see," she added, a proud little smile running across her lips, "I have now nursed four generations."

In the early spring Nanny Shalovchikha died and was buried beside her old friend and contemporary, my great-great-grandmother, Feodosiya from Kaluga.

On the morning of my christening a font arrived from the nearby Church of the Assumption and was placed in the ballroom of Babushka's home. As I was the first child of the eldest son, Babushka wanted to do things in style and invited all her friends and relatives. To accommodate them all, the table had to be stretched from the dining-room into the hall.

Two godfathers had been chosen — my father's uncle and a close friend. The two godmothers were my grandmothers. The Orthodox Church does not permit the parents to be present during the ritual of the christening and that especially applies to the mother. When all the guests crowded in the ballroom, father discreetly remained in the background but Mother was confined to the nursery.

The priest and the deacon took their places beside the font. The two

The Russian household in peaceful days: June 1905 (top) on the arrival of Granny and Grandpa Cameron and Aunt Olga's family from Finland; before the storm, 1913 (bottom), during the visit by Uncle Henry (seated in the centre, between the two grandmothers).

"Bay House", West Ferry 1904 (top) with Vicky, Nelly, Mary and Tammy the terrier; the House by the Dvina (bottom) viewed from the summer house; the Russian–Scottish union (facing page): the author's parents after their (first!) wedding ceremony.

godfathers stood behind them awaiting the entrance of the
godmothers. The double doors opened and Babushka, dressed in
green velvet, the long train edged with sable, entered carrying the
baby. Stepping beside her, Grandma looked equally elegant — her
neat, small figure was encased in a well-cut gown fashioned from lilac
silk and guipure lace. The two ladies joined the godfathers and the
ritual of the christening commenced.

Lying in Babushka's arms, on top of a fine lawn sheet over a pink
quilt, the child was peaceful.

No one had bothered to explain to Grandma the details of an
Orthodox christening. Somehow she vaguely imagined that there
would be a gentle half-immersion of the small body and perhaps a
sprinkling of the water over her head. The baby of course would love
this. Poor Grandma was totally unprepared for what was to follow.

The priest took the naked child. His voice, loud and clear,
proclaimed the solemn words. "In the name of the Father, Son and
Holy Ghost I baptise you Evgeniya." Placing his hand across the child's
face to prevent any intake of water he completely immersed the baby.
Lifting her out, he released his hand and immediately a piercing shriek
of furious indignation rent the air. It was cut short by the second
immersion.

This part of the ritual is repeated three times. Grandma was
completely stunned by the first immersion, and angered by the
second. When she saw the priest preparing for the third, she was
unable to contain herself any longer and, rushing up to him, grabbed
his arm. "Do you wish to drown the child?" she cried.

An astonished silence followed. The priest didn't understand a
single word, but no one before had interrupted this most holy rite. A
hushed whisper ran through the crowded room. At this critical
moment Babushka stepped forward and saved the situation.
"Madame Cameron," she said firmly, "this is very holy and good and
only one more. Please to come." She led Grandma back to her place.
Grandma's habitual self-control took over. She stood in stony silence
until the end of the service. The baby was now handed over to one of
the godfathers for the ritual of the anointing by holy oil. The priest
drew the sign of the cross on the forehead, the breast, the palms of the
small hands and on the soles of the feet. A gold cross and chain was
slipped round the neck, to be worn for all time. Finally the baby was
placed in Grandma's arms.

Meanwhile, isolated in the nursery, Nelly was being torn between
loyalty to her husband's church and agonising anxiety for her child.
She had never heard such frenzied screaming of fear and rage.
Helplessly wringing her hands, she was strongly tempted to run out

of the nursery, but in the end steeled herself to endure her torment until the moment when Grandma ran into the room clutching the infant to her breast. "Take her, Nelly, take her," she said, thrusting the child into Nelly's arms. "Never," she went on bitterly, "in all my born days have I seen the like of such barbarity. Little did I think that I would see the day when a grandchild of mine would be ducked head and all in that fancy font of theirs, not once, mind you, but three times over—and her the helpless wee cratur screaming her head off. I can promise you now, my lass," she concluded grimly, "that there will never again be another christening the like of this one for me. Never, even if I'm spared for a hundred years." She kept her word.

Sometime in February, Granny began to plan her return journey to Scotland. Grandpa's letters were showing signs of impatience with the lack of supervision over their daughters and the haphazard running of the house. Granny was also possessed by a strange urge that overtakes most Scottish housewives with the advent of brighter sunshine and warmer weather. It is known as the "spring cleaning", a time when a surge of unbounded energy and determination propels them to attack all corners of the house, furniture, carpets and curtains, to remove every speck of dirt and dust.

One day Mother suddenly announced that she and I would also go to Scotland. My father was aghast. Nelly was calmly determined. She wanted her father, her sisters and all her friends to see the baby. After all, she reasoned, no one from her side, except her mother, was present at the christening, so it was only fair that they should now have the pleasure of meeting the child. There was also, she pointed out, the advantage of having her mother to help her during the journey. In the face of all these arguments father had no other option but to agree.

And so, in the midst of a howling blizzard, my mother, Grandma and I, some ten weeks old, set off for Scotland.

The journey to Hull was uneventful and after five days we reached the shores of England. The familiar stocky figure of my grandfather was seen waiting on the landing stage. Grandpa did not disguise his pleasure at meeting his wife and daughter. He embraced them warmly and gently pinched the chubby cheeks of his grandchild. "She looks healthy enough," was his sole comment to Nelly.

In Hull they boarded the train for Scotland. Holding me in her arms, Nelly sat in her corner hungrily scanning the fast-moving landscape, the neat and orderly cottages and houses with their gardens, the green fields and the lambs scampering round their mothers. "Was it only a year ago?" she kept asking herself. So much had happened during that time. How different everything had been from Scotland — the customs, the people, but she was getting to know and like them.

She enjoyed the way of life there and was slowly mastering that difficult language; not very correctly, but enough to be understood.

Facing each other in the two far corners, my grandparents were eagerly exchanging their news. Grandma asked questions about the running of the house. "Did the girls remember to make marmalade?" "These lassies," Grandpa began scornfully, "nothing but nonsense in their heads." He lapsed into silence. "Aye, God, aye," he went on again, turning away his head to gaze intently out the window, "you never miss the water till the well runs dry." And Grandma was well content, for that was as big a compliment as she had ever had from him.

Nelly was happy to be back. It was good to be in Scotland and see again the old familiar places that she had missed so much. It was good to meet relatives and friends and take her place amongst them, just as if she had never left them. Good to stroll along the smooth pavements of Broughty Ferry, pushing the perambulator past the old church where she had been married and on to the shops where everyone knew her and to meet friends who would stop to admire the baby and pass the usual flattering comments. All that was fine, but as the spring advanced and an army of daffodils formed a golden border round the lawn and the blackbirds sang their glad songs — there came the knowledge that something was amiss. She had seen everyone, exchanged all news, did all the things she wanted to do and had been happy and content to be in Scotland. Now she began to long for her own home, her husband and all the kind and open-hearted friends she had made there.

In early May, when the waters of the Dvina ran freely to the sea, my mother bundled me up and we sailed from the port of Leith on a cargo ship. It took us round the coast of Norway and the Kola Peninsula and through the White Sea to Archangel. We settled once again in our home and my parents took up the threads of their married life.

In the following spring my mother was expecting her second child and as the days went by she became obsessed with the idea that the baby had to be born in Scotland and nowhere else. Father could not accept this. The child, he patiently tried to explain to her, would be a Russian subject, receive a Russian education, embrace the Russian Orthodox Church and in short become a Russian citizen. Why then was it necessary for it to be born outside Russia? What was her reason? She had no reason, she was perfectly satisfied with the attention and care she received during her first confinement, but this time she wanted the child to be born in Scotland.

Years later she told me that during that distant spring she felt as if some inner voice kept telling her to have this baby in Scotland. She never dreamt that in this way she was doing the best thing possible for her son, as during the hungry twenties when we were in Scotland and when the dark shadow of mass unemployment hung over the whole of Britain, it would have been very difficult for a foreign subject to find any employment. By adopting the country of his birth, a way was open to my brother.

Meanwhile, father gave up pursuing an argument which he knew he could not possibly win. Instead, he decided to take a long leave and combine some business with pleasure in Scotland. We were to leave by ship in early June and take the usual route through Norway. My nanny, Sasha, was to accompany us, as it was thought that she would be a help to Mother on our return journey to Russia.

As the date of our departure drew closer, father was approached by Pavel Tarasoff; the boy employed as a kazachok in our household, which required him to be at the beck and call of everyone, whether it was to clean the stables, polish the harness, deliver letters or hurry for the odd bottle of vodka.

Pavel was an orphan and somewhere along his thorny path he had learned to read and write. From that time he devoted his spare time to reading everything he could lay his hands on. This did not escape my father's attention. He suggested that Pavel should read some of the classics and allowed him free access to them. A new and rich world was open to Pavel. He went through every book my father possessed — all the Russian classics and the translations from foreign writers, especially the English. England especially attracted him. He heard the English language spoken in the house and laboriously began to write down in Russian letters the words he had picked up. At times he timidly approached Mother to ask her to explain the meaning of some words. One day father presented Pavel with a simple Russian-English grammar book and was astonished to see how eagerly the boy began to study the language.

Now, nervously wringing his hands, Pavel begged my father to take him to Scotland. He was prepared, he explained, to work for his passage on the ship. Work in Scotland as well, in the garden, in the house, clean, wash and do anything he was asked to do. He wanted no money, only a little food and a corner where he could sleep. My father could not find it in his heart to refuse him.

It was a happy, carefree journey. Pavel was not required to work for his passage. Instead he spent his time learning as much as he could of the English language and was now able to converse in a halting fashion with the members of the crew. Sasha, on the other hand, picked up nothing at all and when spoken to in this strange foreign tongue, only giggled self-consciously and hid her face behind a corner of her kerchief.

After two weeks we arrived in Broughty Ferry. My grandparents welcomed this invasion. During the last two years the house had become empty. Stephen and Mary were married. Henry was in India. Aggie was soon to sail for Australia and Vicky was only to remain for a little while. Now the house was alive and full again. Sasha and I shared a bedroom overlooking the river. Pavel was accommodated in a room known as "the smoking-room". Grandpa, who could not bear the smell of smoking, which he maintained contaminated the atmosphere, built this room adjoining the house. It had a separate entrance from the garden. Whenever any of the sons, my father or friends wished to smoke, they had to go out of the house and enter this room, where they could do so to their hearts' content.

From the minute he arrived Pavel, true to his promise, was determined to earn his keep. Each morning he could be seen brushing out the courtyard, bringing in the coal, carrying out the ashes. The cook found in him a treasure — he cleaned her grate and peeled the potatoes. Mary, the maid, was thankful to find someone to relieve her from the detested task of polishing the brasses and silver. He worked for hours in the garden, quietly and unobtrusively. My grandparents took to this boy who was always willing to do what he was asked and who in a matter of a few weeks acquired a remarkable fluency in the English language. He was given a little money and at times, in the spirit of adventure, would set off to explore the town. Soon, he was due to travel back with my father, back to the old, drab existence to which he was born. After all he was, as Mikhailo once said, one of the people who walked in the darkness of illiteracy. A village lad for whom there was little hope in the future beyond the promotion to a coachman or perhaps to a worker in the timber mills. He had no education beyond what he gathered from his beloved books.

One day, my father approached a friend who was a flax merchant and asked him if he might employ in his office a boy of unusual ability for a matter of two or three years. The following week the flax merchant called at the house and met Pavel. There was some conversation, a few questions asked and in the end, being duly impressed, my father's friend agreed to take Pavel for a business training in his office. The next day Pavel, completely unaware of what had transpired, was approached by father who in a casual manner enquired if he would care to stay on in Scotland and serve an apprenticeship with a firm of flax brokers, at the end of which, he could, if he wished, return to Russia and find a post in some office in

Archangel.

Pavel never returned to Russia — at least not until as a high executive in a trading firm, he travelled on business to many parts of Europe and like all Russians was drawn to visit the place where he was born.

At the end of three years he had the choice of remaining with his firm, returning to Russia, or accepting a lucrative appointment in London, offering a wider scope and opportunities. He chose England.

I have vague memories of a smart, fair-haired young man calling on my grandparents on a summer's day during one of our last visits to Scotland when I was in my sixth year. He had called to say goodbye before leaving for England. He brought me a doll and conversed freely with my mother and grandparents at the tea table. Pavel would have passed any day for a Scotsman if it had not been for his name and the broad features of a Slav.

I have no knowledge as to what happened in the end to that remarkable man. The war and revolutions intervened, followed by the demoniac reign of the Georgian maniac when even a letter from abroad to Russia could have brought disaster to the recipient. People engrossed in their own worries and tragedies lost touch with Pavel, but, who knows, perhaps his descendants still live somewhere in Britain.

A different cup of tea was Sasha. After the first few weeks of rapturous exclamations over everything she had never seen before — the hot and cold water gushing from the taps, the flush toilet in the bathroom, a special delight in itself, the concrete pavements, attractive little gardens, the shops that offered such a rich variety of things, Sasha began to wilt.

Through the day I kept her occupied. We spent many happy hours on the shores of the sun-drenched Grassy Beach, gathering shells, coloured stones and turning over the seaweed in search of tiny scampering crabs. When it rained, we played in our room. With childlike earnestness Sasha came down to my level and out of bits of cardboard and matchboxes made little shops and houses. She was untiring in all her efforts to amuse me, but at night when I was safely tucked away in bed and sleeping, Sasha became lonely.

Sometimes she sat beside the window doing her cross-stitch embroidery or gazing aimlessly across the river. At other times she would wander outside the gate and stand leaning against the wall, watching the rolling carriages and the pedestrians who in turn would glance curiously at the sad-eyed girl in her unusual dress and kerchief.

She was friendly with Mary, the young maid, who on her day off introduced Sasha to her people. There was a lot of nodding and smiling but the language barrier prevented a closer acquaintance. Aggie and Vicky, who were in the habit of bathing at the Grassy Beach, suggested to Sasha that she might join them and offered a spare swimming suit. Sasha loved swimming and longed to go into the water, but she had been quite overawed by the strange sight of my two aunts emerging from the bathing shed in their navy bloomers, bodices complete with a sailor collar all edged in white braid and frilly mob caps on their heads. Such an unseemly spectacle was not for Sasha. She could take no part in it, nor yet could she understand why anyone should undress only to dress up again to go into the water and come out with these silly-looking clothes wet and sticking to their bodies. Back home no one ever wore bathing suits. They were unheard of. They all went bathing in their natural state just as God made them. The women in one part of the river and the men in another and no one bothered.

Mother tried hard to make Sasha happy. She often took us into town to see the shops and bought prints, ribbons, and strings of bright beads for Sasha. These little expeditions usually finished up in a tearoom famous for cream cakes and hot scones. But the highlight of Sasha's sojourn in Scotland was the day when my mother presented her with a beautiful little hat trimmed with ribbons and glossy crimson cherries. Sasha had never possessed a hat. She was delighted beyond all words and in some way it helped to alleviate the pain of her homesickness. She loved to stand in front of the mirror and smile back at the reflection of the round sweet face, framed by soft tendrils, under the little hat perched on top of her head. She laughed, shrugged her shoulders, made faces, at times lifting her head proudly and looking down her small nose in the manner of a haughty barynya, or suddenly breaking into a gay smile and coyly winking an eye. There were so many variations in her dream world and at the end of each session the hat was carefully wrapped in tissue paper and put back in the box. Sasha never actually wore it.

Another diversion was Jocky the parrot. She liked to sit beside his cage and talk to him. "Oi kakoi ti boltun"—"What a chatterbox you are!" she would say to him and Jocky, his head cocked and his bright beady eyes fixed on Sasha, listened intently to this flow of strange words. But somehow very soon Jocky began to behave in an odd manner. He ran up and down his perch excitedly calling out, "Ship ahoy. Ship ahoy," and still more urgently "Kiss me quick, Mary. Kiss me quick." This was accompanied by the constant rattling of his tin dish. For some mysterious reason Jocky had developed a voracious appetite. No sooner did Grandma fill his dish than she would hear Jocky rattling it as hard as he could and demanding to have it refilled.

Jocky was being a nuisance and Grandma was perplexed by such unseemly behaviour until one day Grandpa, coming in from his office, enquired if Grandma was aware that outside the gate there was an unsightly heap of sunflower husks. Everything fell into place. Sasha had been filching the seeds from Jocky's cage and finding solace in the activity so often practised in Russia. Jocky was having a hard time trying to keep up with Sasha, whose expertise and speed in attacking the seeds would have put to shame any self-respecting parrot.

Father's sailing date drew near. One morning, Sasha, her face swollen and tear stained, came to Mother. "Barynya," she said, "dear kind Barynya, please let me return with the barin back to Archangel. I cannot stand this beautiful country any longer. It is not for me. As God is my witness, it is breaking my heart — please, sweet Barynya, let me go back." What could poor Mother do but agree? A fortnight later Sasha sailed with father. She was last seen cheerfully running up the gangway carrying in one hand a bundle, much larger than the one she brought to Scotland, and in the other the hatbox with the precious hat she was never to wear.

On the day my brother was born, I, protesting loudly, was removed by my granny to the Grassy Beach. Of that of course there is no recollection, but there is, however, a vivid picture, when I was later led into the bedroom, of my mother sitting up in bed, propped up by pillows and beside her an ancient rocking cradle. Inside, under the wooden hood, was a small, red-faced creature wrapped in a white shawl. "This is your little brother," I was told.

A telegram was despatched to Archangel proclaiming the news that at last a grandson had arrived in the family. My brother was named Gherman after our father. When he was six weeks old he was christened in the parish church of St Stephen's where my parents had been married. In this way he was spared the ritual of the immersion, but still had to undergo the anointing ceremony later in Russia.

We sailed from Hull in early December. As there was now no Sasha to assist mother, Granny decided to accompany us as far as Finland where we were to be met by Father. We hoped to arrive in Archangel in time for Christmas.

The crossing was very stormy. Both Mother and I being hopeless sailors were now badly affected by the ceaseless tossing and pitching. Below me, Mother lay prostrate trying to nurse my seven-weeks-old brother who in turn became very ill and never ceased crying. The only person not affected in any way was my granny. I can still see the small sturdy figure jumping off her bunk and being thrown against wall and furniture in her rush over to Mother or myself, changing and soothing the baby, trying to amuse her peevish granddaughter, and attending to all our endless needs. It is only now after many years that I have come to realise how selfless was her decision to take on a journey during the worst time of the year solely for the purpose of helping mother. The snow-clad shores of Finland brought relief. Father was waiting on the landing stage. After a respite of a few days with Aunt Olga we continued our journey to Archangel while Granny returned on the same ship to Scotland.

Archangel was in the grip of an intense frost when we eventually arrived. Babushka, awaiting us at Issakagorka Station, had arrived in a "vozok" — the box-like cab fixed on low runners, lined in thick felt and with two hermetically sealed small windows. Wrapped in blankets and shawls we clambered in.

On arrival, Mother carried the baby to Babushka's bedroom and, unwrapping all the numerous shawls, laid him on top of the bed. Those who may have been expecting to see a good-looking, sturdy child were disappointed. My little brother had been ill and had undergone an exhausting journey. His small face was white and drawn and he neither smiled nor displayed any interest but lay listlessly looking up at the curious faces around him. Someone in the background had picked me up and was heard to pass the tactless comment, "Our one is better." Mother was deeply hurt. Picking up the baby and holding him to her breast she bitterly rejoined, "He is beautiful to me," and stormed out of the bedroom.

We spent some days with Babushka and then moved back to our own home. In a few weeks my brother blossomed into a very attractive blue-eyed, golden-haired child, but somehow from the day of our arrival I was referred to as "Ours", and he as "Theirs", and that is the way it always remained.

For the next few years we shuttled to and fro between Russia and Scotland, either round the coast of Norway or through Finland and St Petersburg, but after my fifth birthday there was a break of some nine years and Scotland became a distant memory. Only the best was remembered. It never rained in Scotland and there were always roses in the garden, apples on the trees and blackbirds hopping around the lawn. The grass on the Grassy Beach was lush and very green, the waters were warm when we went bathing. On Sundays my cousins and their parents came to lunch. Bertie and May, my Uncle Andrew's children, were a bit older than us, but Uncle Stephen's chubby little daughter, Helen, was closer to my own age and I enjoyed playing with her. These were happy gatherings and, looking back, I am inclined to think that my grandparents were rather tolerant with all their grandchildren.

On a hot summer day tea was served in the garden. There were hot, home-baked scones and cream cookies. Jocky was brought out of the kitchen and sat in his cage beside us. Jocky loved the sun and showed his appreciation by stretching out his wings, dancing on one foot and chattering more than usual.

There is one bright scene that seems to stand out, of my brother and I still in our nightgowns, sitting on the lawn one early morning in May and our pretty mother, all in white, gathering the dew on a little sponge and laughingly wiping our faces. "It will make you pretty," she said. Later, still sitting on the lawn, we supped porridge and cream out of little bowls.

In the summer of 1911, my father had to attend to some business in Germany. During our stay, in Hamburg, we lived in a rented furnished house and not long after our arrival my parents decided to take us to the famous zoological gardens.

The day was hot and sultry, and on our return journey we were caught in a heavy thunderstorm. Drenched and miserable, we eventually arrived at our house. As I had been dressed in a light cotton dress, I succeeded in catching a severe chill followed by pleurisy and became very ill.

A telegram had been sent to Russia. Babushka allowed me to see it many years later. It contained only three words. "Jenya is sinking." Jenya, however, did not sink, although our stay in Hamburg had to be extended for a longer period than originally intended. When I recovered sufficiently to travel, we returned to St Petersburg. My parents were to remain there for some time. I was sent to Archangel under the care of our friend Petya Emelyanoff.

PART II

Before the Storm

1

1912

THEY were all there waiting for me, that day in 1912 when I arrived — my two young step-uncles in their black, high-necked uniforms of the Lomonosov Gymnasium, Yura of tawny hair and laughing eyes, Seryozha his elder brother, shy and sensitive, Marga with the round Russian face, large eyes and high arched eyebrows that seem to convey a faintly surprised and somewhat proud expression. Aunt Peeka threw her arms around me and I was enveloped in a powerful smell of tobacco. Aunt Peeka was an inveterate smoker and always carried her cigarettes and matches in a little crochet bag slung over her wrist. Uncle Sanya, my father's brother, tall and fair haired, was also there. He had come up from his quarters to greet his brother's child and, bending over, kissed me with warm affection on each cheek. And there was Sashenka. Young as I was, I sensed that something was odd about this woman in her strange, mannish clothes and was relieved when she didn't kiss me, but instead firmly shook hands with me. "You and I, Jenichka," she said, looking earnestly into my face, "will have to work very hard together." She was referring, of course, to my entrance examination for the gymnasium for which she was commissioned to tutor me.

In the midst of all the hugging and kissing, Dedushka, a giant of a man, arrived from the hospital. He threw me high and kissed me as he caught me and I can remember the touch of his cold cheeks and damp beard, the fresh smell of snow and frost that he brought in with him.

Babushka removed me to her bedroom. For two days and nights I had worn and slept in my sailor's suit and was now grubby and untidy. Mother's strict instructions were, that as soon as I arrived I was to wear the dress laid out on top of my case. I emerged washed and changed into this special dress presented to me by my Scottish granny. It was the style of the Scottish fisher-girl's dress much in fashion for small girls during that time. It consisted of a full tucked skirt in navy-blue serge, caught up at one side to display a blue and white striped underskirt. A fitting jersey was worn with it and a small fringed shawl, crossing over in front, completed the outfit.

We all sat down to lunch. The day was Sunday and the reason I remember it was so was because on Sundays all food was baked in the great oven in the kitchen. Sunday was baking day and the day when only white flour was used, unlike Fridays when the black rye bread was baked and made to last the whole week.

Later, everybody moved into the ballroom. My mother, during our sojourn in Scotland, had taught me to sing to her accompaniment some of the popular songs heard in music halls and pantomimes. Father, full of paternal pride, had boasted in his letters to Babushka about my ability to pick up with speed the melodies and words.

On the scene that followed, I look back with shame as I have an innate dislike of any form of exhibitionism in children. I was asked to sing, and although there was no Mama to accompany my singing, I did not require a second bidding and with perfect nonchalance and style stood in the middle of the floor and presented all the songs I knew — *Daisy, Daisy, give me your answer do* followed by *Yip I Addy, I Aye I Aye* and *Once there lived side by side two little maids*. All this was accompanied by suitable gestures, the stamping of feet, the waving of the hand and a variety of expressions that suited the words and feelings. I was warmly applauded. My repertoire was rather limited, but encouraged by an enthusiastic reception I continued to improvise, inventing words as I went along, secure in the knowledge that they would not be understood, until Babushka decided that enough was enough.

For the first few days I was tremendously spoilt and all my antics were suffered with loving patience, but fortunately for myself the novelty of having me there gradually wore off and I became accepted as the youngest member of the clan, to be teased by Yura, tolerated by Seryozha and, depending on Marga's mood, either petted or brushed aside.

I shared Marga's bedroom. My small bed stood against the opposite wall from hers. The curtains were never drawn across the windows so that it was possible to watch the stars shimmering against the sapphire curtain of the sky. Hanging in the far corner was a large ikon of Mary and the infant Jesus. The holy light of the lampada in front of it burned night and day and gave me a kind of peaceful consolation.

It was Babushka's custom to brush my hair at night. On her dressing-table stood a photograph of my mother sitting between my brother and me. One night when Babushka was brushing my hair, my eyes alighted on the photograph. I suddenly burst into tears. The next night the photograph had vanished.

Dinner was always served at six. When it was over Babushka usually prepared me for bed. Being too young, I was not allowed to sit up and join the family at the evening tea table. At times I lay awake

listening to the voices coming through from the dining-room. I could
also hear the reassuring clicking sound of the watchman's rattle
breaking the frozen stillness of the night. Night watchmen were
employed to walk up and down the streets. The watchman who
walked on Olonetskaya Street was a very old man. Close to our house
on the corner of the street was a small stone hut, known as a "Budka",
where the watchman sheltered if the weather proved to be too severe.
At the same time he was never alone, as he was always accompanied
by Scotka. Every night the old man was in the habit of calling at our
house for a glass of tea before setting off on his round. I can see him
sitting at the kitchen table, in his worn patched coat, thick felt boots
and a shabby, moth-eaten shapka on his white head. At his feet
patiently waiting is Scotka. After warming himself the old man slowly
rises to his feet—"Nu vot poidyom Scotka" . . . "Now let us go, Scotka."
Scotka follows. Through the whole of the night in all kinds of
weather, intense frost and snows, the old Russian peasant and his
Scottish friend walk up and down the lonely street. When they reach
the house the watchman clicks the rattle and it tells us that all is well
and safe. In the early morning they are back in the kitchen. The old
man drinks a hot glass of tea and eats a slice of black bread, rests for a
while in the warm kitchen and then departs for his home, wherever it
might be. As for Scotka, a mass of white needles and dangling icicles,
he immediately vanishes into the warm tunnel below the pechka,
settles down beside the irons and sticks and remains there while the
melting snow and ice form little pools around him. He emerges later,
rested and hungry, and after a good meal is all set to take to the road
once again.

Although at the beginning of my stay there were no playmates, I was
never lonely. Something went on every day in the house and there
was also this constant coming and going of friends and relatives. The
gates leading into the courtyard from the street were close to the
kitchen entrance. There were no bells or knockers on the door so that
visitors usually walked through the kitchen and up the stairs into the
back hall. The front entrance was only used on special occasions, by
strangers and rare visitors; when the front bell rang and the maid
hurried to open the door we would all be overcome by curiosity, and
Babushka, peeping through the dining-room door, would also wonder
who it could be.
   Of Babushka's immediate family there were left only three brothers
and one sister. Aunt Peeka I have already described. She and Babushka
were very attached to each other and could often be seen sitting
together at the round table in the nursery having long conversations,

while Babushka, surrounded by little boxes, paints and brushes, would be engaged in her favourite hobby of creating artificial flowers and Aunt Peeka would sit idly puffing away at one cigarette after another.

Their three brothers were completely diverse in appearance and character; their lifestyles, especially when I tried to compare them with that of my sedate uncles in Scotland, could only be described as rather unusual.

The youngest brother, Vladimir, known as Uncle Volodya, I used to see sitting peacefully on the wooden settle in the back hall where hung all our outside clothing. I would sit down beside him and begin to pull off my felt boots. "Hallo, Jenichka," he invariably greeted me with a sweet but rather uncertain smile. "Hallo, Uncle Volodya," I would return his greeting, but from then on our conversation didn't progress any further. Uncle Volodya was a silent and quite harmless alcoholic not given to many words. Those passing through the hall usually ignored him. He never moved from his corner until the afternoon samovar was brought to the table and Babushka would take him under her wing and place him beside her, at times gently patting his shoulder. Later, when the samovar was removed, Uncle Volodya, back to semi-sobriety, would go to the hall and slowly, with great concentration, begin to dress himself for his return journey to his home. His wife was long since dead; he had no children and only an old servant looked after him.

Babushka's favourite was her eldest brother Ivan. Uncle Vanya, as we called him, was a quiet, unassuming man much loved by all those with whom he came in contact. Like his brother Volodya he had been employed in the Civil Service and, although retired for many years, still wore the faded green, long coat of the civil servant. His longish white hair, the wispy beard and the narrow chiselled features were reminiscent of some ancient saint so often depicted in old ikons. Uncle Vanya, however, was a very ordinary mortal who at one time lived nearby in a pleasant house with his wife and two little girls. His happy married life was shattered by the sudden death of his wife in giving birth to their third daughter. Broken by the loss of his wife and faced with the daunting prospect of bringing up three young children, Uncle Vanya didn't know where to turn.

The midwife, known as Anna Osipovna, had stayed on for a short time caring for the baby and the two small girls. In her, Uncle Vanya decided, lay his deliverance from his predicament and impulsively he married her. Unfortunately, their marriage did not work out and after three weeks of what might be described as a passing acquaintanceship they parted in perfect agreement, without rancour or harsh words.

Anna Osipovna, after her brief encounter with married life, returned to her former occupation. At the same time, what had happened did not deter her from claiming her rights as a member of the family. Determined to be included in the clan and recognised as Babushka's sister-in-law, she came regularly to the house and took an active part in all family gatherings, weddings and christenings. Many decades later, after the death of my beloved Babushka, it was Anna Osipovna who claimed the honour of carrying the ikon at the head of the procession to the cemetery.

Anna Osipovna was a small woman. She possessed an unusually sharp little nose and quick, all-seeing eyes. She was rather aptly named by my father "Osa", meaning "the wasp". As the first two letters of her patronymic Osipovna were the same as that of "Osa" this may have had some bearing on her nickname, but the real reason was because of her waspish nature and stinging tongue.

Anna Osipovna did not mind being referred to as "Osa"; in fact she quite liked it. She and Uncle Vanya often sat at the same table. Between them there was this casual indifference, so that the family were never embarrassed by any display of animosity.

The problem of Uncle Vanya's children was jointly solved by Babushka and Aunt Peeka. Uncle Vanya and his two daughters, Tatyana and Ludmilla, better known as Tanya and Ludmilushka, came to live with Babushka, while Aunt Peeka and her husband, Uncle Kolya, who had no children of their own, adopted the baby Lydia and brought her up as their own daughter. In time, all three girls married and settled down in their respective homes. Uncle Vanya went to stay with his eldest daughter Tanya, who lived across the river near the station of Issakagorka. It was Tanya who was commissioned to take charge of the luggage when my parents arrived from Scotland and mother set foot for the first time in Archangel.

One day, about three years before my final arrival at the house, Tanya came rushing to Babushka and between tears and sobs explained that her darling Papachka had left the house. That morning a group of pilgrims had called and, as they were leaving, Uncle Vanya, having made up a little bundle of clothing, announced to his astonished daughter that he had decided to join them. They were on their way, he explained vaguely, to the monastery of Kholmogor some forty miles up the river and later planned to continue down south to the famous Kiev-Pechorski Monastery. Aghast, poor Tanya begged and pleaded and even ran behind him as he set off along the dusty road, but all entreaties and tears were of no avail. Uncle Vanya was a deeply religious man. This was something, he explained to Tanya, that he had always wanted to do and nothing would divert him from his sacred mission. Tanya had stood on the road helplessly watching her old father walking in the midst of the pilgrims with his stick and bundle, the silvery hair below his peaked hat ruffled by the wind, until he gradually disappeared out of sight.

At first Tanya hoped that her father would return after he reached Kholmogor and that the long trek back would cure all his fancy notions, but she was mistaken. Three summers and winters had gone by and there was still no sight or sound of Uncle Vanya. There were, of course, rumours brought by various pilgrims. Uncle Vanya had been seen in many parts of Russia — Kiev, Vladimirsk, Moscow and even Siberia. After their initial anxiety the family settled down in the firm belief that Uncle Vanya would eventually return to the fold.

The most outstanding and picturesque of the three brothers was Uncle Dmitri — a man of great girth and height towering above all the relatives. His broad cheekbones and strong features are framed by a luxuriant beard and hair that is brushed back from his forehead in unruly waves, tipping his shoulders. He scorns the collar and tie of the usual civilian suit, and favours the Russian style of shirt with the high embroidered neck band and trousers tucked into long boots. He is expansive, flamboyant, generous and violent. He is violent when he is in his cups, and more so if nursing as well a real or imaginary grievance.

His wife, Aunt Liza, was a placid, sweet-faced woman — a typical northerner, fair-skinned and blue-eyed. She wore her blonde hair in a heavy plait wound round her head in a style that aroused my admiration. She was the only child of a well-to-do grain merchant who had built up his business from low beginnings. When he died, Uncle Mitya took over and ran the business on behalf of his wife.

Uncle Mitya very rarely brought his wife to the house and although she was Babushka's sister-in-law she always addressed her by her patronymic of Evgeniya Evgenievna and spoke in a soft sing-song voice. At the tea table she held her cup with her little finger sticking out in a dainty fashion and with each sip bit the sugar with her strong white teeth. The family lived in the northern part of the city known as Kuznichikha — meaning the place of the blacksmiths. It was not a very salubrious district, and there were also certain parts which had an unsavoury reputation, but Uncle Mitya's house was in a quiet street not far from the river. Their two sons, blond and sturdy, attended the Lomonosov Gymnasium. They were friendly boys, but rarely called at the house.

Uncle Mitya was known to be a great "wheeler dealer". There was the time when he overheard me expressing a wish to possess a St Bernard dog. "You want a St Bernard Jenichka," he said. "You shall have your St Bernard." The following day a dog arrived, but it was not a St Bernard nor did it bear any resemblance to any known breed. I was not permitted to keep it, but being passionately fond of all dogs, could not bear to part from it. I kept it hidden in the stables warmly wrapped in Babushka's travelling cloak. I fed it on a special concoction of my own invention — double cream, bought out of my own pocket money from the local dairy, mixed with water, sugar and black bread to thicken it. The pup and the ruined cloak were finally discovered and Babushka was not exactly overjoyed when she saw the irreparable damage done to her prized possession. To escape her wrath and the retribution due to me, I spent a long time hiding behind the sofa in the drawing-room, waiting for calmer conditions, and eventually emerged to receive only a good dressing-down. I never discovered what happened to the dog.

Uncle Mitya was not always so benign. I remember my mother recalling her own confrontation with his wild temper. It happened during her first summer in Archangel. She was calling on Babushka and, while climbing the convenient back stair, suddenly saw the towering figure of Uncle Mitya bearing down like an avalanche upon her. Regardless of her presence, he swept her aside against the wall and continued his mad rush through the kitchen and out of the house.

Upstairs, the rooms were in a shambles. Broken china and overturned chairs were scattered over the dining-room floor. In the ballroom each one of the long wall mirrors had been shattered as Uncle Mitya in his insane rage had lifted the light gilded chairs and flung them with great force, smashing the chairs, the mirrors and the flower pots below them. Earth, flowers, broken ornaments and shattered glass were scattered and trampled into the parquet flooring.

Babushka, shocked into silence, was aimlessly picking up bits of broken glass. Marga, terrified out of her wits, was weeping hysterically in the arms of her governess. It transpired that someone, though no one knew who, had passed some remark which displeased Uncle Mitya and set off this tornado.

The following morning Uncle Mitya was back. Grovelling on his knees and kissing Babushka's feet, he beseeched her forgiveness, swearing in the name of our Mother of God that this would never happen again and that he would make amends for everything. Babushka, being what she was, forgave him.

What she could not forget, or forgive easily, was his exploit during the time of the abortive revolution in 1905. Never involved in any revolutionary activities, he had impetuously decided to join a revolutionary procession which began in his district. In a spirit of bravado and in fine style, his picturesque appearance dominating all the others; carrying a red flag and in full voice proclaiming all the slogans, he marched in the midst of the rebellious workers. The procession was moving in the direction of Solombala and was on the bridge when from the mainland in the distance, galloping along the shore front towards the bridge, a group of horsemen appeared. The procession immediately disintegrated, some running ahead and some back in the hope of reaching the safety of the mainland before the horsemen. Uncle Mitya did neither. He threw aside his flag and leaped into the river. Clinging to the understructure of the bridge, he waited until the thundering hooves overhead galloped on to Solombala. Later, swimming close to the bridge, he succeeded in reaching the shore and eventually the walls of Babushka's garden. There, hiding in the turret of the summer house, from where he could observe the lie of the land, he spent the rest of the day until he was driven by hunger to appear in the house. Babushka, a faithful subject of the crown, was furious, but the call of the blood being stronger than her loyalty, fed her brother and kept him hidden for a few days until it was thought to be safe for him to return to his own house.

From that time Uncle Mitya was named "Mitka Shalai" — a derogatory nickname, never at any time to be used within his hearing. It would be impossible to find the meaning of such a word in any dictionary, but it conveys that the person named as such is reckless, irresponsible and, in short, a hooligan. My great-uncle was never referred to as anything else, but no one would have dared to call him "Mitka Shalai" to his face, for that would have courted disaster. Unfortunately I did not know that and fondly imagined it was just one of the many harmless nicknames bestowed on the various members of the family and friends.

In early December following my arrival, I celebrated my seventh birthday. A big parcel arrived from St Petersburg and inside I found a large doll in a blue dress, wearing a straw hat. What pleased and delighted me more than anything else, however, was my first pair of skis, presented by Dedushka. The following day, during the bright hours of sunshine, I ventured out into the courtyard and donned my skis. Stumbling and falling, I eventually clambered above the snowdrifts and reached a smooth plateau by the garden hedge. There, at first timidly and later with more confidence, I glided up and down until I tired and the short day began to close in. Skiing on a flat surface, I found, was quite simple and prompted a wish to go further afield.

The next day I went out again. In a space, breaking the dark line of the hedge, the garden gate lay deeply buried in the snow. I skimmed over it and found myself in the garden. Still and silent, the trees were in their deep winter sleep. The snow lay thick over everything, masking the flower beds and bushes. It settled in spangled drifts on the bowed branches of the green and blue pines and powdered the glittering twigs of the silver birch. The whole garden sparkled and shone in the dazzling rays of the winter sun. Yet nothing moved — not a twig or a branch. Only the golden beams danced on the lawn and played on the sombre trunks of the wild cherry trees. And there was not a sound to be heard. The snow muffled everything.

Ahead, like a large saucer, lay the pond. After gliding down the rim I circled inside it for a little while and then moved on to a rustic summer house. The steps leading to the glass door inside the verandah were clear of snow. Removing my skis, I climbed the steps and peered through the glass. Inside were Dedushka's beehives, where the bees were kept warm and safe from the frost and cold. Dedushka was an expert beekeeper. It was his only hobby and he was very attached to his bees. I used to see him standing over a small spirit stove preparing a special syrup for them. He would then don his skis and, carrying the container with the syrup, would glide through the garden to the summer house. His bees always survived the Arctic conditions, which was quite an achievement. I never saw any other beehives in our district.

I hurried away to the foot of the hillock on top of which stood the main summer house dominating the garden. It was this mysterious "Fairy Castle" that had fired my imagination and aroused a determination to get inside it, but on drawing closer I discovered that the steps leading from the base of the hillock were completely snowed up. It was beyond my puny strength to reach the platform. The surrounding trees had the closed look of stern sentinels on watch. Perhaps they were guarding their castle and resented this curious interloper and perhaps, who knows, inside there was a sleeping princess who would awaken with the first kiss of spring when she and all around her would come to life again.

When I returned to the house, I discovered that there had been another arrival at the house. My cousin Marina had come from St Petersburg.

Marina was my Aunt Olga's second daughter who had contracted an illness which destroyed her hearing. She had spent seven years in a special boarding school in St Petersburg and still had two years to go before she was finished, but recently a very clever and enterprising lady had opened a small private school for deaf children in Archangel. Babushka had suggested to my aunt that Marina should come to her and join this school as a day pupil and, in this way, have the security and happiness of a family life. And so Marina arrived and, like myself, crept under Babushka's ever protective wings. Marina was seven years older than me, but in spite of the disparity in our ages and her sad handicap, she and I became great friends. She was blessed with a very keen brain and an observant eye. She wrote and read fluently and was an amazing lip-reader as well. I learned very quickly the language of the hands, but Marina never permitted anyone to use their hands in front of strangers or outside, and would brush any movement aside saying one short sentence: "Rukamie ne nado" . . . "Hands are not necessary."

She was given a little room all to herself and, being well trained in St Petersburg, kept herself and her room in immaculate order, allowing no servant to do anything for her. Unlike my young Aunt Marga, who devoted a lot of time to keeping her beautiful hands perfect — and a great deal of patience and energy embroidering handkerchiefs or taking care of her numerous ornaments — Marina followed Babushka like a faithful little puppy, always eager to help, to mend, to sew and in the summer months assist Babushka in every way in the garden. At times Babushka, seeing her engrossed in some task, would exclaim, "My Marinochka has golden hands."

With the approach of Christmas a great activity commenced in the house. The floor polishers came and skated over the parquet floors in their inimitable style. Mirrors and furniture were rubbed until they shone, the chandelier was dismantled and each sparkling piece cleaned and hung back in its place. The same kind of activity went on in the kitchen. On the table, piled high, lay capercailzies, geese and white partridges, waiting to be plucked and prepared for the oven. A special dough, sitting in a crock for a month slowly fermenting and absorbing spices, was now ready to be rolled out and cut into stars, crescents and hearts and finally baked in the oven. Baskets were filled with these biscuits and, along with sweets and other delicacies, despatched to my Aunt Olga in Finland. Every day Babushka set off into town and came back laden with parcels. Presents were sent to each of her numerous granddaughters and all the other members of the family including the nannies and mamkas. No one was forgotten.

Christmas, as well as Babushka's and my own name-day of St Evgeniya, was to be celebrated as usual on Christmas Eve. As the day grew nearer, other more interesting, and for me, exciting and even mysterious preparations began upstairs. One evening immediately after dinner, Babushka produced a big bag of walnuts and placed it on the round table. Saucers of sweetened milk, lighted candles, sealing-wax and strands of green wool were laid out. Then each one of us was handed a small book of gold leaf attached to tissue pages. Marga and

the boys knew the procedure. Marina, once she discovered what was
wanted, worked faster than any of us. I tried to follow the best way I
could. A single leaf, attached to the tissue paper, was held in the palm
of the hand. The walnut was dipped in the sweetened milk and
immediately enveloped in gold. The two ends of the cut wool were
placed on the flat end of the nut and sealed with a drop of sizzling wax.
The nut, now ready for hanging, was placed on a tray.

Apples grown specially for the Christmas trade came next. These
little apples, crimson and white, almost pear-shaped, were the type
often depicted in fairy tales. The stalks on them were long enough to
have attached to them the same green loops for hanging.

I had no idea for what purpose all these loops had to be fixed, nor yet
did it occur to me to enquire. This coming Christmas was to be the
first one I would remember. There was a vague memory of another
one in Scotland, when in the morning I found a stocking full of little
presents followed by other gifts and later by a Christmas party. In my
early days in Scotland there were no Christmas trees.

In the mornings, rosy-cheeked peasant women, carrying baskets,
came to the house offering their home-baked "kazoolies" laid out in
rows between layers of white linen. The "kazoolies" were delicious
spiced cakes formed into shapes of people and animals typifying the
north. There were Eskimos, polar bears, reindeer, all decorated in
white and pink sugar.

The doors leading into the ballroom were locked for some reason.
Yura, Seryozha and Marga kept darting in and out, but gave vague
answers or ignored completely all my enquiries. It was all very
mysterious.

One morning a troika accompanied by the gay jingling of bells
rushed through the gates and halted at the front entrance. Troikas,
with the advent of the railways, were not seen so often. We ran to the
windows and watched two plump ladies scramble out of their kibitka.
They were Babushka's cousins who lived in the depth of the country
far from any railway station. For years they had always stayed with us
over the festive season. They were not married and both were alike,
poured into identical black-lustre dresses, trimmed at the neck and
wrists with lace frills. Their sweet faces expressed cheerfulness and
undisguised delight at being once again in our midst. Adelya and
Verochka were welcomed in the usual Russian fashion, hugged and
kissed on each cheek. They were the only two survivors of what was
once a big and happy family who often exchanged visits with
Babushka's people in Maimaksa. That was long ago when they were
all young, but now, living alone in the depth of the wooded
countryside, they were inclined, like many elderly people, to dwell in

the past. After handing over their many presents to Babushka, who in turn put them behind the locked doors of the ballroom, the three ladies retreated to the peace of the corner room where they sat reminiscing.

A little later a portly gentleman known as Pavel Petrovich arrived from Vologda. A great friend of Dedushka, he was a bachelor and, like Dedushka, passionately interested in bees. No sooner was he in the house than he and Dedushka retreated to the study to talk on their favourite subject. I may add that both gentlemen in due course received a special recognition from the government for the joint invention of a method which enabled bees to survive arctic conditions.

The house by now was rather full, but everyone was happy for in those days people still covered long distances, braving frosts and snowstorms to join family gatherings and above all to enjoy the gladness and warmth of an old-fashioned Russian Christmas.

In the early afternoon of Christmas Eve more guests arrived. Aunt Peeka and Uncle Kolya came with Lidochka, her husband and their little daughter, Polya. Also from Solombala came Ludmilushka, her husband and their young son, Modist. The third sister, Tanya, the three children and her husband, driving their old horse, crossed the river from their house near the Issakagorka Station. Tanya, always willing to help everyone, was very poor so that this yearly Christmas gathering was a special treat and a source of great excitement to her children.

My father's Uncle Adolf, a very imposing gentleman, who was my godfather and the brother of my late grandfather, arrived with his smart wife, Aunt Fanny. There were also young cousins from that side of the family. And then there was Dedushka's only relative, known, strange to say, by her surname of Auntie Doodkina, a sweet and shy old lady who brought some of her lovely baking. Also Aunt Emma, Babushka's dearest and oldest friend from her childhood. Auntie Emma lived alone, but no gathering or celebration ever took place without her.

When Babushka was surrounded by many people or was occupied, Auntie Emma liked to sit alone in some quiet corner with a little glass of something in her hand.

As was the custom, Babushka and I received the usual congratulations on the day of our Saint. The presents that everyone brought vanished behind the locked doors of the ballroom. It was not usual for children to be running around between the feet of their elders, but later, it being Christmas, an exception was made. Meanwhile, the grown-ups adjourned to the corner room while all the children, under Marina's and Yura's supervision, were banished to the

nursery. There we played games and amused ourselves, but I, full of
curiosity, kept opening the door and peeping through to the dining-
room where Babushka, with a preoccupied air, kept rearranging the
hanging grapes on the epergnes and putting finishing touches to the
table. I saw Irisha, the young tablemaid, carrying through to the
dining-room a tray loaded with hot pirozshkis which would be served
with the soup. I passed on the glad news to the others and sure enough
we were soon trooping into the dining-room to take our places with
our elders.

The Christmas dinner bore a resemblance to the one that I
remembered in Scotland except that instead of roast turkey there
were geese stuffed with apples accompanied by partridges cooked in
sour cream. At the end as a special gesture to her half-Scottish
granddaughter, Babushka served a plum pudding. Inside were the
usual trinkets, which surprised and delighted young and old. During
the dinner, there were pauses when someone would stand up and
offer a toast to Babushka and myself in recognition of our name-day,
which gave me a delightful sense of importance.

Towards the end of dinner Yura and Seryozha excused themselves
and disappeared into the ballroom. Soon after, Babushka suggested
we should leave the table and move towards the closed doors. There
we stood waiting. There was an air of expectation. Then, at the
tinkling of a bell, all the lights went out, plunging the rooms in
darkness. The double-doors were flung wide open.

And there, against the background of total darkness stood this
glorious thing, stretching up to the ceiling, ablaze with lights. I had
not seen before a Christmas tree of any kind. The sudden impact of
this amazing sight overwhelmed me.

Everything shimmered and trembled. The beautiful fairy standing
on tiptoes, the snow queen on the sledge driving the silver reindeer to
her ice castle with the little boy behind her, Red Riding Hood with her
basket setting off to visit her grandma, the little mermaid swaying
gently on the edge of a branch, the princess in her gown and diamond
coronet, the evil witch standing beside the cottage which is slowly
circling on hens' feet, the gnomes and the little winged angels, the
tinkling crystal icicles and the sparkling scattered frost. And over all
the glitter, the characters out of fairy tales, the apples, sweets and
golden walnuts, there was the brilliance of candles, each pointed flame
surrounded by a golden halo encircling the tree, layer upon layer of
them, and fusing together into one cascading light of dazzling
splendour.

I still remember saying to myself, "This must be like the heaven
about which Babushka told me — the place where little children

sometimes went to, where they were always happy and never scolded, where everything was bright and golden apples grew on trees."

Happiness is relative — in my days I have had my share, but nothing has ever surpassed those few rare moments of sheer rapture when I stood gazing up at the wondrous sight of my first Christmas tree.

I could have stood for ever. Finally, I turned and walked over to my table. The presents for each member of the family were laid out on small individual tables. On mine there were many gifts. Babushka was distributing presents to all our friends and to every servant. The children were running round eating mandarin oranges and pulling nuts, apples and sweets from the tree.

Later there were slides displayed by a magic lantern on to a sheet hung over the wall of the hall. The scenes portrayed, from fairy tales and nursery rhymes, were accompanied by a running commentary by Seryozha and although we were to see these same pictures year after year they never failed to delight.

In the late evening the sledges of the guests began to glide back to their homes. After the last one left, Yura and Seryozha carried the high steps into the ballroom and began to put out the candles. One by one the lights went out until the tree was left in darkness.

On Christmas morning all members of the family and guests attended the Christmas service. Our church — the Church of the Assumption — lay a short distance from the house. With the exception of Babushka and her plump cousins, who went by sledge, we all walked along the river front. The morning, bright as silver, was filled with the sound of all the church bells ringing in joyful unison. Ploughing through the deep snow, which crunched pleasantly under our boots, we reached the church. In the entrance a row of poor people, dressed in miserable rags, stood begging in the name of the new-born Saviour. Inside, the church was packed. Masses of candles burned in front of each ikon. The smell of beeswax, humanity and incense mingled together. The glorious voices of the unseen choir sang loud and clear.

Two days later Babushka and I set off to the house of my godfather, where we were invited to a family gathering of those related to my late grandfather. We were driven by Mikhailo, who had returned to Babushka's household when my parents went away.

The adults adjourned to the dining-room for their dinner while we children ate at a big round table in the nursery where a young governess took charge and saw that we all behaved ourselves. When dinner was over we were allowed to join the grown-ups in the drawing-room. There we all played drawing-room games. In the corner stood a Christmas tree never to be compared with our own.

Over-decorated, it lacked the artistic touch of Babushka's hands. Instead of the soft candle-lights, small coloured electric bulbs were scattered over the tree — no doubt infinitely safer, but lacking in atmosphere.

In the early evening we said our goodbyes and set off on the return journey. The night was clear and frosty. Our sweet mare, Smirnukha, so named on account of her peaceful and obedient nature, ran cheerfully past the familiar landmarks. As we came down towards the river she suddenly became nervous and shot through the gates. Mikhailo drew up sharply beside the back entrance and, dropping us, went to the gates. "I think, Barynya," he said, locking the gates, "there are wolves about and Smirnukha can smell them."

We went through the back entrance into the hall where we removed our heavy shubas. In the dining-room we found a cheerful gathering round the table. The samovar was singing its welcoming song. Babushka went into the ballroom to pull some nuts and sweets from the Christmas tree. The candles weren't lit. The hanging ornaments glimmered dimly in the moonlight pouring from the windows. I heard her calling me to come and join her. She was standing beside the window. "Come, Jenichka, and see this," she beckoned me. Looking down directly below our windows, which faced the river front, I saw walking in single file what I took to be six or eight dogs. "Why are these dogs walking like that?" I asked. "Those are not dogs," Babushka said. "They are wolves and are hanging around because they can smell our sheep and horses."

We watched in silence as the wolves moved towards the gates, which unlike the gates on the street always remained locked. There they stood, uncertainly looking through the wrought iron and then, slowly turning away, disappeared down the steep incline to the river only to appear again on the moonlit surface, still in single file, walking past the waterhole in the ice and on towards the opposite shore.

This was the first time and only time I ever saw wolves in their natural state. I still remember the strangely sinister and almost uncanny sight of their slinky forms and stealthy approach to the gates.

2

1913

During the first days of the year it became very cold and the frost hardened. We were approaching the festival of Epiphany, when the weather was often referred to as the "Frosts of Epiphany" and when the blessing of the waters in all the rivers in Russia took place. Some hardy souls were known to go into the waterholes in the ice and actually survive their immersion.

Through the week, young friends of the boys and Marga came to the house to take part in the traditional games which were supposed to foretell the future. One of them was to pour melted wax into cold water and try to guess what was prophesied by the shapes which formed. And then there was the game with mirrors. In some empty room, and not within hearing distance of any person, a mirror is placed on a table. A lighted candle is arranged on either side. Draping a white sheet over her shoulders and undoing her hair, a girl sits down in front of the mirror. Directly behind, on another table, is a second mirror. The room is in darkness. The mirrors reflect only the face and shoulders in the flickering lights. The candles, multiplied by the mirrors, form a strange gallery of lights that appears to have no ending. There she sits, not moving or turning her head until gradually some shadowy forms and faces begin to take shape.

I have heard this custom dismissed as an optical illusion, a reflection of a lively imagination or a form of self-hypnotism. I have also known the most incredulous people who swore that they not only had seen objects and faces but whole scenes presented before their eyes.

One of Marga's friends went into Marina's room and followed all the instructions. In a little while she rushed out, deathly pale and frightened, refusing to discuss what she had seen or perhaps imagined.

I was not allowed to indulge in this game, but Marina and I found two saucers and covered the bottom of each with fine cinders and ashes. Water-filled tumblers were placed in each saucer. A wedding ring had to be dropped into the glass. Babushka, who always wore two wedding rings, from her late and present husband, supplied us with them. We had to keep our eyes fixed on the centre of the ring. Although I stared hard and long into the golden cricle I never saw anything except ashes.

Marga for some strange reason was very nervous and could not sleep alone in a room. At times when she was in one of her frightened moods I would be awakened by her calling to me — "Are you there, Jeyna?" — or in a more ingratiating tone — "Are you sleeping, Jenichka?" This of course gave me a certain power over my aunt, ten

years my senior. At times, being irritated at being disturbed or out of
sheer devilment, I pretended that I was sleeping until moved by a
sense of pity I would scold Marga as if she was a little child. "Of course
I am here — where do you think I would be? And don't you know that
our Holy Mother of God is watching over us? Go to sleep and don't
bother me." Poor Marga, comforted by the sound of my voice, would
fall asleep. Well, little did I know that the day would come, a long way
off as yet, when I also would be afraid.

One day, Sashenka informed me I had to work, and work hard, to
make up for the precious hours I had idled away. It was necessary,
before I could be accepted by the Mariyanskaya Gymnasium, to pass
an examination in reading, writing, arithmetic and also acquire some
knowledge of certain passages out of the Old and New Testament.

Having been given the responsibility of driving all this into my
frivolous head, Sashenka didn't spare me. Every day, after she arrived
from her school, tuition commenced at two o'clock. There was no
break until six o'clock, when dinner was served. Immediately it was
over there were further instructions as to what I had to prepare for
Sashenka the following morning. This went on every day, including
Sunday.

There was a thankful break with the Shrove Carnival, or
"Maslinitza", as it is named — meaning "the butter time". For a
glorious week there were no lessons. Holy Russia became the land of
pancakes, of swift horses pulling sledges of every type through town
and countryside, of fancy dress balls and parties and of little children
tobogganing in villages and backyards on home-made chutes.

Mikhailo made a small chute for me by packing the snow with his
spade and pouring water over it. He then swept a path up to his lodge
and poured water over it too. Soon the surface froze and became as
smooth as glass. I spent hours climbing up the little steps and gliding
down to the end of the runway. Masha, Mikhailo's wife, who was not
well, sat beside her window watching me.

The following day I noticed a young boy and girl accompanied by a
soldier standing at our gate looking on at my solitary sledging.
Mikhailo beckoned to them. Volodya, a little senior to me, and his
young sister, Vera, were the children of General Zaborchikoff and his
wife Anastasia Ivanovna, who were our neighbours and lived on the
top floor of a house facing the street. In this house all the servants
were orderlies who cooked, washed, took care of the children and also
served at the table. There was a much younger child called Shurick, a
very attractive little boy bearing a strong resemblance to his lovely
mother. The general, with clean-shaven head, as smooth as a billiard
ball, was a plain, pale-faced man. His unsmiling countenance and

proud bearing inspired fear not only in the children and the orderlies but also in his wife.

I was delighted with my new playmates. After the initial shyness, we spent a glorious time sliding down the chute on the toboggan or on our backs, jostling and rolling in the snowdrifts, shrieking and laughing until it began to darken and the soldier removed my new friends back to their home.

The following day they came back, but after spending some time on my home-made chute we saw other children passing our gate on their way to the river. We ran after them and joined the noisy, cheerful throng sledging down the incline to the river. This was a natural, wide, steep slope, where we could sledge not only down to the edge of the river but a good distance over it.

A young, red-cheeked boy came over and asked me my name. "Jenya," I answered timidly. "My name is Tolya — Tolya Mammontov." He introduced himself with the cool self-possession of an adult. "You are sledging the wrong way," he went on, "sitting there like a baby with your feet sticking out. You won't get very far that way." He then proceeded to tell me that the best way to sledge was to lie flat on my stomach using one leg as a rudder. I proceeded, nervously, to follow his instructions, but halfway down the hill veered to one side and landed in a deep snowdrift. Everyone laughed, but I didn't take offence and was only too glad to be treated as one of the gang. It was a new and happy experience.

During the week, the Samoyeds and their strings of reindeer came driving into our yard. They brought their wares — hats, boots, shoes all made from reindeer skins. They were accompanied by a few snow-white Samoyed dogs, which I much admired, but was warned not to touch as they were not friendly towards strangers and were primarily used for guarding the vast reindeer herds.

The Samoyeds, their cheerful flat faces wreathed in smiles and talking in their quaint style, tried to persuade us to hire them for a run on their sledges even as far as their distant yurtas. Babushka was not keen. It would be bitterly cold on the river, she argued. The sledges were completely exposed and there was the danger of frostbite. In the end she agreed to compromise. We were allowed to go, but not any further than the outskirts of the town.

As the sledges could only hold one or two passengers at the most, two were engaged. Yura and I would travel on one sledge, Marina and Seryozha on the other.

Warmly clad, thick shawls pulled well over our faces, sitting close behind our driver, who held a long pole with which he directed the reindeer, our procession moved slowly through the gates. Each sledge was pulled by four reindeer and, as soon as we went on the river, they set off at great speed.

The sensation of being pulled by reindeer beggars description. The sledges are so light that one has the impression that the runners are flying above the snow. The Samoyed clicked his tongue and prodded his reindeer. I sat a little fearful and excited, clinging tightly to Yura. On and on we raced, the wind whistling past; houses, gardens, the golden domes of the churches appearing for a moment and vanishing away, until we reached the outskirts of the town where there was only a dreary plain, with only a few poor cottages scattered here and there. The snow on the river and the shore changed from gold to crimson and deep lilac. The reindeer turned in a wide circle and raced back towards the twinkling lights of the town and on into our courtyard.

Back in the warm kitchen, we found Babushka, wrapped in an apron, her face crimson from the heat of the range, frying pancakes. On a stool close to the range stood a large crock of buckwheat batter and, in another container, melted butter. A long row of small thick frying pans was strung across the range. Babushka worked deftly with exact timing, her hand speedily moving from one end of the pans to the other and back again. A small quantity of butter was poured in each pan. The batter followed and by the time the last one was filled it was time to turn over the first one and move on to the end and finally back to lift each finished pancake on to an ashet. She preferred to do this herself, repeating each operation over and over again until there was a great golden pile of wafer-thin pancakes, not heavy and greasy, but light and delicious. They were taken to the table to be eaten immediately in several layers. On the table was a bowl of sour cream, caviar, and a variety of other fillings as well as an assortment of jams prepared from wild berries.

Hundreds of these pancakes were eaten. The old honoured Russian custom was kept up throughout the whole week. Only a few other dishes were served to break the monotony.

On the last day of "Maslinitza", Babushka expressed a nostalgic wish to visit Maimaksa — the place where she was born and brought up and spent the first years of her married life. Hardly any of her friends and relatives were left there now, but Babushka wanted to meet again the widow of Pavel Mikhailovich, who had taken care of Babushka and her mother during their journey to St Petersburg for the historic interview with the Tsar. Because this was the Shrove Carnival, combined, perhaps, with some distant associations, Babushka ordered Mikhailo to harness a troika. Yura and I were to accompany her.

The troika has been the inspiration for many songs, tales and paintings. The style of harnessing and the running of the three horses are unique. Only the centre horse runs between the shafts. It trots on two reins, holding its head high, gazing straight ahead. An arch, known as the "duga", often decorated with silver and little bells, surmounts the head. On either side are the two other horses, fixed by a strap and a single rein. They gallop beside their leader with their heads turned outwards.

In the early afternoon, sitting close together inside the wide padded sledge, and tucked in by rugs, we set off. It was frosty and snowing gently, but the festive season had brought the people out and sledges of many types were racing up and down the broad fairway. A horse, harnessed to a small, elegant sledge, came racing towards us. Inside the sledge was a young man, his arm round the waist of a pretty girl muffled in furs. She laughed and waved as they passed us by and vanished towards the lights of the city. Then, further along the road, a troika full of young people singing, with someone playing a concertina, came alongside and for a short time we travelled abreast with all the bells jingling in unison.

We reached the part of the river where the great mass of Solombala divides the river, leaving the narrower stream hugging the shores of the mainland. It had stopped snowing and the moon, clear and white, lit up the great expanse. "Now then," Mikhailo called out and raised his knout. The horses immediately broke into a gallop and swept round the island. On our right were the orange lights of Solombala and on our left the dull shores of Maimaksa where lay all the structures of the timber mills. On these bleak shores the great wealth of the timber industry was founded. The troika raced on passing one mill after another until it climbed ashore and drove up to a single-storeyed house completely surrounded by trees. Climbing up the steps to the entrance, we were welcomed by a chorus of barking dogs and a young servant girl who opened the door and showed us in. Inside, all warmth and light, the house was full of young people and little children.

Mariya Egorovna, the widow of Pavel Mikhailovich, threw her arms round Babushka. Now quite old, she lived with her married son and his family in the same house where she had spent her married life. Her three lively grandchildren, the youngest a boy named Sasha and a classmate of Yura's, demanded that we should go with them into their garden.

Behind the house was a steep ice chute built on a solid wooden foundation, with strong steps leading up to the platform. On either side of the chute and the long runway to the house were planted small

The Bridal Group (top), taken at "Bay House" 1904; Aunt Olga, 1905 (bottom left) – lovable and a little eccentric and her husband, Oscar Semyonovich Yanushkovski Councillor of State for the Russian Civil Service in Helsinki. The author's parents visited them on their honeymoon and travelled to Russia with Olga.

pines all lit up by colourful lanterns. Lanterns were tied too to the
stark branches of the birches, lighting up the trees and throwing
splashes of crimson, gold and green on the snow.

We spent a very happy time gliding down on sledges and rugs. I set
off with Yura and Sasha on a rug, but lost the two of them on the way
down and careered on my own in giddy circles to the end of the
runway, where we all collided and shrieked with excitement. This
went on until the servant girl came running to tell us that the barynya
wanted us all back to the house as supper was now ready and the
samovar was on the table.

Another mound of pancakes awaited us.

After supper, Babushka decided that it was time to go. There was a
long road in front of us and it had started to snow again. Having said
our goodbyes, we climbed into the sledge and drove on to the river.
When we reached Solombala, Mikhailo took the road diagonally
across the river to our own street. This was the quickest road. Already
visibility was poor and getting worse. At first the snowflakes drifted
slowly but gradually came thicker and faster. The moon vanished in a
milky whiteness; sledges and horses appeared as dark formless
shadows moving through a snowy haze. As we made our way home,
the sledge moved slowly, swaying gently from side to side and the
muffled tinkling of the bells was like the repetitive singing of a sweet
lullaby.

Lent followed the Shrove festival. The faithful religiously obeyed all
the austere laws, but the average family, such as ours, observed only
some of them. Sunflower oil was used for cooking instead of butter
and animal fat. Eggs were avoided. Fish dishes, of which there was a
great variety in this land of seafarers, replaced meat and fowl. To
break the monotony of the forty-nine days' diet, the law was
occasionally discarded and a joint of venison or a roasted capercailzie
accompanied by cranberry sauce appeared on the table.

A new member of the household arrived from St Petersburg as
housekeeper. Kapitalina Semyonovna, always referred to as
Kapochka, was at one time brought up, along with her sister, by
Babushka's family in Maimaksa. When the girls grew up they went to
St Petersburg, where they eventually married. Kapochka's husband,
however, became ill and died and she was forced to look for work.
Kapochka's life had been rich and colourful. For some time she moved
in the world of the stage, and, although in a lowly position, knew
many famous people such as the great singer Feodor Shaliyapin and
the immortal ballerina Anna Pavlova. Later she worked in the
household of the well-known singer of Russian folksongs,

Plevitzkaya.

Kapochka was something very special. She helped Babushka, dealt out the required amount of ingredients in the preparation of food, mended linen, repaired clothing and did many unseen tasks that helped to keep the house in running order. She was beloved by everyone with whom she came into contact, for she possessed an elusive quality which is rare and difficult to describe. I only know that no matter where she went or whom she met she radiated warmth and affection.

I can see her standing in the old nursery dressed in a dove-grey, loose-fitting dress girdled by a silk cord. I can even recognise the soft texture of the dress, the little lace collar, the large pockets which I know are filled with small oddments — keys, reels, thimble, glasses and so on. Her hair, gold and grey, is rolled in a little bun on top of her head. I cannot tell how old she might be for Kapochka is ageless. Her skin is flawless and the eyes are like brown velvet.

One evening, after dinner, as I was sitting over my books with Sashenka, Mikhailo came rushing into the house in deep distress, Masha was now seriously ill and, after a severe fit of coughing, had taken a sudden haemorrhage. Dedushka followed by Babushka ran to the lodge. Dedushka did all that he could and for the time being saved her. Babushka sponged her and brought clean sheets from the house.

However, gradually Masha's health became worse. Dedushka, after a thorough examination, told Mikhailo that Masha had tuberculosis. Masha was doomed, for in those days there was no known cure for this terrible scourge that took such a toll from all classes of society in Russia. Mikhailo, driven by despair, began to drink. There were times when Dedushka, called out in the evening to some patient, would find Mikhailo incapable of either harnessing or driving the horse. Vassily would harness the single sledge and Dedushka would hurry off, driving himself.

A few days before the holy week of Easter, Masha died. She had died in the early hours of the morning and in the evening the first Requiem took place in the lodge. The whole family attended and stood crowded round the coffin placed on the table. In the soft glow of candlelight Masha's young face was peaceful. Across the forehead was a white band on which was printed in gold letters a tract from the New Testament. In her folded hands lay her white and gold marriage candle with the crushed orange blossoms still attached to it. On her breast was a small ikon. Two peasant women, standing beside Mikhailo, wept bitterly, constantly crossing themselves, bending low and going down on their knees, their foreheads touching the floor.

At the end of the service everyone moved to kiss the ikon. Mikhailo,

tears streaming down his face, kept stroking and kissing his wife's
hands. I was pushed over to kiss the ikon and, as I did so, my cheek
came in contact with Masha's ice-cold hands. Involuntarily I shrank
back. This was my first acquaintance with death.

The following morning I went up to the lodge again and, removing
my skis, entered the room where Masha's coffin lay. An old monk,
sitting at a table in the corner of the room, was reading in a quiet voice
the prayers for the dead. He didn't even turn round. I stood for a
moment gazing at Masha. Her features looked sharper and there was
a bluish line between her lips. On all the walls of the room were
posters depicting the evils of drink. One showed hungry children
sitting around an empty table and a weeping mother with her head
buried in her arms. Another, children begging on the streets, and still
another, a man prostrate on the snow and beside him an empty bottle
of vodka. They had been pinned up by Masha in a vain hope to shame
and cure her husband.

A few days before Palm Sunday, Yura and Seryozha put on their skis
and set off across the river to the willow woods. They came back laden
with bundles of pussy willows which were then divided into sprays,
tied with ribbons and decorated with Babushka's lifelike artificial
lilies.

On Sunday there was a steady procession of people winding their
way to the church carrying the sprays of the silvery catkins. In Russia,
Palm Sunday is known as the Sunday of the Pussy Willows, there
being no palms about. The service was followed by the holy week of
Easter when the monumental preparations commenced for the great
day of the Resurrection.

Even as far back as the early summer the preparations had begun. A
little pig was bought and put in a stable where it was fed on special
food and treated with great care until the late autumn when a little
stout German gentleman arrived in his cart equipped with some
unpleasant-looking instruments. He came every year and I used to
think that his rosy, plump countenance and ginger hair bore a certain
resemblance to the poor victim he and Vassily slaughtered.

A long deal table was placed outside the kitchen and Dunya, the
cook, along with her assistant, Grusha, were kept busy carrying out
buckets of boiling water. The German expert and Vassily worked the
whole day and in the end the cart was loaded with the biggest part of
the pig. Some time later he brought back strings of delicious smoked
sausages, bacon, hams and other parts of the pig. Everything was
eaten and enjoyed except the two hams which were hung in the garret
beside the strings of dried mushrooms and herbs.

The hams were now brought down to be prepared for the Easter table. They were baked in the great oven inside a crust made from rye flour and water. Then there were the sweet Easter cheeses known better as "pashka". Some ten and more pyramid-shaped forms had to be filled. A large tub was brought into the kitchen. Into it went the curds, first drained of every drop of whey, pressed and put through a fine sieve. Beaten butter, whipped cream, sugar and vanilla were added and then the hard work of mixing began. A long pole which widened at the foot was used. Everyone in the family took a turn at mixing. This went on until it reached the texture which pleased Babushka. It was then poured into the muslin-lined forms and taken to the larder. I have since tasted many cheese cakes and, having the form, attempted to produce one myself — but nothing ever had the elusive flavour of those prepared during my childhood.

The colouring of the eggs and the baking of several "kulich" and "rumbabas" were left to the end of the week. The "kulich" is a raised round cake prepared from flour, raisins, peel, numerous eggs and flavoured with vanilla and cardamom. Later it is iced and decorated with the first letters of the words "Christ has risen". Rumbaba is also a cake raised with yeast. It has to stand about ten inches high and is baked in a special form. The word "baba" in Russian means a peasant woman. The cake with the rum icing poured over it does have a certain resemblance to the figure of a woman dressed in a full sarafan.

Meanwhile, the various rituals followed one after the other. During the week every member of the family and all the servants set off to the church for their confession. They went at different times and prior to leaving went round begging everyone to forgive any sins that they may have committed. I, not having yet attained the wisdom of a ten-year-old, was not included in this ritual, but graciously forgave all those who had sinned against me — including Sashenka.

On Thursday of Holy Week it was usual for the whole family to attend the evening service in the church. The Passions of Our Lord were being read according to the Gospel, in twelve parts. We stood listening, with lighted candles, to the words. In between the reading of each apostle, the candles were put out, and prayers and the beautiful poignant singing of the choir took over. With the exception of the glorious midnight service of the Resurrection, this particular service has always remained my favourite. Yet, much as I loved to listen to it, standing there in the heat of all the lighted candles and dressed in my heavy shuba and felt boots, I invariably, halfway through the service, would begin to feel an intolerable pain across my shoulders which would spread across my back, gradually getting worse, until in the end I was forced to go to the back of the church and find a corner on a bench especially placed there for all the old babushkas and dedushkas who were also unable to bear the strain of standing throughout the whole service. And there, to my shame, I would sit beside them all.

The following afternoon we went back to the church. Christ's Body was now brought down from the cross. A lifesize ikon lay in front of the sacred gates leading into the Holy of Holies which no woman was ever allowed to enter. Worshippers coming and going brought artificial flowers and reverently laid them beside the ikon. Babushka, who grew hyacinths in pots, made up a spray from these blooms and laid it on the ikon at Christ's feet. Real flowers were a rarity in our parts at that time of the year.

On Saturday morning, I was awakened by the noise of intensive activity. Mikhailo and Yashka were bringing down from the garret small tables and placing them against the walls of the dining-room. The main table was extended. Kapochka and Irisha, standing at opposite ends, were spreading the snow-white damask tablecloth. Everybody was bustling around. Even Marga, not given to straining herself, was carrying in on a tray the dishes and wine glasses and arranging them on the serving table.

Downstairs in the kitchen, where Babushka's expertise was required, hams were being decorated, joints of veal glazed, baby sturgeon arranged in aspic jelly, salmon laid out on ashets and dressed with great artistry, and caviar, pickled mushrooms, salted herring and all the other zakuskis placed in their dishes. Helped by Dunya and Grusha, Babushka worked fast, with intense concentration, her experienced hands moving from one dish to another.

As the Easter feast was to last for several days everything had to be prepared in duplicate and passed on to Irisha who carried it upstairs to the "buffetnaya" — a long, narrow room adjoining the dining-room. In this room was a trapdoor below which were steps leading down to a cold larder lined with stone shelves. The dishes not required immediately were placed there.

In the late evening the preparations rose to the final crescendo when each dish had to be arranged on the table in the correct place. In the centre stood the great pyramid of coloured eggs — blue, crimson, gold and green, dominating the table. Around them were the various ashets and dishes. The delicate pink of the ham, the creamy tenderness of veal, the black and orange caviar, the rich paskhas, kulichies and rumbabas, and finally the glowing colours of the liqueurs and various vodkas. As an extra touch there were bowls of blue hyacinths.

To this day the scent of hyacinths invariably conjures up the richness of the Easter table. There would only be a few more of these

Easter tables. They grew poorer with each year and in the end vanished for ever.

As the last hours of Lent drew nearer all began to get ready for the midnight service of the Resurrection. Only Babushka was to remain behind to receive the guests who would arrive straight from the church. I, anxious to join the others, in the end was promised that if I went to bed early I would be awakened in time to go to the service. With this promise secure, I went off to my bed and soon fell sound asleep.

And as I slept I dreamed that there were some other people moving around the house. Their voices seemed familiar but I could not place them. Then my mother appeared to be standing at the foot of my bed. She was in a crimson dress trimmed with cream lace and was holding an Easter egg. She looked beautiful. I wanted this dream to continue. "I don't want to go now to the service," I said. My mother laughed and bent over me. "Khristos Voskryese — Christ has risen," I heard her say in her own accent. I opened my eyes. There she was, kissing me and holding out the Easter egg. My father was standing behind her. "Khristos Voskryese, my darling," he said and picked me up in his arms. "Where is Ghermosha," I asked him. "Ghermosha is sleeping," he said.

It transpired that Babushka knew all the time that my parents would be arriving, but she wanted to surprise me. It was to be like an Easter present. They were due to arrive on Easter day, but somehow left St Petersburg earlier than they planned and arrived after I was asleep. I had heard nothing and by now the Easter service was over.

My father carried me into the dining-room. It was packed with all our friends and relatives, milling around the table. They were all kissing me and saying "Khristos Voskryese, Jenichka," and I was answering them as I was taught. "Voistinu Voskryese — Truly He has risen."

Later I was taken back to my bed. In the morning, when I awoke, I found my little brother sitting at the foot of the bed. We both laughed.

On the first Easter day, Marina, Yura, Ghermosha and I set off to our church to ring the bells. During that time children, and anyone who wished to do so, were allowed to climb up to the belfry and ring the bells. I led Ghermosha up the steep steps and found other children were already there, pulling the ropes as hard as they could. When our turn came, Marina joined in and assured us that she could hear the chimes. I spread the good news at home that Marina was not entirely deaf and could hear certain sounds, but Dedushka explained that Marina did not really hear the sound of the bells but only felt their vibration. There was a constant flow of relatives and friends. They all brought Easter eggs and the pile of eggs grew higher with each day. Some were chocolate, some sugared, others of wood or fine porcelain, and many were simply boiled eggs painted in colourful designs.

Uncle Volodya, perhaps a little less inebriated than usual, brought to his sister an ordinary egg completely painted over with beautiful wild flowers, minute and perfect in every detail, created with fine artistry and loving patience. Babushka was quite overcome. He partook a little of what was on the table and then as usual slipped away quietly and unnoticed. Uncle Mitya came. "Khristos Voskryese, Jenichka," he called out to me kissing me thrice and lifting me off my feet. "Voistinu Voskryese," I rejoined timidly, feeling as if I was being embraced by a great bear, all dressed up in a crimson silk shirt and velvet trousers.

All the mamkas, of course, also came from their various villages bringing little gifts to their own particular child. Seraphima, my father's mamka, came and presented Ghermosha and me each with a wooden Easter egg painted in crimson. When opened, it disclosed a succession of eggs in different colours progressively becoming smaller and culminating in one the size of a peanut.

Having handed over to us our presents and exchanged the Easter greetings with all the members of the family, and after enjoying what was offered on the table, Seraphima turned her attention to my father. She spent the rest of her time sitting beside him, calling him her "synok" — her little son — asking him many questions, and having a long, earnest conversation accompanied by numerous glasses of cherry brandy. She had no eyes for anyone else.

Spring came back. The river lost its pristine whiteness and became tinged with a dull lilac hue. A fast-flowing stream like a dark ribbon appeared in the middle and widened. Suddenly, as if possessed by a wild fury, the river began to shatter her fetters. The broken floes, carried by churning waters, began their journey to the sea. With ever-increasing speed, clambering over each other, rising high on end and crashing down, colliding, sending showers of splintered ice, they rushed ahead carrying everything with them, destroying all obstacles. On their surface could still be seen the tracks of sledges, the discarded debris and circles of small pines surrounding the waterholes where only recently women gathered to rinse their washing.

Gradually the pace slows down. The river, sparkling in the spring sunshine, now flows serenely on her way. A few small isolated floes, like swans, sail in the wake of others and vanish in the Arctic depths.

In the garden, the grass is pushing through the melting snows.

Beside the steps of the summerhouse, clumps of blue Siberian anemones have struggled to the surface and are nodding their dainty heads to the sun. A tender green is intermingling with the black twigs of the birch; the buds of the wild cherry are swelling.

Spring is short in the north. One week there are hard frosts and blizzards and the next the thaw arrives and moves swiftly. Snow on the rooftops begins to slide and crash onto the pavements. Snowdrifts shrink and vanish. A merry bubbling can be heard coming from the torrents running below the wooden pavements. Everywhere there is slush, and streams hurry down to the river. All the back streets are quagmires, until the sun dries them out.

Inside the house, the inner frames of the windows are removed, and all the outside noises come in. Gone is the deep silence of winter, the gentle creaking of the sleigh runners. The wheels of carts trundle over the cobbled streets. The ears are assailed by a shrill chorus of chirping sparrows, cawing rooks and the excited sounds of dogs who in their joy appear to bark at nothing at all. The crowing of the cock awakens the whole household in the early hours of the morning. He and his hens have been removed from their dark winter quarters to a more congenial habitation and are allowed to stroll in the courtyard. The hens, like fine ladies walking on tiptoe, step carefully, lifting their feet high over the lush grass of the drying green. They blink their amber eyes up to the sun and emit peculiar drawn-out sounds of sweet contentment.

There is an old Russian saying: "Open wide the gates — here comes trouble".

Soon after the arrival of my parents, I noticed that there appeared to be some discord between them. There were disagreements and angry exchanges at the end of which my mother wept bitterly and her eyelids remained swollen for days on end. I didn't ask any questions. In any case the tragic truth was beyond my understanding and only reached me many years later.

My father was a generous man — he was also gullible and a soft touch for anyone who cared to come along to him with a hard-luck story.

Perhaps a year or more earlier my father was introduced to a pleasant gentleman who had arrived from Riga and whose name was Ganneman. My father was always pleased to make new friends and especially with anyone from Riga, where he had spent such a big part of his childhood and youth. Being hospitable he brought him to his house and introduced him to my mother. She did not take to him.

At that time the timber trade was flourishing. Father, who was in partnership with his uncle, was doing very well. His uncle was a hardheaded businessman with a wide experience in the timber trade so that Father, being young and with very little practical knowledge, had to defer to him.

One evening while sitting in the club with my father over a glass of vodka, Ganneman casually suggested to him that he ought to start up a mill of his own further up the river. To begin with Father paid little attention, but the more he listened the more the idea of being sole owner of a mill appealed to him. Ganneman sounded a very knowledgeable man. He also had contacts with people with whom arrangements could be made at a reasonable price for all the equipment, the buying of the land and the building of the new mill. In fact all that was required for the success of this enterprise was money.

Full of this scheme and bright hopes, Father came home and spoke to my mother. Mother was not a very clever woman and was therefore blessed with plain common sense. She firmly believed in the adage that the bird in the hand was worth two in a bush and was perfectly happy with everything as it was. They were comfortably well off, wanted for nothing, and were free from care. Why was this gamble necessary?

Disappointed by this lack of co-operation Father went to his mother. Babushka threw up her hands in horror. In a matter of a few years, she pointed out to him, his uncle might be retiring and then he would be the senior partner. His future was assured, as was that of his son. There was also this house and grounds and all that they entailed, which was his inheritance. Disappointed with Babushka, Father finally spoke to his uncle. My great-uncle and godfather did not waste any time in idle persuasions. Sternly and in a few words he warned Father that if he embarked on this venture and removed his inheritance he would forfeit the right of partnership left to him by his own father and would be fortunate to have even a minor position in the business.

It is a well-known fact that if anyone is determined on a certain course of action, advice and threats are useless. He will only hear what he desires to hear and if that does not coincide with his own wishes he will go his own way. The details of the catastrophe which followed are lost in the mists of time. I only know that my father withdrew the largest part of his inheritance and by doing so lost his partnership in the business, being replaced by his uncle's son, Adya. Father was given a minor position in the firm which deprived him of any say in the running of the business. No mill materialised and only a small part of the fortune was salvaged. The trickster vanished without a trace.

The results of this tragedy were far-reaching. My father was broken by the betrayal of the man he trusted, by the knowledge of his own foolishness and above all by the loss of his previous position and hopes for the future of his son. His whole personality changed from a man who was good-natured and given to laughter to one who could not joke any more and went about with a permanent frown. There are no more terrible words than "I told you so". For a time he heard them often, not only from my mother, but from his own as well.

We never went back to the house in Technical Street. All our furniture and belongings were brought to the house in Olonetskaya Street. The various pieces were scattered over the house and all the china, silver and ornaments packed in cases were taken to the garret. Never before had I seen my mother weep as she did that day.

And then there was the time when we watched sadly as the mare Plutovka was being led out the gates. Plutovka was not really needed and had to be sold. She was my mother's favourite and sometimes when my mother was quite old she liked to talk about her.

My mother was neither ambitious nor covetous. She never wanted more than she had. The big house which my parents might have possessed one day held no attraction for her. Everything was too big, the house, the grounds and garden. The constant coming and going of friends and relatives and the generally expansive way of life was something she could not see herself fitting into or controlling effectively. She preferred her own compact style. Yet she loved the Russian people and followed their customs along with those of Scotland.

To the cleaning and preparations for Easter she added the Scottish "spring cleaning". Curtains and carpets were taken out into the hard frost, shaken and beaten, and the whole house turned upside down to the astonishment of the servants. She baked scones and Scotch shortbread and bought oranges and made marmalade, a thing unheard of in our arctic regions. During the summer when jam was made from the golden wild Moroshka berry, she followed suit but in the Scottish way, stirring vigorously and breaking down the berries, which horrified Babushka. The Russian method was to boil the syrup first and then gently lower the berries in so that they would remain whole.

The house in Technical Street had been her world and now the bottom had fallen out of it. There was nothing to do in a house where everything ran like clockwork. She began to go out, make new friends and accept all invitations. My parents were drifting apart.

3

1913

One day Sashenka and I set off for my entrance examination to the Mariyanskaya Gymnasium. In the hall were other girls of my own age, each one accompanied by an adult person. There was an air of nervous expectation. A teacher appeared and, after calling out our names, shepherded us into a spacious classroom. We were placed behind individual desks and the examination began. A dictation was read. I scribbled furiously in my atrocious writing and somehow managed to keep up with the measured pace. The papers were then removed and others placed in front of us. This time it was arithmetic.

I found some of the sums difficult, but with surreptitious help from my ten fingers carried on the best way I could. A bell rang, the papers were removed and we returned to the hall where we were immediately surrounded by our eager escorts. Sashenka bombarded me with questions, but didn't appear to be enthralled by my answers.

After an interval of some twenty minutes we were escorted upstairs to a large hall for the final examination, on scripture. This time all those who escorted us were admitted to the room and sat together with their charges on chairs lining the walls. At the other end of the hall, sitting behind a long table, was a group of people including a priest and the headmistress. On the table stood a box containing small rolls of paper.

The surname of each girl was called out in alphabetical order. The more I watched, the more apprehensive I became. At last I heard my name being called and walked up to the table. The instructions were to take out one of the slips from the box and read out the question, loud and clear, so that everyone in the hall could hear it. I did as I was told and read out the question loud and clear. But that was all — I had not the faintest idea what the question was about, except that it had something to do with the Virgin Mary. A dead silence followed — all eyes were upon me. Suddenly from the back of the hall the black figure of Sashenka stepped forward, her hand raised in a peremptory gesture. In a voice that brooked no opposition, I heard her saying, "This is not a question for a seven-year-old child. No one of her age can possibly understand the meaning behind it."

This was followed by consternation and a hasty consultation at the end of which Sashenka was informed that her objection was upheld and that I was allowed another chance. I removed another slip of paper from the box and read out the question. To my great relief I understood it and answered correctly.

The examination was over. I danced and hopped on the wooden pavements all the way home. There would be no more lessons, no more Sashenka and slaps over my hands. I was free to play with my brother in the garden, free to go down to the river, to splash with my playmates and learn to swim, for the water of the Dvina close to the shore was now warm, heated by the sun-baked boulders.

In June the tender white nights returned. Sunset and sunrise met — there was no darkness. People strolled on the river front and in parks where the bands played well into the night. Once again ships skirted the island of Solombala and the fishing fleet in full sail hurried seaward. Once again there were midnight picnics to the islands and the sounds of voices floating across the river.

My Uncle Sanya joined in these midnight excursions as part of his merry-making, but now that the white nights of high summer had arrived there was an additional craze as a finishing touch to his parties. Draped in towels the guests would all go down to the river and splash and swim around until they sobered up before dispersing.

One night, in the early hours of the morning, I was awakened by the noise of a great commotion coming from the courtyard. I ran to the window. In the yard close to the gates four men were holding the corners of a sheet on which lay the naked body of a man. They were throwing it up and down, the old Russian way of reviving a drowned person. Dedushka, half-dressed, appeared on the scene and ordered them to place the body on the grassy verge. Going down on his knees, he began to apply the professional method of artificial respiration. He worked hard and long to the stage of utter exhaustion, perspiration pouring down his face, until another doctor arrived and took over.

Standing around, watching helplessly, were all the guests and Uncle Sanya. On the grassy verge, still with a towel draped around him, his head buried in his arms and his entire body shaking with convulsive sobbing, was Petya Emelyanoff.

It was his father whom the doctors were trying vainly to bring back to life.

Petya's father was a man not given to merry-making. He had called casually, with his son, on Uncle Sanya and found himself involved with the others. When, in the early hours of the morning, they all decided to go down to the river, he joined them. Petya's father had been a powerful swimmer in his day and while everyone was frolicking in the shallows he struck out from the shore into deep water where he was suddenly overtaken by cramp. Uncle Sanya and his friends, shocked into sobriety, brought him ashore. It was too late.

Later in the morning the police arrived and came back again to ask many questions. The whole family were upset by this tragedy. Father, who had always been very close to his only brother, sided with Babushka when she accused Sanya of reckless behaviour.

A few weeks later, Sanya left his flat and rented a house in a street nearby. There he engaged a young housekeeper to administer to all his wants. I was sorry when he left us, although he regularly came back to the house and in time there was no ill feeling between him and Babushka or my father. He was a kind man, with a slightly absentminded air about him who had always welcomed me when I called on him. He was usually to be found reading a book or newspaper, lying stretched out on a large shabby sofa covered with faded chintz.

There was an enormous tiger-like cat whose amber eyes were intently fixed on the numerous squirrels that Uncle Sanya kept. These animals, with their bushy tails, leaped about the furniture, cracked hazelnuts laid out on the table, made little clicking noises and amused themselves by running up and down the walls, tearing off strips of paper.

There was also a large cage which housed several black-beaked, red-breasted bullfinches. At times the door of the cage was open and the little birds flew out to have a bath in the flat dish on the table, where they chirped happily while hopping about and scattering the water all around them.

When Uncle Sanya left, his squirrels, birds and the cat went with him. The flat remained empty and silent for many years.

The days were unusually hot during that summer of 1913 and the nights sultry. No breeze stirred the curtains of the wide-open windows and not a ripple was seen on the glassy surface of the river. The servants, in search of a cooler place, carried their mattresses out of the house and slept on the balcony beside the hayloft.

I remember being awakened early one morning by the bright sunlight pouring into the nursery, where for some reason the curtains were never drawn. Already from the street below our windows could be heard the rumbling of the carts rolling down to the river. Feeling rather bored, I decided to waken my brother, sleeping soundly in his small cot next to mine. We lay for some time talking quietly and watching the strange shadows appearing and gliding along the wall opposite the windows.

"What are these shadows?" asked Ghermosha, secure in the knowledge that his sister was bound to know the answer. "These," I enlightened him carefully, "are the reflections of the little men going back to the mountains." "What mountains?" he enquired, doubt creeping into his voice. "Their own special mountains," I replied firmly and, before he had time to ask any more questions, suggested that we should go out into the garden. We dressed and, tiptoeing through the silent house, ran into the courtyard and from there to the garden.

I remember with great clarity the joy of that early morning. The welcoming shrill chorus of the little birds, mostly sparrows, the shimmering gauze of the dew spread over the lawn, the crimson carpet below the old balsam tree, lazily shedding its scented catkins. We gathered these catkins, held their sweet softness close to our faces, scattered them over the grass and chased each other until we tired.

Nearby the stone steps, flanked by hawthorn and wild roses, led to the summerhouse. After the snows had melted, the door leading into it remained locked for some time, but now it was open. Inside there was nothing but the prosaic furnishing of a plain table, some chairs and, in a glass cupboard, cups and saucers. But through the coloured diamond-shaped panes of the Gothic windows, light filtered in rainbow splashes. "Look, Ghermosha," I called out, peering through a crimson pane, "the garden is on fire." "Look through the purple glass," he called in turn. "All is dark and 'Baba Yaga' is hiding in the bushes." We ran in great excitement from window to window, seeing the garden in all the different hues — the sinister dark green; the golden yellow, when the trees, the flowers, the butterflies and even the birds turned gold. It was all strange and mysterious.

An outside stair led to the platform above the room. Here on the east side the tips of the trees were level with the shallow walls. The white heads of the rowan trees and the scented racemes of the wild bird-cherry spilled over the side.

We climbed up to the turret. From here we could see the sparkling waters of the Dvina, sweeping down to the north, the shores of the opposite islands, strung together in a long dark line, the golden domes of the churches, the houses, the leafy gardens and the wide cobbled streets.

As we stood on this high platform, almost afraid to move, we saw Babushka bending over the flower beds and hurried down to join her. It was now time for breakfast, so we started to stroll back together. It was then that we noticed an old man walking along the path in our direction. He was dressed in the faded uniform of a civil servant. He had a thin straggling beard and below his shabby peaked cap the snow-white hair tipped his shoulders.

Babushka halted and then began to run. "Vanya, Vanichka," she cried, throwing her arms around the old man, tears streaming down her face. "I always knew you would return, always knew it."

The news of Uncle Vanya's return spread fast. By lunchtime his two daughters, Lidochka and Ludmilushka, and their children along with Aunt Peeka had arrived together from Solombala. Tanya was already there. Uncle Mitya and Uncle Volodya also came to join in the celebrations. Everybody was mildly surprised to see Uncle Vanya's estranged wife Osa appear on the scene as well. After formally shaking hands with him and expressing the hope that he was none the worse for his long walk, she took her usual place at the table.

Uncle Vanya, a man who was never talkative, sat smiling benignly at everyone. It was Tanya who did all the talking. It transpired that the day before, when she was preparing the midday meal, her papachka walked in and calmly sat down at the table, "Just as if he had never been away," she concluded happily.

Uncle Vanya's momentous trek through Siberia earned him the nickname of "Siberiyan — the Siberian", and from that day I never heard him referred to as anything else. He was a gentle and deeply religious man who had a great love for all wild animals, birds, trees and flowers. I never heard him talk about his experiences except that he did once express his opinion that the great "Mother Volga", about which so many songs were sung, was not nearly such a beautiful river as our own "Dvinushka", with her crystal-clear waters.

On another occasion, while admiring some of the flowers in the garden, he described the wondrous sight of the steppes in the early spring, when as far as the eye could see the whole great expanse became a flowered carpet. But, he added sadly, this colourful mass of flowers didn't last very long and was soon burned into dry whispering grass by the merciless rays of the sun.

He had gathered seeds and bulbs in Siberia and brought them to Babushka, who planted them in the garden where they flowered successfully year after year. To us all he brought little carved crosses, small ikons and souvenirs from the monasteries.

That day, as we were all gathered round the table, a letter was delivered to my father. He impatiently tore open the envelope and scanned the pages. "Our Jenya," he announced, "has passed her examination and is accepted by the Mariyanskaya Gymnasium." Everyone kissed me. Sashenka received a special vote of thanks. Not given to praise, she merely commented: "Strange are the ways of God. This is a miracle!"

Miracle or not, I had been accepted. The following week Nastenka, our dressmaker, arrived at the house and took my measurements for the school uniform.

Uncle Vanya's homecoming was followed by the arrival of my Scottish

granny and Uncle Henry from India, whom my mother had not seen
for eight years. They were accompanied by Pavel Petrovich, the
beekeeper, who had come to keep an eye on the precious bees while
Dedushka, Marga and Seryozha were on vacation in the Crimea.
Granny, now a seasoned traveller, had come via St Petersburg, where
she had arranged to meet Henry who had come by a more adventurous
route — by sea to Vladivostok and then across Russia on the Trans-
Siberian Railway.

Mother was overjoyed at seeing Granny and Uncle Henry again. It
had been such a long parting — she could not stop talking to them in
between listening to all the news from Scotland. As for Uncle Henry,
all friends and relatives took this young man to their hearts. Uncle
Henry was young, good looking, debonair in his well-cut tropical
suits, but above all generous and friendly. The servants vied with each
other to clean his shoes and to carry the cans of hot water into his
bedroom every morning. Ghermosha and I followed him about
wherever he went. Like Uncle Stephen of earlier days, he was invited
to all the houses and lavishly entertained.

A trip up the river, of a few days' duration, was organised on one of
the more luxurious passenger paddle-steamers. The whole family
went, including Babushka. The weather was pleasantly cool. The
steamer meandered gently around the winding shores. On the
landing stages barefooted children surrounded us, offering baskets of
wild strawberries. At night we ate these fragrant berries with cream.

To us children the trip was a novelty of absorbing interest. We liked
to watch the foaming wake from the paddles, the tying up of the boat
to the landing stage and the lively scenes that followed when the
motley crowd, with their bundles and baskets, surged on to the lower
deck.

We returned back in time to attend a garden fête held in the
Summer Gardens in aid of some charity. Before leaving for the fête
Babushka decided that we should all have our photograph taken
together, as a record of Grandma's and Uncle Henry's stay in
Archangel.

The delay caused by the taking of the photograph (and by Yura's
insistence of having his bicycle in it) resulted in us arriving at the
Summer Garden when the fête was almost over. The stalls were
empty with the exception of one, where stood an enormous doll. I had
never seen such a large doll before and asked my father if he could buy
it for me, but Uncle Henry stepped in at this point and said that the doll
would be a present to me from him. Unfortunately, the doll was not
for sale and would be raffled. Disappointed, he bought the few
remaining tickets and we all went strolling through the leafy avenues

in the garden up to the stage where a band was playing. There we found a table where we sat eating tubular-shaped waffles filled with cream, and listened to the music. Someone came over to our table and congratulated me on winning the doll. "I told you," said Uncle Henry laughing happily.

Triumphantly I carried the doll back to the house, but as the poor thing only had a pair of shoes and a pink shift I wrapped it up in a shawl and tucked it in its cot. A few days later it mysteriously vanished. To all my enquiries I received vague replies to the effect that the doll was away being fitted out with some clothing.

Somehow I soon forgot about it as other events occupied my time. There were trips into town to buy a schoolbag, a pencil case, books, jotters and all the things that are new and exciting for the beginning of one's first schooldays.

On the day of Granny and Uncle Henry's departure, we all got into the carriage and were driven to the docks. Permission was granted to board the ship. Normally this would have resulted in we children romping around the decks, but there was this heavy sadness in the air which transmitted itself to us. When we had to say our goodbyes and leave the ship, Mother clung to Grandma, weeping bitterly, and she in turn lost her habitual calmness and broke down. There were tears in Uncle Henry's eyes when he embraced us and shook hands with my father. Seven years were to pass by before I saw Granny. As for Uncle Henry, never again was there to be another meeting.

The house was quiet and empty. Dedushka, Marga and Seryozha were still in Yalta. Marina had gone to Finland to visit Aunt Olga, and Yura left to stay with friends up the river.

Mother went to her bedroom and, throwing herself on her bed, turned her face to the wall. The following day I noticed a change had come over her. She was withdrawn and spoke very little. She often went into town, sometimes taking Ghermosha and me to the shops or visiting her friends. On other days we played in the garden and fished for tadpoles in the pond, while she sat nearby watching us. When she went off into town on her own she brought back numerous little packages — brown ribbons to match my uniform, stockings, gloves, handkerchiefs and small gifts which were meant to surprise us.

About three weeks after Grandma's departure, Mother came in from town and presented me with a thick bar of chocolate. I vividly remember the confectioner's name, "George Borman", emblazoned in large gold letters on the blue wrapping.

She went over to the wardrobe and, taking out my school uniform, asked me to try it on. The universal brown uniform of all gymnasiums was a plain dress with a long bodice, high neckband and pleated skirt.

Over it was worn a black-lustre apron. Perhaps a little sombre, but neat and practical.

Mother fastened the dress down my back and after twisting my unruly hair into two plaits and fixing the ribbons, told me to stand back in the middle of the floor. She wanted, she explained, to see how I would look in this new outfit. I was quite pleased to do this and did a few pirouettes in front of her. To my surprise, I saw her suddenly lift her hands to her face and burst into tears. "Why are you crying, Mama?" I asked, feeling this awful tightness in my throat. "It is nothing," she said, turning away her head, "nothing at all."

Kapochka came in. She was holding a small bundle of broderie anglaise neckbands which had to be worn round the high neck of my uniform. "Elena Avgustovna," she addressed my mother by her patronymic, "Nastenka has just brought them. Would you like me to sew one on?" "No, Kapochka," Mother rejoined, "I should like to fix this one myself." Kapochka placed the small bundle on the dressing-table and left the room.

I undressed and handed over my uniform. Mother, threading a needle, sat down on the edge of the bed and began to sew with serious concentration while I changed back into my usual dress.

When she finished sewing, she handed the uniform back to me to be hung in the wardrobe. As I was struggling with the coathanger, she came over to help me and, throwing her arms around me, held me close and kissed me. "You will look very pretty in this," she said, and again I saw tears welling up in her eyes, but before I could say anything she hurried out of the room. I did not see her again, nor yet my young brother, until almost two years later.

Mother went to St Petersburg, a place she always loved, a place of happy memories. She lived with people named Sabinin, friends of long standing, the head of the family being a native of Archangel. They were close to my parents when they were living in St Petersburg and they had entertained Grandma and Uncle Henry there.

I do not know when my mother decided to go away, but I suspect it was after the departure of my grandmother and Uncle Henry. Disillusioned and bitter that my father, heedless of all advice, had embarked on a venture which ended in the destruction of their way of life, she may have hoped that her mother and Henry would provide a solution to her problem. And when one didn't materialise, she lost heart and decided to get away — perhaps for just a little while.

I do not blame Mother for leaving me the way she did. Prolonged farewells would have been more painful. She knew I was in good hands and that the plans for my education could not be changed.

What she didn't know was that I was already absorbed into the family, the way of life, the very house itself, and would never have chosen to go to St Petersburg.

Father, having arranged an allowance for my mother, went to St Petersburg to plead with her to return, but his journey was in vain. Some six months later Babushka, who had never quarrelled with Mother, visited her before going on to Helsinki to stay with Aunt Olga. Before she left, she half-promised me that she would bring Mama and Ghermosha back with her. I dreamt a lot about this but in the end there was no Mama and no Ghermosha.

The autumns in the distant north are harsh, if brief. No Indian summers ever come to give some cheer before the winter. A moaning wind keeps beating against the windows and rushes through the plundered garden, angrily flaying the last leaves still clinging to the branches. The leaden skies are pitiless — a steady drizzle, never ceasing, soon transforms the gravel paths into quagmires. The days are dark and dismal. But soon the scene changes. Frosts take over, followed by the first of the snows blanking out all that was bleak and ugly.

Before the winter came, Kapochka wakened me early one morning. This was the beginning of my schooldays. She helped me to dress, braided my hair and tied the ribbons.

In the dining-room the boiling samovar was humming a cheerful song on the round table. Yura, in his immaculate black uniform, and with well-brushed hair, was already seated beside Marina. Babushka in her dressing-gown was engaged in preparing coffee over a small spirit lamp. Dedushka always took coffee with his breakfast and Babushka allowed no one else to prepare it. Seryozha came in, half-asleep. Then, of course, there was Marga, now in her final year at school. The girls in her class were permitted to have their hair up and wear grey dresses. Our Margachka was rather vain and kept admiring herself in the mirror hanging opposite the table. She was a perfectionist in everything she did, especially for herself. She possessed beautiful hands, which were never allowed to do anything that could mar their delicate softness. Kapochka, presiding over the samovar that memorable morning, was passing round the cups, but I, in the grip of excitement, could hardly drink the tea or eat the little white rolls which were normally my favourites.

When I was ready to leave Babushka came over to bless me. "You are starting on a new road — God be with you," she said.

The gymnasium was only a half-an-hour's walk from the house, but on that morning Kapochka and I set off in a small carriage on our own.

At the school I was directed to my classroom. Kapochka, after kissing me and giving a quick sign of the cross, left me. At the door of my classroom stood our headmistress, Nataliya Pavlovna. Each girl curtsied before her and she in turn had a few words of welcome to every one of us.

In the classroom, Lydiya Nikolaevna, our dame de la classe, took over. We were all formed in pairs and waited. A bell rang, shrill and loud, as a signal for us to be led out of the room along the passage and up the stair towards the hall. Other classes, one after the other, followed on our tail.

Upstairs in the big hall a narrow carpet in the middle of the floor led to an altar where stood the priest waiting to begin the service. On either side of this carpet, the classes, still in the same orderly formation, took their place. Away to the right I was able to catch a glimpse of my tall, rosy-cheeked aunt, her hair piled neatly on top of her head, standing amidst the senior girls dressed in grey. At the back of the hall stood all the teachers and the dames des classes, dressed in navy-blue dresses.

At this point, the girls in the choir stepped forward and took their places on a raised dais. A short service followed, accompanied by the sweet singing of the choir, at the end of which, after a brief order, the whole school turned to face the teachers, curtsied and then, led by the senior class, marched back to their classrooms. This formal procedure was repeated every morning.

In the classroom we were allotted our desks. Each desk, divided down the centre, was shared by two pupils. My neighbour, Vanda Derboot, was a Polish girl, red-haired with fine features and a rather proud expression on her little face. We became very friendly. She was the daughter of a high-ranking officer who by some strange coincidence lived in the house which had been our home and where I was born. Thus began my schooldays.

The day at school began at eight o'clock. I remember well Kapochka's light touch on my shoulder and hearing her saying, "It is time to get up now, Jenya." Behind the frozen panes not a glimmer of light would be seen — only the darkness as dark as pitch.

After a hurried breakfast, there followed all the preparations for our short journey. Felt boots pulled over thick stockings, a shawl crossing the cheeks and chest below a fur hat securely tied under my chin, mittens fixed to tapes and finally the heavy fur-lined shuba. Babushka invariably came forward to make certain that the shawl was firmly tucked around my throat — that, she always maintained, was the most vulnerable spot.

Outside, Mikhailo and the mare, impatiently shaking her mane, were waiting. The four of us would pile into the sledge to be dropped at the doors of our respective schools. After removing all my heavy clothing and changing into light shoes, I would join my classmates and await the ringing of the bell which summoned us for morning prayers.

There were two breaks during our lessons. During that time we were allowed to buy kalachi, the doughnut-style rolls displayed on a sideboard. There were no playgrounds, no doubt due to the climatic conditions. We strolled around the hall or sat on forms eating our rolls. At times, standing at the wide window-sills, we played "Kamushki", meaning "Little Stones". Five small stones were spread on the window-sill. One had to be thrown up in the air while the player gathered up one or more quickly in time to catch the stone coming down.

School finished at half-past one during my first year, including Saturday. During the extreme frosts there was an occasional bonus when the temperature dropped to minus 22. Then, flags were hoisted on high government buildings sending out messages that all schools were closed.

Often when wakened early and having a pleasant dream cut short, I would enquire hopefully if the flags were up, only to receive the reply, "No, Jenichka — it isn't cold enough today."

Not that I disliked the school; on the contrary I liked it a lot. I was a gregarious animal, and happy to be one of the flock. As for the teachers, I naturally preferred some to others. Our headmistress, Nataliya Pavlovna, was a respected and lovable figure. Small, plump, her white hair piled high on top of her head, always immaculate in her blue dress and neat collar, she was completely dedicated to us girls. Her eyes, kind and thoughtful, always gave the impression that she could see into the heart of each one of us and understand our griefs and failings. At the same time she stood no nonsense and expected a certain standard of behaviour.

It was her custom, every morning after prayers, to stand on the landing outside the hall. Smiling a little, she watched the procession of some three hundred girls filing past her. The eyes of Nataliya Pavlovna missed nothing — the soiled neckband, untidy hair, a piece of jewellery or anything that could offend the eye. A girl who broke the rules was gently reprimanded.

Discipline was strict — the rules laid down had to be observed. Hair was not allowed to be worn loose hanging around the shoulders. It had to be braided and if wished the braids could be placed on the crown of the head and tied together. Uniform had to be tidy and spotless. No jewellery of any kind, with the exception of a watch, was tolerated.

The relationship between the teacher and pupil was formal. When addressed by the teacher only the surname of the girl was used —

never the first name. Vanda Derboot was just Derboot, Evgeniya Scholts — plain Scholts.

Physical punishment in any form was unheard of in either the girls' or the boys' school. The usual punishment consisted of being kept behind after school hours for a period, depending on the misdemeanour and the mood of the teacher. The discipline at school was perhaps assisted by the parents, as each week we had to take home a kind of a diary known as the "dnevnik" which had to be signed by a parent and returned on Monday. In this book were written comments and the marks we received in various subjects during the week. The mark on behaviour was also included. The highest mark was five, so that a minus five for behaviour was a matter for concern for the parents, followed by an enquiry, if there was no explanation written, as to what offence their offspring had committed.

The only time I was afraid of my father was when I had to present this book to him. On seeing a mark less than three, such as for arithmetic, which was my weakest subject, he would mince no words and would coldly enquire if I wished to be like Nastenka, our sweet little dressmaker, who was illiterate.

The marks were certainly important. A succession of less than three in one or two main subjects resulted in being kept back for another year. The name of "ftorogodnitza", a girl in her second year in the same class, had a derogatory sound. The thought of being left behind all my classmates was quite unbearable. It spurred me on to steer a course which allowed me to move forward from class to class to the end of my time in the gymnasium.

Our French teacher, Mademoiselle Zaizeva, dressed in a blue suit, never in a dress like the others, complete with a snow-white pleated blouse, her hair arranged in a smart chignon, was a stylish lady who was fond of giving us the full benefit of her sarcasm. Against such clever witticisms the nine-year-old is helpless. The class was therefore not enamoured with her. She liked to teach us all the various phrases in French, which was only natural. I soon acquired a fine fluency in one which has remained with me ever since. It became the custom for me, soon after the class began, to stand up and with due respect say, "Permettez-moi de quitter la classe," to which I usually got the response of, "Allez, Allez," accompanied by an impatient sweep of her hand towards the door.

There was no necessity at all for me to leave the class, but the ten minutes' respite helped to shorten the lesson and brought a little enjoyment. I liked to stroll along the corridors peeping through the glass partitions of the doors into the other classrooms.

This ploy of course could not continue. One day as I stood up to say my piece, Mademoiselle Zaizeva interrupted me. "Do you not think," she enquired in the sweetest of tones, a faint smile hovering on her lips, "that it is rather a strange coincidence that you should require the toilet each time with the commencement of my lesson?" I didn't answer. She still allowed me to leave as, after all, how was she to know that my reason wasn't genuine?

As I went strolling along the empty corridor I paused outside the preparatory class and became engrossed watching "the little ones", as we, now being one class above, scornfully referred to them. The door suddenly opened and I was dragged inside. "Sit down and welcome," said the teacher pointing to a desk. "Here we have someone," she addressed the giggling children, "who cannot bear to leave this class and wishes to start all over again." Each lesson usually lasted for forty minutes, so that I was kept sitting and having to answer all the questions until the bell rang for the interval.

Our teachers were a group of women about whom we knew very little and they in turn made no attempt to know any of us personally. They were there to instruct us, broaden our minds and inspire us with an inner strength to face up to the world. They therefore commanded our respect. On meeting any of the teachers in the corridors or rooms, the pupil had to drop a quick curtsy in front of them, but when meeting Nataliya Pavlovna, who on occasions stopped to say a few words, we sank in a curtsy, known as the "réverénce", when the right leg went back and the left was drawn up to it in a slow motion.

Some of our teachers were able to inspire us to give of our best. Others lacked imagination. There was, for instance, Mariya Arkadievna, our sewing mistress. Why was it, in a land where the most beautiful embroidery and handwork was done, each one of us had to labour over a long winter term sewing a pair of coarse cotton knickers meant for giants, doing minute stitches, herring-bone, and button-holes? I gave up halfway through the term and used the knickers for polishing the brass lid of my inkwell instead. At the end of the term I had the brightest inkwell of them all, and a minus three for sewing. Mariya Arkadievna displayed my ink-stained knickers to the class and sorrowfully told me, "Scholts — you will never be a seamstress." I have to add modestly — in my defence — that she was completely mistaken.

The teacher who stood head and shoulders above them all was Mariya Osipovna, who taught us Russian grammar, literature and history. Plain, serious, her greying hair pulled back into a small bun, she was a gifted teacher. From the moment she stepped into the classroom, she held the attention of every one of us, even the dullest and laziest. She was endlessly patient and, when explaining the difficult rules of the Russian grammar, never used unnecessary words, so that everything she said was made quite clear. But it was in her lectures on literature that she excelled herself.

We listened spellbound as she opened the door to a world of books. All our classics, the poetry and prose of Pushkin, Lermontov, Turgenev and others. We learned the translations of the English, American, French and German classics. In Russia literature always held an important place and nowhere more than in our provincial city of dark days and long winter nights.

Mariya Osipovna has long since gone with all the others, but if it were possible for us to meet again, I should like to thank her for all that she had taught me and to add that I believe it is through her that I have never forgotten my beloved language.

There was a tradition in the gymnasium to have in every class a "dame de la classe", as the class mistress was known. These normally pleasant ladies usually joined the preparatory class and remained with it throughout the school life of the pupil. It was therefore natural for the class mistress, after shepherding her flock from year to year, to form an attachment to her girls and to be closer to them than any of the teachers. In the end, no doubt, there was a void and sadness when they went out of her life and she was left to start all over again — provided her age and circumstances allowed it.

Our class mistress, Lydiya Nikolaevna, appeared to differ from the others. At no time did she ever display the smallest glimmer of affection or any attachment to her class. Lydiya Nikolaevna was there to do her duty. She did it with efficiency and the exactitude that was demanded. She did no more. Even the punishment of ordering the pupil to stay behind was done with just a calm detachment and not a trace of any anger.

During the last month of the year the frosts hardened and the days grew darker.

Earlier, in the late autumn, Mikhailo, assisted by Vassily and young Yashka, brought the heavy window-frames down from the garret. They laboured all day long fixing them again on all the windows in the house. Between the double frames they spread white cotton wool on every window-sill and sprinkled them with borax, which sparkled in the wintry sun. The logs inside the stoves burned and crackled merrily spreading their warmth and the pleasing smell of pine and birch throughout the rooms.

The winters weren't easy for those who laboured in the cold outside. Keeping the house supplied with water was especially hard, as only in government buildings such as schools, hospitals, and public baths was water laid on. But later, there was an innovation which spared Mikhailo and the others in our district from going to the river to fetch the water from the waterholes.

In a nearby street a small kiosk was built to which water was laid on by some device. You slipped a metal disc into a slot, which was collected by a girl sitting inside. She then turned on a tap, filling barrels, buckets and all kinds of containers. That was a great boon.

I have heard it said that hardship sat lightly on the shoulders of our northern people. That is not altogether true. Hardy they were, but many times the burden almost reached the limit of endurance. There was the monumental task of washing-days, which came once a fortnight. A tub standing on legs, named the "koryto", fashioned like an oval table surrounded by an edge just deep enough to hold the water, was brought into the kitchen. The work had to begin early so as to finish before the daylight vanished. Buckets of hot water were carried from the boiler and emptied into the tub. A woman engaged to do the laundry soaped and scrubbed the clothes, bending over the koryto until the white mountain of the laundry gradually diminished. At times Grusha relieved her. All the soaped clothing was placed in baskets and carried out on to the waiting sledge. Mikhailo drove both women on to the river close to the waterhole. The worst part of the work was still to come.

Going down on their knees and leaning over the blue depth, where often newly formed ice had to be broken, they began to rinse. No gloves could possibly be worn and there was nothing to protect their hands. The worst part was the wringing, of sheets, tablecloths and towels. I once saw Grusha standing in the warm kitchen rubbing her hands, which had lost all feeling, tears streaming down her face.

The frozen laundry, stiff as boards, was carried to the garret to hang until the following day. The ironing which followed, went on all day and in the evening the finished bundles were placed in drawers and presses.

With the blessed coming of the spring, the waterholes were carried out to sea. The pier became the meeting place where once again the women rinsed their laundry and gossiped in the sunshine.

A new member of the family often came to visit Babushka. Sometime in the autumn, Uncle Sanya and his young housekeeper Shura decided to get married. There was a quiet wedding attended by all the members of the family except myself. I had succeeded in catching chickenpox and was forced to stay behind, lying in bed.

Uncle Sanya and his young wife called at the house after their wedding and came to see me. "This is your new aunt," Uncle Sanya said. I thought my aunt, standing smiling back to me, dressed in her snow-white wedding gown, a veil and wreath of orange blossoms, was pretty, but nothing as pretty as my mother.

Now that Aunt Shura was not the housekeeper but mistress of the house the first thing she did, to Uncle Sanya's deep distress, was to get rid of all the squirrels and little birds flying and leaping from room to room, tearing the paper off the walls and fouling the floors and furniture.

A decorator was engaged who painted and repapered all the doors and walls and generally put the house in order. The tomcat, Vaska, still remained. My uncle, who adored his cat, flatly refused to part from it.

In early December I attained my eighth birthday. There were several presents and a parcel arrived from St Petersburg. Inside was a gold locket and a book. On the fly-page was written in English, "To Ena with love from Mama". Mother never called me anything else but Ena. About the time of my birth, Princess Eugenie, the granddaughter of Queen Victoria, married the King of Spain. She was often referred to as Princess Ena. The name appealed to my mother, as it came easier to her tongue than the diminutive Jenya of my full name Evgeniya. From that time on I was always called Ena or Eugenie in Scotland, and Jenya or Evgeniya in Russia.

Christmas back again — the time of gathering round the table, gilding the walnuts, fixing loops on sweets and apples. Again we heard the jingling bells of the troikas as they ran through the gates bringing old friends. The scent of spices, tangerines and pine pervaded the house. This year, the Christmas tree could not surprise me. I knew that it was being decorated behind the locked doors of the ballroom which for some reason I was not allowed to enter, and more mysterious activities went on in the boys' bedroom.

On Christmas Eve the numerous guests arrived. Uncle Vanya, our wandering "Siberiyan", arrived with Tanya and her family. Uncle Sanya brought my new aunt Shura. Aunt Shura had a large stomach — I wondered if there might be a baby, for I had noticed in the past that a large stomach was followed by the appearance of a baby. The mystery of how it succeeded in getting out, or for that matter getting in, remained unsolved for some time to come.

After the Christmas dinner the lights went out, and Babushka, according to her custom, rang the little crystal bell. The doors into the ballroom opened — and there it was again, this glorious vision of all the glowing candles, the sparkling decorations, the swaying fairies and the gnomes.

I moved across the room — there, sitting on my table was the doll won by Uncle Henry, by now almost forgotten. No longer the doll dressed in a simple shift, she was transformed into Red Riding Hood, all set to go on a visit to her granny. Every detail is there — the full embroidered skirt over a frilled petticoat, white blouse, black velvet bodice and the crimson cloak over her shoulders. In her hand is a little basket holding tiny replicas of a loaf, a bottle of wine, oranges, apples and a napkin.

She is resting on a little patch of grass and growing at her feet are wildflowers, all cleverly contrived. She is oblivious of the wolf hiding in the pine branches behind her. Only his head and glowing eyes are visible. It was Yura and Seryozha, I discovered later, who had worked in their bedroom, secretly creating the realistic head of the wolf. Outside this sylvan scene were presents and a small replica of an old chest complete with copper bands. Inside was everything a doll could wish for — little boots and shoes, dresses, coats and hats.

Who conjured up all this? No one but Babushka. For months, unseen by me, she had laboured, sewing out of bits and pieces all the garments with meticulous attention to the smallest detail. Even the tiny flowers and the grass had to have the realism and perfection she demanded of herself. Later, after all the excitement subsided, we children watched once more the coloured pictures on the wall. We had seen them all the year before, but that did not detract from the enjoyment of seeing them again.

In the late evening, the sledges of our friends glided away, the boys put out the candles on the tree and closed the door behind them. So passed Christmas of 1913 — the last Christmas of a peaceful era. Each year the peace diminished until, in the end, it vanished for ever.

4

1914

On New Year's morning I was woken by Mikhailo dropping his heavy load of firewood on to the floor. "It is a hard frost the New Year has brought us," he said, arranging the logs inside the stove.

Outside the frost was bitter. A thick rime like cottonwool hung over the river and the empty streets. Nothing stirred. That day, as the frost

hardened, no one left the house and no one called. Our guests and
Babushka whiled away the time playing cards, sewing, knitting and
reminiscing for hours on end. It was a peaceful beginning to the year.

At the end of January, Irisha, who had been with us since my
brother was an infant, left to be married. A young girl — Marusya —
joined the household after a short interrogation by Babushka,
followed by an adroit scrutiny of her person and especially her hair.
Babushka had an innate fear of lice being brought into the house. This
fear, amounting to an obsession, sometimes drove Babushka to
extreme measures. I remember how on one occasion a visiting relative
left her little daughter, Varya, in our care while she went shopping.
Babushka, sitting watching us at play, suddenly observed the tell-tale
signs in Varya's hair and promptly proceeded to use the infallible cure
of dousing her head with vodka.

Marusya, according to the prevailing custom observed in all
households, had to give her passport to Babushka. Without a passport
no servant could obtain employment. Marusya was attractive. Dark,
curly hair framed a round face and clear complexion. Brown eyes,
unusually large, held a serenity seen often in the eyes of grazing cows.
She was compliant, doing everything that was expected of her, but she
moved slowly and in a manner which, now, with hindsight, I recognise
was sexually provocative. The boys, for some unknown reason,
rechristened her "Marietta". One day, soon after her arrival, Yura,
who was a talented painter, decided he would like to paint a portrait of
"Marietta" and she obligingly complied. The paints and canvas were
all set out in Yura's bedroom. I do not know what form this painting
was to take as it never got under way. Babushka, discovering
"Marietta" in the bedroom, promptly despatched her to the kitchen
and Yura was told to stop his nonsense.

However, Babushka was too preoccupied these days to worry about
Marusya. Marga, now in her last term at school, was planning to join
the university in St Petersburg the following autumn. Meanwhile the
girls in her class were giving coming-out balls and parties. The whole
household revolved round Marga. Nastenka was hardly ever away
from the house, measuring, sewing, fitting and crawling on her knees,
pins in her mouth — sorting the hem, letting out or taking in. Marga
had to have several dresses, as not a week passed without her
attending a dance or party. Kapochka, through her experience as a
dresser in the theatre world, was an artist in hair styling. She spent
hours arranging Marga's coiffure, while Marga, difficult to please, sat
gazing into the mirror and Babushka anxiously hovered around.

And then there came the great occasion when it was Marga's turn to
have her ball. Invitations to all her friends were delivered by hand to

the various parts of the town.

Preparations on the day of the ball began at daybreak. Flowers forced in the hothouse were put below each long mirror in the ballroom. Marga herself supervised the setting of the table. With anxious concentration, she kept arranging and rearranging all the place cards. No one was allowed to interfere in any way. This was her ball and, with the exception of Yura and Seryozha, the family were to remain in the background. Yura, being more self-assured than Seryozha, was chosen to be the Master of Ceremonies.

In the early evening an old lady, Clara Antonovna, arrived. She always played the piano at all our parties. On this occasion she was accompanied by a violinist and cellist.

One by one the guests came. The girls in Marga's class, young and fresh in their evening gowns, the boys from the senior form of the gymnasium, others no longer schoolboys, and, from the local garrison, a sprinkling of officers, young and debonair in their smart uniforms.

When the dancing started, I hid behind the curtains hanging over the double doors leading from the hall into the ballroom. From there I had a clear view of the dancers. They were doing the figure-dance. Yura, his voice clear and resonant, was calling out the commands. The dancers formed pairs, gliding hand in hand round the ballroom and on through the arch into the drawing-room and corner-room beyond, turning and moving back into the ballroom to form a great circle and finally breaking into pairs to waltz until the music died away.

I stood watching, wishing I was old enough to be dancing to the haunting music with them all. Now, they were dancing the pas d'Espagne, that fashionable and lively dance we were being taught at school. Marga, in a cloud of white chiffon, flashed by with an officer holding her hand and smiling down at her. I had never before seen our Marga look so beautiful.

Kapochka crossed the hall and came up to me. "What are you doing here?" she asked. "Come." She led me away to my bed and tucked me in. For a long time sleep eluded me. I lay listening to the strains of the Viennese waltzes, the voices and the laughing in the dining-room and somehow felt strangely sad.

Early in March, my suspicions about Aunt Shura proved to be correct. A baby son made his appearance and was named Evgeny. Jenchik, as he became known, grew to be a flaxen-haired, delightful child. His christening which took place in April was attended by all the family. As Uncle Sanya's house was only some fifteen minutes' walk everyone walked there with the exception of Babushka, Kapochka and I, who went by sledge.

Yura was given the honour of being godfather. We all gathered round the font while Aunt Shura, according to the custom, retreated to her bedroom. During the immersion little Jenchik, not unnaturally, protested loudly, but that was considered to be a good omen as it went to prove the child had strong lungs.

After the service everyone congregated in the dining-room to a plentiful supply of food and drink. Halfway through the speeches and toasts, our young godfather rose and begged to be excused. It was necessary for him to return to the house, he explained, as an important essay had to be written for the following morning. The party continued, but a little later, Babushka suddenly announced that she also had to go back. She left on her sledge accompanied by Kapochka.

When Marga decided that we should wend our way home, Father remained to continue the celebrations along with Uncle Sanya's cronies. At the house we found Babushka in her bedroom, sitting on the edge of the bed, tears streaming down her face. At her feet, on his knees was Yura, beseeching Babushka to forgive him. Kapochka was gently patting Babushka's face with a damp towel. Behind them, Dedushka was preparing a dose of Valerian to tranquillise Babushka's nerves. He looked serious but remained silent. Sashenka, on the other hand, kept running out and in, muttering "Bezobraziye, bezobraziye . . . Disgraceful, disgraceful."

It transpired that Babushka, on returning home, had found Marusya and Yura lying together in Yura's bed. She promptly dragged Marusya out, chased her downstairs and then ran into her own room, where she burst into tears.

I was bewildered. Certainly it was wrong for Marusya to go sleeping in another person's bedroom — and in the afternoon too. Babushka had reason to be angry, but why the fuss? What else did she discover? I could only think of one thing. "Babushka," I said, stroking her tear-stained cheeks, "why are you going on so? If Marusya has got lice, all you have to do is to buy a little bottle of vodka and then all will be well." "A little bottle of vodka," Babushka repeated slowly, looking puzzled. "Oh, you dear innocent child," she cried, starting to weep again.

Marusya, timidly, appeared in the doorway. "Barynya," she said, "please let me have my passport — I must have it." The very sight of Marusya infuriated Babushka. She rushed to her dressing-table, pulled out the drawer, took the passport and, snatching the wet towel, made for Marusya. Marusya fled to the back stair and down to the kitchen. "Shameless wretch," Babushka called after her, throwing the passport and the towel.

That was the end of our Marusya — named "Marietta". After gathering her few belongings, she vanished like the snows in spring and was never seen again.

Marusya was replaced by a young girl named Glasha. Glasha was small and quick. Everything about her was fresh and tidy. The flaxen hair, braided neatly round her head, her cheerful face, the ready smile when spoken to, won everybody over. She arrived in the midst of the Easter preparations, in which she energetically joined, working with efficiency and speed the whole day through.

That Easter I was determined to attend the Easter midnight service, and refused to go to bed. Shortly before midnight the whole family set off for our Church of the Assumption. The night was warm. Already there was a touch of spring — the smell of melting snows. Although the river had not moved yet, the murmuring of the little streams running below the wooden pavements could be heard quite clearly.

The church was packed with worshippers. Spread on a table, waiting to be blessed, was all the Easter fare — the plates of coloured eggs, white pyramids of Easter cheeses, decorated kulichies.

Just before midnight a procession, led by the priest and choir, left the church. At midnight, as if from a distance, came the sound of singing. It grew louder, rising, spreading and then entered the church, triumphantly proclaiming, "Christ has risen — Christ has risen from the dead." A great light, from all the blazing candles, flooded the church.

I see it all again. The crowded church, the radiance on the faces of the people standing with their lighted candles, our gentle priest in his white vestment facing his flock, repeating in ringing tones, "Christ has risen", and each time the whole congregation, young and old, responding in one voice, "Truly He has risen."

Throughout old Russia, across the length and breadth of this great land, in every village and great city, in humble and rich churches, at that very moment, people were saying the same immortal words, embracing each other — singing.

We walked home together, carrying our lighted candles. Everywhere — walking towards us or following behind, was this mass of moving lights.

A young boy came up to me. "Little girl, may I have a light?" he asked. "Mine has gone out." I relit his candle. "Christ has risen," he said and shyly kissed my cheeks. "Truly He has risen," I rejoined — and we both continued on our ways.

The following day I joined all the children in the ringing of the church bells. My playmates, Volodya and Vera, were there as well.

Yet, that Easter day was not the same as that of the previous year. I had secretly hoped that I might awake on Easter morning and find again my brother sitting on my bed — but that was not to be.

The trouble was that I couldn't write in English and Mother, although she spoke quite well in Russian, could not follow the written word. At times my father wrote little notes in English, which I laboriously copied, but they were my father's words and not what I might have written. In this way slowly the gulf widened as the days and months went by.

In the early summer, it was noticed that Mikhailo was courting Glasha. They were often seen in the evenings strolling together on the river front or in the garden. Mikhailo never drank now and his appearance had improved. One day they approached Babushka and told her that they were intending to get married. Babushka was pleased. It was arranged that Glasha would settle with Mikhailo in the lodge, but at the same time continue with her duties in the house.

Glasha and Mikhailo were married in our local church. Glasha's dress was simple — she wore a veil and a wreath of small white flowers, made by Babushka. The wedding celebration took place in the flat once occupied by Uncle Sanya. A long table, covered with a white linen cloth, was laden with food and drink. Everybody helped to make the wedding a success as both Glasha and Mikhailo were orphans.

Before sitting down at the table, the newly-weds went down on their knees and Babushka, who took the part of the mother, blessed them with an ikon. Father, who was to perform the traditional ceremony of welcome with the bread and salt, stepped forward, but, as he raised the bread with the small salt cellar sitting on top, his arm trembled — the salt cellar rolled on to the floor, shattered in smithereens and scattered the salt. Everyone gasped — there is no more unlucky omen than this. Glasha covered her face and wept. Mikhailo was aghast. Father was equally distressed. A second salt cellar was brought and the ceremony repeated, this time without any mishap. But somehow it was not the same.

There was silence round the table until someone fortunately remembered the traditional call of "Gor'ko, Gor'ko" — "Bitter, Bitter." The party livened up and as the night wore on the unlucky incident was pushed into the background. An accordion appeared, one of the guests began to sing a folksong, others joined in and later there was dancing. And when the last of the guests had departed, Glasha and Mikhailo walked across the courtyard to the lodge and began their married life.

The author's grandparents: Babushka (top left) Evgeniya Yernett Scholts, 1881; Dedushka (top right) Aleksandr Scholts, 1885; Granny (bottom left) Helen Cameron . . . all set to embark on her journey to Russia in 1905; Grandpa (bottom right) Augustus Stephen Cameron.

The author: aged 2 (top left) in Russian national costume; at home in Archangel (top right) in 1908; with her mother and younger brother (bottom left) in 1911; the Russian schoolgirl (bottom right), – with Uncle Henry's doll.

PART III

The Darkening Skies

1

1914

THE days of that sunny summer went by very quickly. I, with my playmates, Vera and Volodya, spent hours swimming and splashing in the river, sitting on the warm boulders, drying ourselves, having long discussions and going once again into the water. Sometimes we played in the garden or went fishing in the pond. The pond abounded with two kinds of fish — rather repulsive looking carp and little nameless specimens. We fished with rods we made ourselves from branches, string, cork and hooks. The carp were impossible to catch, but the smaller fish eagerly snapped up the dangling worms. On account of their unpleasant taste none of the fish was edible, but we usually had an interested audience of cats who would appear from nowhere and readily devour the discarded victims.

In the middle of July Dedushka decided to take a trip to the famous Solovetsky Monastery on the White Sea. He took with him Marga and Seryozha. As at this time of the year the monastery was visited by crowds of tourists and pilgrims, Babushka thought she would prefer to go to a quiet village on the other side of the river where Yura's wet nurse lived. Yura, Marina and I were to accompany her, along with Father, who decided at the last minute to join us. We took the ferry to Bakaritza and went on to Issakagorka to spend the first night with Tanya. Tanya lived in a simple wooden house near the station. Attached to it was a shed housing a horse and cow and, above, a hayloft. A few hens, contentedly scratching for worms, ambled about in the yard, and in front of the house was a tiny garden where Tanya grew some vegetables and flowers.

Tanya welcomed our invasion. She had baked the traditional fish pie, a large cheese cake, and produced a bowl of crimson berries known as "polyeneeka", which she served with cream. The berry itself is like a raspberry, but there the resemblance stops. No other berry can be compared for flavour or scent to the polyeneeka. Tanya's eldest boy, Mitya, had gathered them and offered to take us to his secret place. As gathering berries and mushrooms is one of the greatest pleasures I have known, I eagerly went off with Tanya's children to this mysterious place.

After walking along the railway line for the best part of a mile, we climbed the steep embankment at the top of which was a small clearing, broken by mounds and groups of slender birches. The mounds were covered by these crimson berries. We began to gather them.

One of the mounds, covered by a profusion of the berries, appeared to have a deep fissure from which protruded a wooden board. Curious, we knelt to examine the opening and immediately leapt to our feet. The board was part of an open coffin and inside was the black mass of a decaying corpse. After that shattering experience we lost all desire to continue gathering the luscious berries and returned home.

It transpired that the mounds were the graves of Chinamen who had been employed on the railway the year before and had contracted some mysterious disease — suspected to be cholera. The thought that these delicious berries were nourished by the dead bodies of Chinamen cancelled any wish that I might have had to go back to that strange place.

That night we children slept in the hayloft. Tanya had spread a sheet and pillows over the hay. I enjoyed the novelty of sleeping in the loft, the company of my young relatives, smelling the scented hay and hearing the gentle stirring of the animals in the shed below us.

The following morning, our little group set off for the long trek to the village lying some seven miles beyond the Issakagorka station. The day promised to be kind, with the sun shining from a cloudless sky.

Soon after leaving Tanya's house we came to a peaty moorland stretching far into the distance. The ground, dotted by clumps of heather, cranberry bushes and mossy humps made the going uneven. Yura and Marina, taking long firm steps, were ahead. I, hopping from hump to hump, my hat dangling from my wrist, was following. In the rear were Babushka and Father.

Turning round, I saw my father sitting on a hump with Babushka standing over him. I hurried back to them. I heard my father say, "It's impossible for me to go on further — my legs can't carry me." His face, bathed in sweat, was deathly white. I remember clearly being overcome by some nameless fear. It was as if the skies darkened and the brightness of the morning vanished.

"Please go on without me," he was saying. "I will rest here for a little while and later take the ferry back to town." We left him sitting and walked away in silence. For some time I kept turning and seeing him waving back with his hat on the end of his walking stick, but gradually the white blob grew smaller and eventually I could see it no more.

After traversing the moor, we took a path through a wood. There, inside, were shade and coolness, the pungent smell of earth, mushrooms, birch and pine all mingling together. Shafts of sunlight threw golden splashes on the sombre branches of the pines, the white trunks of the birches, the trembling leaves of aspens. We sat down to rest. Around us was the enchantment of the forest, the sweet cooing of the doves, the distant call of the capercailzie, the little unseen animals scurrying through the rustling leaves. Mushrooms grew in abundance. No Russian can ever pass a mushroom, and as we continued on our way Babushka took her kerchief and, tying the four corners, began to gather them.

The trees gradually thinned out as we came out on to a clearing. In front were smooth green fields where cows and horses were peacefully grazing. To the right lay a row of cottages and a small wooden church. We saw coming towards us the plump figure of Yura's mamka, dressed in a sarafan. Ulyana had seen us and was hurrying across the field to meet us. She was a sturdy, smiling woman who adored Yura. From the time she left him to return to her own son, when Yura was two years old, she kept trekking back the long road to see him and always brought her own special brand of baking which she knew he liked. Ulyana hadn't done too badly. She and her husband owned a bit of land, a few cows and a solid clean "isba" decorated by carved gables.

Waiting at the entrance were her three children, including Yura's "milk brother", Vanya, now a tall, strong boy, who had been left in the village soon after he was born so that his mother could earn money by suckling another child. The isba was spotless — the floors scrubbed white with sand, the table covered by an embroidered cloth, and set with bowls and wooden spoons. Babushka, Marina and I were to share the "gornitza" — the best room, the walls of which were decorated with pictures of the royal family. In the corner was an ikon and, draped over it, an embroidered linen towel. As usual, the pride of place was occupied by an enormous double-bed piled high with feather mattresses and pillows. Yura and the children slept in the hayloft.

Ulyana fed us with her simple meals. Bowls of yoghurt topped by a thick layer of "smetana" (sour cream), buckwheat porridge and her baking. Especially good were the "kolobki", which are made from fine oatmeal and butter, formed into balls and baked inside the pechka. Their fine, crumbly texture melted in the mouth. Little meat, if any, was eaten in our northern villages, but from the river there was a plentiful supply of fish, and the fish soups were delicious.

We spent a happy week in this peaceful village. I was accepted by the children and spent the time gathering berries and mushrooms in the wood or swimming in the little river. A slanting path led down to the sandy shore where all the children gathered. The river was very narrow, which enabled us to swim across and play with children from the opposite side.

We were now in August. The villagers were harvesting the crops. Yura, Vanya and Marina were assisting them, working the whole day through in blazing sunshine. On the 3 August, a stranger arrived in the village and pinned a notice on a post. The people gathered round it and those who were able to read passed on the terrible news.

On the 1 August, Germany had declared war on Russia — in every town and village mobilisation was taking place. There had been a rumour earlier to that effect, but now it was confirmed and, like an ant heap disturbed by clumsy feet, it brought turmoil and anxiety. Babushka immediately decided to return to town and after packing our few belongings we left the following morning. This time we took the road that led us to the railway and walked along the line until we reached Issakagorka station. All I remember of that weary trek were the never-ending sleepers, the big steps we had to take across them, standing aside on the embankment until a train rushed by, and trudging on again. Late in the afternoon we arrived at the station. Troops were embarking for the front. A packed train was on the point of leaving. Inside, the young faces of the soldiers were cheerful. They were singing rousing marching songs — songs that had been passed from one generation to another. The platform was a milling throng of mothers, wives, sweethearts and children seeing off their men to some distant front.

The whistle blew. The great wheels commenced their churning, gradually gaining speed. The women ran along the platform and along the track, hoping to catch that final glimpse of a loved face — until the thin wisp of smoke vanished in the distance and they were left standing, wiping tear-stained faces with the ends of their kerchiefs.

It was a relief to be back in Tanya's house. I remember Babushka telling Tanya that we had covered seven miles along the railway line in the heat of the day.

We all slept late the following morning and after breakfast took the ferry back to town. On the landing stage we found Father and Mikhailo. Father, although still pale and leaning on his walking stick, was jubilant. "Britain," he announced, "is on our side — yesterday she declared war on Germany." On account of Mother being Scottish the family had been wondering on which side Britain might come in — Father's news brought great relief.

When the carriage arrived at the house, I rushed out and bounded up the back stair to the hall. The first person I met was Sashenka. "Sashenka," I cried out triumphantly, "Britain is on our side." "No one is on our side," she replied scornfully. "Each one is for himself."

A wave of fervent patriotism swept over Russia. Never, during these hot August days, was the Tsar loved more — and never were the soldiers so willing to fight and if need be die for him and their beloved country.

On the same day of our return from the village, Kapochka and I went off to the shops to buy things for the soldiers. I remember the excitement of packing the parcels with socks, soap and most important of all the little square packets of "makhorka" — the cheap tobacco so prized by soldiers. With one I enclosed a little note saying, "This is from a schoolgirl called Jenya — come back safe."

All over the town women were congregating round tables laden with clouds of gauze and piles of wool to knit and make bandages. Marina, no longer at school, dedicated herself to this work and went off every morning. Marga, due to join the university in St Petersburg, surprised everyone by announcing that she had decided to take a training as a nurse, in the hope that she might be later sent to the front.

Babushka became a member of a committee formed to raise funds by arranging sales of work, concerts, dances and other activities.

Meanwhile, school had begun again. To our morning prayers was now added the national anthem — "God save our Tsar — strong and all powerful — may he rule to confound his enemies — and render glory unto us." On the walls the portraits of the Emperor and Empress took on a greater dimension. The eyes of Tsar Nicholas II looked down benignly — a faint smile on his lips. The face of our beautiful empress was coldly distant.

In the late autumn, when the red-breasted bullfinches arrived again to devour the crimson berries of the rowans, and over the garden lay the sadness of fading flowers and falling leaves, our Mikhailo received his calling-up papers. No one had expected this to come so soon. Mikhailo left, and Glasha, grieving for her short-lived happiness, returned to the house. A new coachman came to live in the lodge. He was called Nikolai — a tall dark man with a saturnine expression.

A few weeks later, Irisha arrived at the house. Her husband had also been called up and she, with her little baby, had to vacate their quarters. Driven by despair, with no one to turn to, she came to Babushka, and Babushka took her under her wing. It was decided that Irisha and her little boy would live in the lodge, while Nikolai would join Vassily in his quarters. Young Yashka, who had been the kazachok at the beck and call of everybody, left to better himself. Things fell into place.

Not long after, I attended a performance organised in aid of funds for the war effort. It was held in the largest theatre. Every seat was occupied and people were standing in the passages. The scenes were numerous and varied — dancing, singing, recitations; but the superb final *tableau vivant*, representing all the allies, was the most memorable. Five girls were chosen, each representing one of the allied countries. My young Aunt Marga was chosen to personify Russia.

When the curtain went up, a sigh rippled through the audience. Against the background of all the flags on a raised dais stood Marga, dressed in the style of the ancient nobility. Her tall, statuesque figure was encased in a fitted dress of gold brocade. The front panel, studded with jewels, sparkled in all the colours of the rainbow. From the high headdress, trimmed with pearls and jewels and framing the typical Russian face, a gossamer veil fell in soft folds down to her feet. On either side were the girls representing Britain, France, Belgium and Italy, all wearing traditional costumes. As they stood motionless, illuminated by the constant changing lights of crimson, gold and green, the orchestra played the various anthems. The audience, rising to their feet, immediately responded by singing with great fervour and, long after the orchestra ceased playing and the curtain dropped for the last time, the applause continued. Never before had they witnessed such a scene of exaltation.

Meanwhile, after the disaster of Tannenberg where a quarter of a million men laid down their lives, many of the wounded were being sent to Archangel. Dedushka worked well into the night operating on the broken bodies of the soldiers. I was once taken by Marga to the hospital, where in a large sunlit room were two long rows of beds. Many of the soldiers were heavily bandaged. I saw the stamp of patient resignation on their faces. War was not the glorious thing I imagined it to be.

That year Father engaged a music teacher for me — an old lady known as Madame Susanova, who had spent her youth in France and had attended the Paris Conservatoire of Music. Father had also asked that her tuition should be conducted in French. With undue optimism he imagined that in this way my knowledge of the French language might improve.

In spite of her age, Madame Susanova was a formidable lady who had the nasty habit of striking my fingers with her pencil each time I played a wrong note. I enjoyed learning to play simple little pieces and detested the practising of scales. Madame Susanova came three times a week and, when I was finished with her, a young tutor, Nina Andreyevna, took over to assist me with my homework. Father, who was possessed by a strange fixation over my education, feared, not unjustly, that I would neglect my homework if there was no supervision over me. The homework kept us occupied until six o'clock when I joined the family at the dinner table.

During these winter nights, after dinner, everyone was engaged in doing something. Babushka went off to her committees, Marga and Dedushka, back to the hospital so that often I was left to my own resources with only Kapochka to keep me company. We would then retreat to the nursery; she with her mending, I with my books and little bits of sewing. A lamp overhead would cast a bright pool over the table. Except for the holy light in front of the ikon, in the corner, the room would be in darkness.

Outside, the snow and wind might beat against the windows, the frost increase until the rafters cracked above us in the garret, but we sitting together were safe and warm.

Kapochka, a good story-teller, would talk about her childhood or the times she spent in St Petersburg. Sometimes, lifting a piece of mending, she would begin to sing. She sang with the ease of a nightingale or blackbird in the early spring — there was never a jarring note and there was not a Russian song that she didn't know. Her voice was in a low key and held that special caressing timbre that is so often found in Russian voices.

During these winter nights the weekly excursions to the banya were also something I enjoyed.

I liked, too, to watch the preparations. Fresh, sweet-smelling linen packed in a basket along with soap, sponges and brushes, and, in another small basket, the crisp pasties, the bottle of "morse", a cooling drink prepared from cranberries.

Outside the vozok awaited us. Square-shaped, like a box on runners, it had a special appeal as if it came out of some fairy tale. In front, dressed in his cumbersome coat and shaggy fur hat, sat the coachman, huddled like a bear.

The banya, a brick, two-storeyed building, was only a few streets away. A wide stone staircase led to the second storey, where a long corridor with numbered doors branched out on either side. We were shown into our rooms and each presented with a dried, leafy switch made from the thin twigs of the birch. The dressing-room was sparsely furnished with a table, chairs, and horse-hair sofa, over which were thrown clean white sheets. After removing all our clothes we entered the tropical heat of the washing-room. Basins of water were thrown over the hot stove in the corner, creating clouds of steam. Hot water was also poured over the birch twigs to make them soft and pliable. My elders used them, whipping one another to increase the circulation, and bring to the surface of the skin any impurities. No one was ever allowed to indulge in that custom on my person and any advance was met with loud protests.

Polished copper basins and small wooden tubs were placed on forms running round the walls, and there were also several hot and cold water taps. Beside the stove were shelves in the form of wide steps. The higher one climbed the greater was the heat. The top step was very popular with elderly people and considered hot enough to drive out many ills, from rheumatism to alcohol.

A curious feature were the small arches, some eight inches high above the floor, cut out from each dividing wall above the grating covering the drain. The stone floor gently sloped towards these drains, which were shared by adjoining rooms. These small arches had a strange fascination for the young. By lying flat on the floor, it was possible to peep through and see the bare feet of our neighbours. Being taken to a banya from an early age, I had no inhibitions and the naked body did not present any mysteries, but there was a lot of fun derived from trying to guess the owners of the various feet. On some occasions a person in the neighbouring room would be imbued with the same idea, and I would suddenly be confronted by a pair of curious eyes staring intently into my own.

I was usually dealt with first, thoroughly and efficiently. When the ordeal was over I was handed a basin and told to do as I liked. From that moment I delighted in a happy orgy of splashing and throwing basins of water over everybody. Babushka, with a cold cloth over her forehead, lay stretched out on the top shelf. Kapochka stood in the middle of the floor and chastised herself with her switch until she glowed like a boiled lobster. The small leaves stuck to her body and she emptied countless basins removing them. Everybody sweated, soaped and scrubbed, and all around us was this hazy curtain of heat and steam.

It was pleasant to be back in the dressing-room. I can still feel the sudden coolness and general well-being as I sat wrapped in fragrant towels, drinking cranberry juice and eating the pasties.

Back in the house all was light and brightness. Sashenka, our self-appointed major-domo, would be bustling around, cutting lemon into transparent slices, spooning jam into small individual glass saucers, ordering Glasha to bring the samovar. We, now in our white sleeping jackets, our damp hair hanging loosely, would gather round the table.

Nothing unusual ever happened during our visits to the banya, but one evening a strange incident did take place there — so strange that the description of it received a column in our local paper.

Some time before this incident, an Italian family came to stay in our town. It is difficult to imagine what possessed this son of warm climes to move to our northern city of frosts and snows, but no matter, he came, settled down and in time prospered. However, I vaguely remember that he ran a profitable restaurant.

One night Dedushka received an urgent call to the house of the Italian and on arrival was met by a small group of weeping children, a distraught mother and an anxious father, who led him into the nursery to a small cot. Dedushka bent over and gently lifted the cover to examine his young patient. There, curled up and wrapped in a shawl, was a small monkey!

Dedushka, in spite of his serious exterior, was at heart a kindly man with deep compassion and a gentle sense of humour. He hid his astonishment and proceeded to treat the monkey. In time she recovered and later, as a mark of esteem and gratitude, the Italian called and brought Fifi the monkey with him.

A monkey in our arctic city was as strange a sight as a polar bear might be in the tropics. There was no zoo in our parts, we were therefore excited beyond words watching this intelligent and almost human little animal.

One frosty night, soon after Christmas, our Italian friend decided to take his wife and children to a Russian banya. He looked forward to a new and what he hoped would be a memorable experience. He was not to be disappointed. The family were shown into their room. No one noticed or paid any attention to the small bundle muffled in a shawl. The Italians undressed and, unwrapping the monkey, proceeded into the washing-room. In clouds of steam, our Italian friend and his wife sat soaping and scrubbing themselves accompanied by the singing, in full voice, of their native songs, while the children scampered about, splashing each other in happy abandon.

The doors were closed — they were secure in their privacy and no one noticed the small archway leading into the adjoining room — but not so Fifi. She examined the opening. Before her stretched a long vista of similar archways leading into other washing-rooms and offering endless possibilities.

The room she entered was occupied by an old couple from the country. The man was lying stretched out on the top bench. His wife, having scrubbed and beaten him with the birch switch, was now sitting on the lower bench washing her hair, meanwhile keeping up a continual flow of small talk. Unable to see clearly, she was groping for the cake of soap beside her when, suddenly, her hand came in contact with what seemed alive, soft and furry. She opened her smarting eyes. Something dark and strange leaped down and scampered past her into the opening in the opposite wall. There it appeared to pause. Surprised by the sudden silence, the peasant glanced at his old woman. Her frightened eyes were focused on a long tail curling gently on the damp stone floor. A simple man, surrounded by woods and fields, he had seen many tails. Yet now he was confronted by one he could not place anywhere at all — unless . . . unless . . . it was something he was afraid even to think about. At this point the tail, giving one final, jovial flick, vanished. All at once the sound of crashing basins, frenzied screaming, broke out in the adjoining room. Fear is infectious. Half-carrying his terror-stricken wife, the peasant dragged her into the dressing-room. From there, hastily draping some sheets over their bodies, they rushed into the corridor. Simultaneously, the door next to them opened and three hysterical young women ran out, completely nude, with streaming wet hair, soapy bodies and birch leaves sticking to their rosy bottoms.

Inside the room, further along, on the highest bench, reclined a giant figure of a man. A cold, wet towel lay across his forehead where a thousand tiny demons were driving red-hot needles into his skull. He was in the throes of the worst hangover he had ever known.

His wife, a sturdy figure, was quietly intent on her own ablutions, ignoring her spouse and treating him with silent contempt. Standing in the middle of the floor, she was chastising herself in the usual manner, now and again casting a baleful glance at the top bench. Beside her in readiness for further use stood a row of filled basins.

Impervious to everything, her husband lay sweltering in the heat. A bottle of some refreshing drink to quench his thirst stood near him. His languid gaze travelled around the immediate surroundings, up to the ceiling, stove, walls and down to his feet. There, sitting, staring curiously — was a monkey. He closed his eyes and turned away. It was impossible for such an animal to be here. It could only mean one thing — the dreaded symptom of delirium tremens. He glanced again. It was uncanny how real it looked — real enough to be now sitting calmly drinking out of his bottle.

The sudden frenzied screaming of his wife rent the air. She had also discovered Fifi. Fifi, terrified out of her wits, leaped from shelf to shelf or flashed in crazy circles round the room. The woman, fat and heavy, floundered in all directions. The inevitable happened. She slipped and landed on her posterior. The monkey vanished.

On his high bench, her spouse sat watching the scene below him. Waves of relief surged through his being. He didn't question the monkey's presence. His wife had seen it. His body shook with uncontrolled mirth and he was still laughing when he joined the others in the corridor.

And now like a snowball rolling down a hill, gathering momentum and increasing in size, Fifi, traversing from room to room, succeeded in spreading utter fear and astonishment. Men, women, children, in all stage of undress, were milling up and down the corridor, gathering in groups, laughing, crying, shouting. In their midst was our Italian friend with his wife and children. Gesticulating wildly, all speaking at once in their broken Russian, they were endeavouring, with no success, to explain the situation to the bewildered manager. People surrounding him, not understanding anything, were nodding in agreement.

At that moment a door at the end of the corridor burst open and a young woman ran out. In her white, frothy pantaloons, slotted with crimson ribbons, a fur jacket over her shoulders, barefooted, she presented a titillating picture. Behind her, red faced and embarrassed, hurried a young officer. In their wake was Fifi, wearing a small fur hat, with its lace veil dragging behind her like a bridal train. She was wet and frightened and had lost all her bravado. Someone laughed. Laughter like fear can be infectious, and what a few minutes before puzzled and terrified became simple and even an object of adulation. The children laughed, people crowding round made friendly overtures and cooing noises reserved for babies and small animals. Fifi clung to her owner and wanted none of it.

Gradually the normal routine took over. The young woman retrieved her hat and shawl and vanished with her companion. The naked and half-dressed likewise retreated. The Italian, with Fifi and his family, thankfully returned to their room

2

1915

The first Christmas of the war came and went. There was again the Christmas tree, the usual gathering of friends and relatives. Stamped in my memory is a picture of my little cousin, Jenchik, now ten months old, held in his mother's arms. Adelya and Verochka arrived in their kibitka, drawn by a single horse. The requisitioning of horses for the war put an end to troikas. The sisters had lost their liveliness and were still grieving over the loss of their only nephew, a young officer, killed at the front during one of the battles in the beginning of the war. Nothing, that year, was quite the same as the past happy Christmases.

The days slipped into the New Year of 1915. One morning in early January, a peasant came to the kitchen and asked to see my father. The man was my father's "milk brother" who brought the news that his mother, Seraphima, had suddenly died. Father immediately ordered Nikolai to harness the sledge and the three men set off for the village across the river. Father spent the night in the isba where Seraphima had lived with her son and family, and the following day, after attending the funeral, returned with Nikolai.

The crossing of the river in the intense frost proved too much for him. Cold and exhausted, he succeeded in catching a chill and had to take to his bed for the next few days. For some time Father's health had been gradually deteriorating. He was losing the power in his legs and now walked slowly, supported by two walking sticks. Although I did not know it at the time, I discovered much later that his condition was diagnosed as disseminated sclerosis — a deadly illness for which, to this day, there is no cure.

Children, unlike their elders who weep and pray, will accept what is inevitable. From that day when we were crossing the moor in Issagorka and I was overcome by a heavy foreboding, seeing my father sitting on the small hump unable to join us, I gradually became reconciled to the knowledge that he would never walk again. Deep in my heart I knew that I would never see the familiar figure striding along our street or on a summer's day go strolling in the garden.

One evening after dinner, at the beginning of the year, everyone gathered round the circular table in the dining-room, engaged in their own particular hobbies. Babushka was creating beautiful flowers, Marga embroidering her handkerchiefs, others knitting and sewing, and I nibbling sweet pine-kernels, listening to Seryozha reading one of Pushkin's entrancing stories.

Becoming thirsty, I interrupted Seryozha and asked him to stop while I went for a drink. Hurrying from the dining-room and through the back hall, I entered a long narrow corridor. At the far end was a window and against the wall a wide staircase going up to the garret. Under the stair was a sideboard on which stood a row of samovars and a tray with tumblers. In one of the samovars boiled water was kept for drinking. Lifting one of the tumblers I turned the tap — and with that heard quite clearly a voice coming from above me saying my name. Holding the tumbler, I stepped out and glanced up at the staircase. There, leaning on the banister, was a woman — an ordinary woman, plain faced with no outstanding features. Over her head and shoulders was a shawl such as was worn by peasants. "What do you want, who are you?" I asked her. There was no answer. Vaguely alarmed, I repeated my question. She remained silent, but then suddenly smiled. It was a terrible smile, venomous, frightening.

Horror stricken, paralysed, I dropped the tumbler. The sound of breaking glass set off a screaming — shrill, prolonged and heard throughout the house.

Downstairs, the servants heard me screaming and rushed upstairs. "The woman, the woman," I kept repeating through my sobs. "She is hiding in the garret, find her — catch her." Certainly it was impossible for her to be elsewhere — she never passed me and, if she had, she would have run into the servants or the others all rushing into the corridor from the hall.

While the garret was being searched, I was led away to Babushka's room and given the never failing sedative of Valerian drops. Babushka never left the bedroom. Father came in and sat talking to her. Both spoke in whispers, yet I overheard Babushka asking if they had searched the garret well and Father saying that they had, although they knew it was impossible for anyone to be there, for when they rushed up to the door, they found that it was locked as usual and the key hanging on the nail outside. That night I slept between my grandparents — in their large twin beds joined together. Protected on either side, I eventually fell asleep.

She was never found — the mystery of her appearance remains unsolved. Yet she has not vanished entirely and still haunts me. She comes in various guises, young and lovely, old and pleasant, but always frightening in the end. Once, years later in India, I dreamt that I was back in the house, bending over a basket in which we kept our fancy dresses. A strange young woman joined me and, dreamlike, I saw nothing unusual in her presence until I recognised the evil smile and woke up bathed in sweat screaming for my mother. Always my mother.

Later I went back to sharing the bedroom with my aunt. Marga was never able to sleep alone. I knew that at one period of her life Marga had been frightened, but by what I never discovered. The days when I could scold my aunt for being afraid and bothering me were over. It was she who comforted me now. "All is well," she would assure me, gently stroking my head, "there is nothing to be afraid of, the holy light is burning. Try and think of happy things — think about a Christmas tree."

With the beginning of the war the Tsar, conscious of the humiliating defeat Russia suffered during the Russo-Japanese war in 1905, was determined that such a disaster would never be repeated. He issued many edicts including one prohibiting the sale of alcohol. Although widely welcomed, this measure also created problems.

As the purchasing of alcohol was confined only to those who could obtain a prescription from a doctor, Dedushka was besieged by persons clamouring to obtain one. A man of high principles who abhorred the effects of alcohol in any form, he refused to be cajoled, bribed or threatened.

Many citizens, unable to appease their thirst, turned to the nearest substitutes. Our coachman Nikolai, finding the answer in denatured spirits, was soon rechristened "Denaturka", a name to which he responded with calm detachment. A close friend of my father, Pavel Stepanovich, became known as "Rosachka" on account of his addiction to "White Rose" perfume which, he asserted, was as good as any vodka. He was quite devastated when due to unprecedented demand it vanished from all shops.

Father and Uncle Sanya got together to prepare a special concoction. The ingredients, which were not divulged to anyone, were placed in a large square tin and left in the warmth of the kitchen. Mystified, with eager anticipation, we waited for what promised to be a brew par excellence.

The result came sooner than expected. One evening we were startled by a loud explosion coming from the kitchen. Rushing down, we found a mass of twisted metal, still in its death throes, bouncing on the floor, and the evil-smelling contents splashed on the walls and ceiling.

By a sheer miracle the kitchen was empty at the time. I need hardly add that no further experiments took place.

One morning a letter and a small box arrived for Glasha. With cold detachment, the letter stated that Mikhailo had been killed in action. As somehow no one imagined that Mikhailo would be killed, we were all shocked. From the day Mikhailo left there had been no letters. Glasha had hoped and prayed day after day for the war to finish. Now there was no hope, no future and the only thing to remind her of their fleeting happiness was the small cross of St George, posthumously awarded for some brave action on the field of battle. No one knew what or where it was. The cross meant nothing to Glasha and offered no consolation.

A Requiem was held in our Church of the Assumption. We all went to it, even Father, ill as he was. Mikhailo was something special. He had been with the family from the time he was a young boy. Standing with my lighted candle I kept remembering so many things — that perfect frosty morning when he and Babushka met me at the station on my arrival from St Petersburg and we drove across the silver river with the little dogs running beside us — the day of his wedding and the salt cellar rolling off the bread. No wonder Glasha wept — it had proved to be unlucky.

Shortly after Easter, Father came into the nursery where I was sitting, lost to the world, engrossed in a book. "Jenya," he said, sitting down beside me, "today I have received the wonderful news that Mama and Ghermosha will soon be with us." Overwhelmed, I rushed outside to tell my playmates all about it. For a long time they had been hearing about my brother. Everybody had a bigger brother or a sister; only I was alone. But my brother, although living far away, was bigger and stronger than any of them. He could outrun, outswim, outfight them all. Now, on hearing my exciting news, my friends waited, full of curiosity, to meet this wonder boy.

At last, in May, the day arrived. Dressed in a sarafan which Babushka had ordered for me, a wreath of flowers on my head, I spent the time running up and down between the house and the top corner of our street, waiting for the carriage to come along. It was a very special day, as it coincided with the first tramcar to appear on our main street. Groups of people gathered all along the street and stood waiting. Beribboned, decorated with flowers, the tramcar, travelling slowly, came into view. Inside were seated the governor and other leading figures of the town. Crowds cheered as it passed our corner, and I, distracted by this sight, missed the carriage turning down into our street, until I saw it driving through the gates. I rushed behind it and up the red-carpeted stair into the front hall.

There, surrounded by the family, were Mother and Ghermosha. Perhaps the shock of suddenly seeing them again, after the long absence, proved too much. Overcome by shyness and the familiar tight feeling in my breast, I could not speak or show any signs of gladness. Mother put her arms around me and kissed me. Ghermosha smiled, and still I stood staring in silence. "Show Mama all your treasures," Babushka suggested and in this way broke the tension. We went into the nursery where I produced my books, the doll that Uncle Henry won for me, dressed as Red Riding Hood, and all the presents Mother had sent me.

Outside, waiting at the gate, a small group of my friends had collected. I led Ghermosha to them and proudly introduced him. They stood, staring in amazement. Conditioned to expect someone out of the ordinary, a champion, a strong defender if need be, they saw a timid little boy dressed in a sailor suit. I read their thoughts. "Although he's small, he's also strong," I quoted, in defiance, the old Russian saying and, to prove my words, gave him a gentle little push.

My little brother fell sprawling to the ground and, scrambling up, ran screaming back to Mother. "Some big brother," Tolya Mammantov remarked.

Ghermosha had disgraced me, and, what was even worse, when I ran after him, there was an angry scolding from both parents. I rushed out of the house into the garden and for a long time sat below the overhanging branches of an ancient pine. "Why did this have to happen?" I asked myself, weeping my eyes out.

But everything passes. The following morning, when we awoke, I took Ghermosha to the garden. It was a beautiful spring morning, the trees and lawns flooded in sunlight. We went back to the old places, up to the turret of the "fairy castle", to the white jetties on the pond from where we watched the dragonflies skimming over the water, little fishes darting by. The garden was still the same. The apple tree was in full blossom with the blue scillas grouped around it; the poplar was again shedding its crimson catkins. It was as if Ghermosha had never been away.

Life in the house, however, was not just quite the same — Mother had changed. The happy carefree laughter I used to hear in my early childhood when she would chase us round the lawn in Scotland, or take us paddling to the Grassy Beach, was never heard again. My father's health was gradually deteriorating, and I still clung to Babushka and Kapochka and was given to running with my problems to them rather than to my mother. Yet slowly everything took on a certain pattern to which we grew accustomed. For, after all, as our poet Pushkin said: "Sufferance is sent to us from heaven; it takes the place of happiness."

In the years to come, Mother rarely referred to her long absence, but I gathered that she led a busy life in St Petersburg, and made new friends, some of whom wanted lessons in conversational English. When the war came, she joined a circle of ladies to assist the war effort. Eventually, the problem of my brother's education, the longing for her other child, and my father's illness compelled her to return. They came back. That was the main thing.

In July we received a letter from the Sabinin family, the friends with whom Mother stayed during her sojourn in St Petersburg, now renamed Petrograd. They were inviting Mother, Ghermosha and I to their summer residence in the village known as Dobroye Selyo, meaning "The Kind Village".

We journeyed to Petrograd and from there changed to another train which took us to the small town of Luban. A carriage drawn by a lively dappled horse awaited us at the station. We drove what seemed to me for some considerable time. The little sturdy horse saw no reason for hurrying and ran in a playful manner, shaking its mane and swishing its tail to chase away the flies. At times it snatched a little grass from the lush edges of the fields flanking the narrow dusty road. The driver, a good-natured peasant, sat sprawling sideways, lazily flicking the reins while keeping up a steady flow of friendly conversation, sometimes with us and sometimes with the horse. We eventually drew up beside the dacha, as that type of house is normally known.

From the glass-enclosed verandah steps led down to a charming, if neglected, garden where paths in all directions were flanked by sweet-scented jasmine and lilac bushes.

The family, waiting on the steps, welcomed us with the usual Russian hospitality. On the verandah a table had been set and a young girl carried in the samovar. The whole set-up had the air of a bygone world, something perhaps out of one of Chekhov's plays.

We spent a month in Dobroye Selyo. The curious name went back to the days of Peter the Great, when Peter, walking through the village, stopped at one of the humble isbas and asked for a drink of water. The peasant, not recognising the tall stranger, asked him to come in and rest a while. He also invited him to share his simple meal. Peter accepted and when leaving is supposed to have said "I shall call this village 'the kind village' — Peter will remember."

In August we returned to Petrograd before leaving for Archangel. We spent two days in the Sabinins' house. While strolling along the Nevsky Prospekt, Mother pointed out the imposing palace where she along with other ladies had gathered in the ballroom at a long table rolling bandages and tying parcels for the soldiers. It was often remarked there that Mother bore a curious resemblance to the Empress Alexandria, perhaps due to them both having the same fine features.

One morning as they were all busying themselves, the Empress came, accompanied by her two eldest daughters. The girls, smiling shyly, dressed in identical velvet dresses, followed their mother. The Empress was seldom known to smile. Mother confirmed this. While slowly passing the table, at times stopping to speak to some of the ladies, the Empress remained coldly distant with never a vestige of a smile.

Summer yielded to autumn. I was back to school, now in my second form. Each autumn life at school began anew. We moved into another classroom, there was the novelty of a new subject, new books, new jotters, pens and pencils and spick and span fresh uniforms.

Seryozha left for Petrograd to join the medical faculty in Petrograd University. We missed Seryozha. Quiet and sensitive, dominated by his younger, flamboyant brother, he remained always in the background, intent on his books and hobbies. He returned during the Christmas vacation, looking well and happy and more self-assured. The lifestyle of a student appealed to him. He loved Petrograd and talked largely of his distant plans to remain there after he qualified.

During the Christmas holidays, Yura, now a passionate hunter, donned his skis and went across the river to the woods and brought back a capercailzie and partridges. They were cooked for our Christmas dinner instead of the traditional goose, and served with buckwheat and cranberry sauce. There were plenty of sweet dishes and a Scottish plum pudding especially prepared by Mother to her own recipe. Presents on little tables were spread out as usual and although there were no golden walnuts or small red apples from Crimea hanging on the Christmas tree, the candles burned just as brightly as before.

By the end of that year many commodities were becoming scarce. Our shoemaker who made fine shoes for the whole family found it difficult to obtain the best leather and was forced to cancel many orders. We were in a more fortunate position than many others. Father, foreseeing the coming shortages and being in touch with the crews and captains of some of the cargo ships from Scotland, arranged to have footwear and clothing to be brought from there. Granny was commissioned to choose these articles from the various shops in Dundee. Parcels arrived containing shoes, materials for dresses, suitings for coats and, from Granny herself, a bonus of two leather schoolbags, hand-knitted woollens and, what pleased Ghermosha and me most, tins of shortbread and molasses candies. At least for the time being we were shod and clothed.

Father, who now found walking more difficult than ever was compelled to order an invalid chair. It arrived with our parcels and greatly pleased him. Made in Britain, it enabled him to move with ease throughout the house and even along the garden paths.

3

1916

Walking home from school one day I was tormented by a terrible headache and felt very thirsty. Some icicles were hanging from an iron pipe. I broke one off and, although warned by my schoolfriends, continued sucking it until I reached the house. By the late evening I was very ill and was put to bed. Dedushka came in and after examining me I heard him say to Mother: "No, Nellinka, this is not influenza — it is typhoid." I gradually became worse and remember very little of the critical period. Later, I was told, I became capricious and wanted no one near me but Kapochka. From Mother, however, I demanded a lemon jelly. When she personally prepared it and brought it to me, I, after tasting it, accused her of not giving me what I wanted. To prove to me that this was what I asked for she took a spoonful and earnestly assured me that it was indeed a delicious lemon jelly. I do not know if using the same spoon had any bearing on her illness which followed shortly. She became far worse than I was. Dedushka's colleague, a Doctor Grenkov, was sent for and a young nurse arrived from the hospital. By that time I was out of danger. My bed was carried into Babushka's bedroom so that Mother would have a little peace. Poor Father kept moving in and out our bedrooms, anxiously watching us, but soon I reached convalescence and spent the time demanding food, eagerly enquiring what was the menu for lunch and dinner.

One morning I got out of bed for the first time. Weak and hardly able to walk I went to see Mother. I hardly recognised her. Her skin had a peculiar yellow tinge, her fine features stood out sharply and the eyes had sunk into deep hollows. She was unconscious and did not recognise me. Terrified that she might die, I kept going to her bedroom — but the crisis came and went and she recovered.

Fate, as if not satisfied that she had done enough, struck down Ghermosha with diphtheria. Mother, although still a shadow of her former self, was convalescent and insisted that Ghermosha's bed be placed beside her own. She never left his side, watching despairingly as he lay battling for breath. Babushka, resorting to the old custom in Russian, kept waving a pillow-slip above him to create a current of air. When she tired Marina took over, but in the end it was Dedushka who saved Ghermosha. Slowly, we three returned to ourselves.

As both my mother's and my own hair was coming out in handfuls, Dedushka advised us to have it shorn close to our heads, warning us that if we didn't do so the hair would never grow well again. Both at first categorically refused but later agreed to have it shortened to just below our ears. On the appointed day the barber, a suave young gentleman, came to the house. Mother's hair was cut in the style she suggested. I then sat down and firmly gave the order that my hair was to be cut level with my ear lobes and on no account shorter. The family gathered round to watch. The barber moved behind me and, before I had time to stop him, ran the clippers up the back of my head. Infuriated by such perfidy, I leaped from the chair and ran up to the mirror. Sure enough — there was a long bare patch running through my hair. All this of course had been cunningly planned, for out of nowhere a little mob cap, trimmed with ribbons and lace, appeared which Babushka assured me would be very becoming. Resigned to my fate I wore this nonsense on top of my head, shorn of its locks and as smooth as a billiard ball.

Dedushka proved to be right. Mother's hair was never the same while I, by the end of the summer, was blessed with a thick mop of curls. When I was able to go back to school I was pleased to discover that so many of the girls who had also been ill were now forced to have their heads covered by mob caps or turbans.

One day, on my return from school, I found Babushka deeply distressed and everyone worried. It transpired that during the morning Dedushka collapsed and was brought back from the hospital. He had been for a long time under a great strain, working for hours with hardly a break. During the epidemic of typhoid, the hospitals became overcrowded and mattresses had to be spread on the floors. Dedushka, forced to go down on his knees to attend to his patients, eventually caught the infection.

He was seriously ill. The nurse returned and remained beside him, installed in the adjoining bedroom. Doctor Grenkov called twice a day and we all walked on tiptoes. To Babushka this was reminiscent of the time when she lost her first husband, my grandfather. Now she was again undergoing the same despair, never leaving Dedushka's bedside — but he, possessed of a mould stronger than his predecessor, after fighting for weeks, in the end recovered.

When he was up and about again Babushka sent for our "batushka", Father Aleksandr, who came to the house and held a thanksgiving service, sprinkling each room with holy water. We had reason to be thankful. Out of our family, four had been at death's door, but by some grace were saved.

There is a strange sequence to what I have described. A half-century later, while attending a service in the Russian Orthodox church in Edinburgh, I was approached by a small frail lady. "Is it true," she enquired, "that you are from Archangel?" "Yes," I said. "I am also from Archangel," she told me, "and was employed as a nurse in the main hospital there assisting Doctor Aleksandr Egorovich Popov — you may have heard of him?" "He was my grandfather," I rejoined. "In that case," she went on, "you must be the people who owned the beautiful garden. I remember during one hot summer when we were working day and night, the doctor told me and my friend, also a nurse, to go to his house where his wife would provide us with tea and take us to the garden to rest a while. Your grandmother had the tea brought to the garden and we sat together for some time. It was a perfect day, bright and sunny. I have never forgotten that peaceful place nor the lovely flowers and wished I could have stayed for ever. During the epidemic of typhoid when the doctor was so seriously ill I stayed in the house to take care of him, but I also remember being sent some time earlier to nurse an English lady who was desperately ill and not expected to recover. There were two children there who had been ill as well. I believe the lady was the daughter-in-law." "Yes," I agreed. "The boy was my brother and I his sister — the lady was our mother." "The world indeed is small and our roads are strange," she remarked.

Liza, as I knew her, died shortly after our conversation. The paths that she had trodden were indeed strange. In 1918 she escaped from Russia on an icebreaker, disguised as a young boy, and after many adventures eventually reached the shores of Norway and from there sailed to Scotland, where she settled down and later married.

In early June of 1916, our town was in the midst of preparations for an event of great importance. Lord Kitchener was arriving in Archangel from where he was to travel to Petrograd to meet the Tsar. No one knew what the mission was to be about, but great hopes were expressed that it might bring about an early conclusion to the war. Russia, having lost millions of her sons, was sick at heart and prayed for it to end.

A civic reception was to take place. A triumphal arch was being erected and the great man was to be met with the traditional welcoming symbol of bread and salt. The inexorable hand of fate intervened. On 5 June, the ill-starred *Hampshire*, carrying Kitchener, struck a mine near the shores of the Orkney Islands and he was drowned. This tragic disaster was followed by others. Earlier the allies had applied to the Tsar for help. During the great offensive by General Brusilov, Germany was compelled to withdraw several divisions from the west and so abandon her riposte against the Somme offensive. Brusilov's attack, although effective, was prolonged. In sacrificing herself for her allies Russia lost a million men — a loss that undermined her materially and, more important, morally. The flame of patriotism which burned in every soldier's breast began to waver and eventually went out. Revolution and anarchy followed.

During that summer no one to my knowledge, although concerned with the war, was heard to express any fears of a revolution. Everyone was kept more than usually busy as the house was overflowing with a steady stream of visitors who came to stay for weeks on end.

My cousin Militza, Aunt Olga's eldest daughter, came with her husband to spend part of her honeymoon with us. She had married within months of leaving school a young officer — Volodya Pasternak. Militza was something special, blessed with an elusive charm difficult to define. Although all her sisters were pretty and attractive it was Militza who possessed this mysterious charisma — the way she moved, the way she smiled, the way she spoke and the endearing habit of being able to raise one eyebrow while slightly narrowing her eyes when listening to someone talking.

Aunt Olga with her two younger daughters, Zlata and Jenya, arrived as well. My cousin Zlata, a few months senior to me, was a golden blonde with large eyes like black cherries, thick dark eyelashes and finely arched eyebrows, which of course was considered unusually beautiful. She was Aunt Olga's only fair-haired child and my aunt, determined that Zlata's hair should never darken, washed it constantly with camomile flowers.

I was never again to meet Aunt Olga, but in 1949, after two wars and a revolution, Zlata, Jenya and I met each other in the Gare du Nord in Paris. After the second war, I got in touch with my cousins in Finland and discovered that Jenya, now married, was living in Paris, a member of the large community of Russian emigrées. Zlata was staying with her.

My husband, our two young sons and I, travelling to Scotland after a holiday in Switzerland, decided to meet my cousins in Paris. It was arranged that they would recognise us by our style of clothing, our sons wearing their kilts, and that Jenya and Zlata would have white button-holes. They forgot to do this but I, running ahead of my husband and the boys, never hesitating, driven by some strange compulsion, recognised my cousins amongst a multitude of people. We had a happy reunion which was often repeated until such time as they both died, Zlata in Finland and Jenya in Paris. Jenya had become my dearest friend and my last link with our distant past.

That last summer before the revolution there were several naval ships of our allies lying in the harbour. We entertained many of the officers. To the young officers of the ship *Champagne* our house became their second home. French was spoken comparatively freely, especially by my father, and this delighted them being so far from their own homes.

In return for our hospitality, Mother and other members of the family were invited to a dinner party aboard the ship. To my annoyance I was not included and the following morning, listening to the glowing account of the gay time they all had, tried to pretend I wasn't jealous. Volodya was one who took no pleasure in the party. Being possessive over Militza, he became annoyed with one of the officers openly flirting with Militza in the best French style. There was some altercation when they returned to the house with Militza pointing out with her usual sweet charm that she should not be blamed if other men admired her.

Their marriage did not last. After a divorce she married the Finnish Consul called Laurison and for some time lived with him in Germany and later in Russia, which enabled Militza to travel to Archangel at a time when it became a forbidden city to all visitors. In this way she was able to pass on information about members of the family.

One evening at the table, Seryozha, who had arrived for his vacation, suddenly announced in a manner that brooked no opposition that he had given up the university and was going to join the army with the hope that he would soon be sent to the front. Russia, he pointed out, was in a bad way and was more important to him than his career or for that matter his own life. Being an idealist, he wanted to enlist as a private, seeking no privileges and sharing all the hardships. When he finished speaking everyone fell silent and no one attempted to dissuade him. Shortly afterwards he left for preliminary training at the recruitment centre.

In the kitchen changes had taken place. Dunya, who had been our cook for many years, was now failing in health and decided to return to her village. She was replaced by a sprightly little widow named Yenichka. Yenichka, long past her youth, had a married daughter and a granddaughter of my own age called Leedka who, when visiting her babushka, liked to come upstairs to play with me. Unfortunately she had the quaint habit of skilfully removing any little object that took her fancy. This involved Yenichka having to go through her granddaughter's pockets before Leedka returned home.

One morning, Ghermosha, dressed in the black uniform of a gymnasist, complete with leather belt and buckle, grey overcoat and military style peaked cap, set off accompanied by Yura to the Lomonosov Gymnasium. Memory has kept a picture of a small boy bowed down by his heavy coat, proudly striding out whilst trying hard to keep pace with his tall uncle. Life for Ghermosha as a full-fledged gymnasist had begun in earnest.

In early winter we were surprised by a strange soldier at our door. It turned out he was Irisha's husband, discharged from the army. Vakhonin, as he was called, had been wounded in the hand and had lost two fingers. Irisha, who was still living in the lodge with her little son, was overjoyed. She and her husband resumed their married life together.

He called one evening to see Father, who wanted to hear a first-hand account of what he had witnessed at the front. Vakhonin was bitter in his condemnation of bribery and corruption, the desperate lack of supplies and above all the wanton loss of life. Words flowed from his lips like an angry torrent. Rumours were rife amongst the soldiers of the "Nemka" (the German woman) influencing the Tsar through the evil monk Rasputin — they blamed her for all their ills.

"Gherman Aleksandrovich," I heard him say, "some of us were defending mother Russia with only our bare hands — lucky to lift a rifle from a dead comrade." He went on to describe how his contingent was ordered to advance and hold a certain position. After fierce fighting and an appalling loss of life, they took it and held on, waiting for the relief and more supplies — but nothing arrived. In the end forced to retreat, only a handful of men reached their lines. "I am glad I've lost my fingers — I've had enough, the stink of death, the rotting bodies, flies, maggots — and all for what? For nothing, Gherman Aleksandrovich — for nothing — Russia is finished."

No one doubted Vakhonin's vehement account, for rumours of a similar nature were reaching Archangel all the time. Yet in spite of his barely healed wounds, the missing fingers, the ravaged face, there was also something about him that didn't endear him to us. It was also openly said that his wound was self-inflicted.

He settled in the lodge with Irisha and his little son and all might have gone well if it had not been for Nikolai. He had been courting Glasha for some time and had hoped to marry her and settle in the lodge which had always been the married quarters for a coachman. Vakhonin, meanwhile, was settling down in a comfortable home, with free light and fuel. Babushka, of course, would never have had the heart to turn out a wounded soldier, his wife and child, when they had no place to go to.

All this irked Nikolai as he was not happy living with Vassily, it being winter and all the hens wandering around his feet. So he found another job in the timber mills and left us.

Nikolai was replaced by a young, good-natured giant of a man called Arsyeny. Unlike his taciturn predecessor, Arsyeny with his ready laughter, his little earthy jokes, his willingness to work on anything outside his own tasks, repair a sledge or fix a new strap on my skis, was very popular with us all. To our new cook, Yenichka, he held a special attraction, the full implications of which were as yet a closed book to me.

Yenichka, a grandmother, old enough to be Arsyeny's mother, was overtaken by a passion that blossomed like a crocus in the winter of her life. For Arsyeny coming to the kitchen there was always a little bit of something to appease his appetite, saved by Yenichka out of her own portion, or pilfered from the larder. And, after all, who was he to refuse such offerings if it made Yenichka happy? The one who wasn't happy was Glasha. Having to share her bedroom with Yenichka, she resented this intrusion.

Once, while assisting Kapochka with sorting out the laundry in the nursery, and quite oblivious to my presence, Glasha gave vent to her resentment. "Kapitalina Semyonovna," I heard her say, "all these goings-on are really shameful — the other day I found the bedroom locked and heard Yenichka saying to Arsyeny, 'Would you like it with my stockings on or off?'." At this point Glasha was interrupted by a sharp nod from Kapochka in my direction. After Glasha left the room I, overcome by curiosity, asked Kapochka what was it that Yenichka was going to give with her stockings off. "You just be quiet," Kapochka retorted, "your ears are now so long you could tie them under your chin." I was mortified and could not understand why Kapochka should wound me so.

Shortly after this conversation Glasha left to get married to Nikolai, who was making good money in the timber mill and had found a little house in the vicinity of Maimaksa. A peasant girl named Katinka replaced her. Yenichka and Arsyeny continued working for us, but their affair, I think, must have died a natural death.

In November, Seryozha was granted a short leave before departing for an unknown destination. We saw a great change in him. He looked as if he had been through a serious illness—his face was white and thin, the coarse uniform hung loosely on his shoulders. Yet he was undaunted and never mentioned the hardships he had undergone, with the exception of criticising the abhorrent custom of having two or more men eating out of the same bowl. Finding this repellent and difficult to bear he at times preferred to do without.

His mamka, Vera, who lived in the historical little town of Kholmoger, came to see him off. Vera was deeply attached to him. I remember seeing her sitting beside Seryozha on the edge of his bed. Seryozha was earnestly trying to explain something and she, gently stroking his sleeve, was listening, tears streaming down her face.

As the dark days of December approached Christmas, startling news reached Archangel. On 16 December, Grigory Rasputin, the Siberian peasant who wielded great influence over the Empress to the detriment of Russia, had been murdered.

Much has been written and said about this illiterate peasant. Some thought he was a saint, others that he was possessed by evil. He was known to be a lecher and a drunkard, but at the same time to have the gift of prophecy and healing. The prophecy may have been coincidental, but the strange power of healing has never been denied or explained. His fame as a miraculous healer travelled far and eventually reached Petrograd where he was introduced to the Empress. The young Tsarevich Alexei had haemophilia, a disease for which no doctor ever found a cure or was able to alleviate his suffering. In desperation the Empress turned to Rasputin in the hope that he would save her son and his future throne. Certainly many reliable witnesses had testified that the strange power Rasputin possessed saved the Tsarevich from the brink of death, not once but several times.

What was this power? Some have said it was a form of hypnotism. Hypnotism may have alleviated the suffering, but how could it remove the ominous dark spots on the body, the swellings in the joints, the high temperature, the symptoms of approaching death? To this day no one had been able to give a convincing answer.

It has been said that haemophilia was one of the links in the chain of disasters which brought on the revolution and changed the face of the nation. Some guardian angel may have watched over the throne of Britain, for Queen Victoria, the carrier of the deadly gene, only passed it on to her youngest son, Leopold. The future King Edward and his other brothers escaped it, but two of her daughters were carriers and succeeded in spreading haemophilia over the royal courts of Europe.

The Tsarevich was the only son and heir to the Russian throne. The Empress cannot be blamed for turning to the only man who could save her child. If only Rasputin's activities had been confined to curing the child! But power corrupts and the miracle worker overreached himself. He began to interfere with the running of the country and the war. Men of integrity and high ability, who disliked Rasputin, were constantly being removed and replaced by men of a lower calibre and less credibility. The Empress, firmly believing that this was the voice of God speaking through the "holy father", followed his advice and rebuked those who criticised him adversely. With a determination which brooked no opposition she demanded that the Tsar should obey Rasputin's recommendations. The Tsar, weak and uncertain, gave in to his neurotic wife for the sake of their child.

There was only one solution. Rasputin had to be destroyed. Enticed to the house of Prince Yusupoff, the husband of the Tsar's niece, and assisted by other conspirators including Prince Dmitry, the Tsar's first cousin, Rasputin was murdered. His body, pushed through the waterhole under the ice, was found two days later.

There was great rejoicing in Petrograd and a general feeling of relief over the country. Yet, there was something ominous in the fact that members of the Royal family were implicated in the murder. It was as if in this Royal hive, the queen bee herself was being attacked by her own kind. An act that seemed to indicate an approach of a greater disaster.

Christmas came and went and there was still no news of Seryozha's whereabouts, but with the dawning of the fatal year of 1917 a brief message arrived saying he was well, but was expecting to be moved to another destination. From these words it was surmised that it might be the Silesian front.

4

1917

I remember one early morning in March walking along the slushy pavements to school. The snows of a hard winter were disappearing. Only the high snowdrifts flanking the footpaths, overlaid by a fine tracery of soot, remained, slowly shrinking.

As I approached the school a procession of men and women tramping on the road overtook me. A forest of crimson flags fluttered in their hands to the triumphal strains of the *Marseillaise*. They passed me by and vanished in the direction of the Cathedral Square.

Inside the school, upstairs in the hall, there was the usual assembly for morning prayers. Each class, formed in pairs, stood facing the altar. Behind us were the teachers grouped around the principal, Nataliya Pavlovna. Members of the choir took up their position on the dais. The priest stood waiting for the sign to start the service. All remained still, aware that something unusual was taking place. Nataliya Pavlovna spoke to us: "Girls, most of you perhaps have heard that a revolution has taken place in our country. There will be no more singing of the national anthem at the end of the services. That is all," she added, unable to continue. On the walls where only the previous day had hung portraits of the Tsar and his family, were blank spaces. A new era had begun.

In our house the news of the revolution was received with mixed feelings — sadness, uncertainty and resignation to the inevitable. Overriding all emotions was the fervent hope that, under a democratic government, the war would be brought to a successful conclusion, bringing an end to the frightening slaughter.

During the first months of the revolution there was great excitement and optimism in our town. Processions, concerts, plays took place and in our largest cinema a film on Rasputin and his evil influence on the Empress ran to packed houses.

In one of the concerts organised in aid of funds, the boys and girls of the gymnasiums took part. Dressed in our national costumes, we stood in groups around the stage. When the curtain rose "Old Mother Russia", portrayed as an old witch — the wicked "Baba Yaga" of our fairy tales — was seen slowly sinking through the floor and as she vanished a beautiful young girl, dressed in a red sarafan, rose through the same cunningly disguised trapdoor. The new young Russia unfortunately had some difficulty scrambling through, clutching her unwieldy crimson flag. No sooner did her pretty head appear above the floorboards, than we, the chorus, burst into a fervent rendering of the Russian version of the *Marseillaise*. Various scenes followed. I was chosen to take part in one of them, where the girls linked together and faced the boys on the opposite side. It was one of those bantering songs and dances — the girls advancing, teasing the boys, retreating back, with the boys following suit. The dance, accompanied by a balalaika orchestra, was vigorous and joyful, only slightly marred by my petticoat becoming undone and slipping below the sarafan. This aroused unseemly mirth in the audience and helpless fury in my mother's breast, forced to watch her daughter in gay abandon galloping up and down the stage with the petticoat flopping around her ankles.

At the end of the concert all the performers gathered on the stage to receive a standing ovation. The *Marseillaise* was sung once more with the same fervour as was sung the national anthem for the Tsar three years earlier when my young Aunt Marga stood resplendent in the traditional dress of old Russia, surrounded by her allies.

Meanwhile, with each passing day, Russia, like a rudderless ship, was moving closer to disaster. The renowned oratory of Kerensky failed to inspire the troops to go on fighting. Soldiers continued to desert. Estates and houses were being plundered, owners murdered and officers shot out of hand. These excesses had not, as yet, reached our part of the country, so that the minds of the people tended to be occupied by their own immediate problems. The shortages of the barest necessities were more acute than ever. In the market the peasants still offered milk and butter, at a price, but there was a great scarcity of flour, meat, sugar, tea and even soap. Our family was luckier than most, for as long as we had our black-faced ewes we didn't have the same meat problem as others and were even able to help our friends.

However, we had had an unexpected blow when the ram died and, because of the war, could not be replaced from Scotland. No one in the family, or anywhere around, knew anything about sheep farming, as only cattle were kept in the district. Mitka Shalai came to the rescue. "You want a ram. I'll find you a ram."

A "ram" duly arrived. It was enormous, smooth-coated, and with a peculiar head and long, flapping ears. The ewes recoiled in horror. Though scorned and rejected, the ram trotted eagerly behind them to their haunts by the river. One day, finding the ram more bothersome than usual, the ewes simply tossed it over the boulders and down into the river. That was the end of the story. The silly things paid for their conceit. One by one they perished, and for a time there was a surfeit of mutton.

During the summer of the first revolution, Babushka decided to spend a short holiday in the historic small town of Kholmogor, lying some thirty miles up the river, beyond Archangel.

Kholmogor is also known as the dairy of the north through her famous cattle, first brought there from Holland by Peter the Great. Babushka, believing that an abundance of fresh milk, butter and better feeding would do Ghermosha and me some good, took us with her.

As Vera, Seryozha's mamka, lived in Kholmogor, it was arranged that Ghermosha and I would stay with her for a few days and then join Babushka in the guest house of the ancient convent.

Vera, in her early days, after losing her first child, took on the job of nursing Seryozha. She and her husband saved all the money they earned. Later, out of their joint capital, they bought a two-storeyed solid house and turned the ground floor into a profitable eating-house. The entire floor was devoted to kitchen premises and one large room, where, on a long sideboard, stood a bubbling samovar and trays laden with a variety of Vera's baking — curd cakes, pirozhkis filled with mushrooms, chopped eggs or cabbage — all protected by fine clean linen. At the beginning of the war, Vera's husband, a shrewd peasant, seeing the coming shortages, purchased various commodities — especially sugar, tea and flour. Glasses of tea were still accompanied by jam prepared from wild berries and served in little portions — a luxury no longer available in Archangel. There were also barrels of "kvas" — the cool drink made from rye bread. On each of the small tables at all times sat containers filled with salted squares of crisp black bread. Vera's daughter, Shura, had to prepare them daily. I enjoyed helping her, cutting the bread into tiny squares, drying them in the oven and sprinkling them with salt. Patrons nibbling these salty titbits became thirsty and drank more kvas and that in turn helped to swell the kitty.

We spent several days with Babushka in the convent's guest house. The convent was a hive of industry as all the work, the tending of the cattle, the labouring in the fields, was done by nuns. Every room was spotless, scrubbed and polished every day. We were allotted a spacious and comfortable room which we shared with Babushka.

The meals, served in the refectory, were only allowed to be attended by women and girls. Men and boys were not admitted. Their food was brought to the guest house, where Ghermosha joined all the male guests.

In the refectory stood long tables with stools placed round them. In the centre of the room, standing at a praying desk, a nun read passages from the Bible throughout the meal. The first course, I remember, was a rich fish soup known as "ukha", with pieces of the fish and potatoes floating in it. I might well have enjoyed it if it wasn't that each bowl had to be shared between three and more people. I didn't mind so much sharing the soup with my immediate neighbour, a fresh young nun, but facing me sat an old and not particularly clean-looking pilgrim, who dribbled and loudly smacked her lips as she went on pulling out the best pieces of the fish. This course was followed by two bowls — one containing buckwheat porridge, with a little well in the centre filled with melted butter; the other filled with rich, fresh milk. There again we had to share the bowls. Although fond of buckwheat kasha, there came a moment when I decided that such delights were not for me, and quietly laid down my spoon. From that day I joined Ghermosha and the boys for meals. Babushka, being deeply religious, succeeded in overcoming her repugnance and continued attending the refectory. "We are all God's little children," she reproached me later, a statement, like the kasha in the refectory, I found difficult to swallow.

The kindly Abbess invited us to tea one day. In her sunny room, the table spread with an embroidered linen cloth was laden with an abundance of fine baking accompanied by bowls of wild strawberries and cream. The gentle soul insisted that we should take something from each plate until we were more than satisfied.

This was the time of the sacred festival of the Assumption. Attending the morning service we found that because of the great mass of worshippers, it was difficult to move inside the church. Leaning against the wall was a small, shrunken old woman. On the black cloak and hood covering her frail body were embroidered skulls and crossbones. She was one of those saintly beings, entirely

Postcards sent by Nellie and Gherman: to Uncle Henry in India (top); to Nellie's parents (bottom) showing the market in Archangel.

Sergei, the author and Ghermosha with their nanny in the garden, 1910 (top); the same view 51 years later (bottom) – all is destroyed; only the lake remains. Shura (Sanya's wife) stands alone, the last survivor of her generation!

dedicated to God, living somewhere in the depths of the convent, praying all day long, sleeping in a coffin and existing only on bread and water. The shrivelled, parchment-coloured face, half-covered by her hood, already had the stamp of death upon it. People were coming up to her begging to be blessed. She did it mechanically, her claw-like hand making the sign of the cross over them, never raising her head.

In the evening there was a torch procession. Led by the priest, the chanting nuns and people circled round the convent carrying high their lighted torches. The white nights were already over. The mass of flaming shafts reaching out to the skies, the showering sparks like clouds of flitting fireflies and the floating pools of light upon the smooth waters of the moat, lit up the gathering darkness. Young people, children running to and fro, their shadows dancing on the walls, were laughing and calling to each other. Fascinated and absorbed by this ancient ritual, we ran behind them.

The news on our return was not cheerful. General Brussilov's victory on the Austrian front had brought hopes only to be dashed when defeat followed, the Germans bringing up reinforcements.

Kerensky's oratory was useless to inspire the exhausted troops to continue fighting in the face of the slogan coined by the Bolsheviks — "Peace, land, all power to the Soviet". There was a general rout, the soldiers casting aside their guns, rushing to get away from the fields of carnage; the officers tearing off their epaulettes, and those trying to rally the men being murdered. "Po kolyenam" . . . "Aim for their knees," was the brutal order as they shot the officers through the knees and finished them off with bayonets.

In late August, Kapochka left our house. In the town there was a well-to-do businessman named Ukropov whose wife and lover had run off, leaving him with two small girls and a boy. Their father, not knowing to whom to turn for help, was in complete despair. The sad bewildered children required someone special to love and care for them to fill the void left by the heartless mother. Kapochka was approached, and Babushka as well. Kapochka was offered a far higher salary than she had at present, but what was more important she would be taking charge of the entire household, all the servants and, in short, be her own mistress. Furthermore, her future would be assured and when the time came for her to retire there would be a home of her own and with it a liberal pension. In all fairness to Kapochka, Babushka advised her to accept this post. Kapochka, being only human, did accept it.

At first it was unbelievable to me that Kapochka could ever go away. How could Kapochka leave me, I argued with self-centred egotism? Kapochka who, when mother left, took care of me. Brushed and braided my hair, sewed the white bands around the neck of my school dress and laid it out night after night. Kapochka who on a winter's night sat beside me telling wonderful stories or singing softly in the gentle light of the lampada — it was she who taught me all the songs.

In the end all the promises and plans by Ukropov came to nothing for the Bolsheviks confiscated his business and house. Kapochka eventually left for Petrograd to live with her sister. Two decades later, during the Second World War, both perished in the siege of what is now known as Leningrad and were buried with other countless thousands in an unknown grave.

One day, returning home from school, I found Mother upset and weeping. In the morning a telegram from Scotland had arrived, sent by Grandpa, saying that Grandma was seriously ill and asking Mother to come to Scotland. After great difficulty in trying to contact various sources, help came from high places. A berth was found in one of the British ships preparing for a return trip to England.

In early October, as the river was beginning to show signs of freezing, Ghermosha and I, with Babushka and Marina, went to the landing stage to see our mother off. The day was grey and a bitter wind was blowing. Ghermosha, like myself, was most unhappy. As the ship was not due to leave until the cover of darkness, we had to say our goodbyes and stand watching our mother, tears streaming down her face, climbing up the gangway. At the top she turned and waved before disappearing inside. During our drive back to the house, Babushka tried to cheer us up by saying that Mother would probably return on an icebreaker in time for Christmas, but that was not to be. Late in the evening we kept watching the windows and were eventually rewarded by seeing the dark shadow of the ship gliding past our house, before vanishing behind the island of Solombala.

As there was now no Mother or Kapochka, father engaged "Osa" to help Babushka in taking care of us. This pleased Osa immensely, as it enabled her still to continue her work as a midwife, have a comfortable room and increase her income. Her duties were to be quite simple — seeing that we were tidy, and doing necessary mending and a little sewing, such as fixing daily the white bands on my school dress, a task I eventually did myself.

Osa did nothing whatsoever. She smoked incessantly, stealing my father's cigarettes, and as for darning our stockings, which were now scarce, she used the expedient of dropping them down the chute of the toilet, to the great astonishment of the men who came in the early spring to remove all refuse.

Meanwhile, Mother had arrived safely in Scotland after a stormy crossing. Grandma, who had succumbed badly to the prevalent epidemic of "Spanish influenza", was now slowly recovering, but all Mother's enquiries about an icebreaker were fruitless and became even more so after Christmas, with the now raging civil war and other hazards.

By the end of October, Russia was virtually out of the war. The great orator Kerensky fled in disguise, leaving the young cadets and the brave women's army to defend the Winter Palace. It was a futile attempt. The defenders were arrested and the Bolshevik government, led by Lenin, took over.

In November Seryozha returned from the front. The war for him was over. He had been carried with the flood of men rushing back to the land they were promised, pillaging the estates on their way and murdering the owners. He had witnessed frightening scenes and was heard to remark later with a cynicism foreign to his nature, "Our gentle peasant is hard to beat when he embarks on his sadistic tricks." Seryozha had walked for days on end, travelled on trains crowded with lice-ridden soldiers. Typhus was rampant. In every station the sick and dying were unceremoniously thrown out. Eventually, on reaching Vologda, he found the same chaos. After pushing and fighting, he succeeded in scrambling into the train bound for Archangel. He was lucky. Many were left behind. Others travelled clinging to the roofs, from which some of them, overcome by cold or carelessness, fell off or were killed by overhanging bridges. Exhausted, Seryozha slept in the corner of the corridor and did not waken until the train reached Issakagorka. From there he walked, crossing the ice-bound river and at last entered the gates of his beloved home.

Seryozha was back — but where was the young boy of high ideals and fervent patriotism? In his place now stood a man in a tattered uniform, filthy and unkempt. The hollow-eyed, ravaged face bore the stamp of extreme suffering. The old zinc rocking bath was brought down from the garret. The women were chased out of the kitchen. Yura lovingly cleaned and scrubbed his brother. Seryozha had not eaten for days and after his first meal slept the whole day and night.

Christmas was approaching. Although the means with which to celebrate it were more scarce than ever, we were still in a position to offer up a Christmas dinner to our friends. The last of the sheep was slaughtered — there at least would be roast mutton on the table with a blueberry tart, made from last year's jam, which had been carefully treasured in the larder.

Meanwhile, as the days went by, Ghermosha and I still clung to the hope that Mother might return in time for Christmas. We wrote little notes which I don't think ever reached her. Yet, long years after, in going over Mother's belongings following her death, I came across one letter I had written soon after she had arrived in Scotland. It was the only one. Although she must have had difficulty in making out my scribbling, never having quite mastered the written word in Russian, she had treasured it throughout the long decades. On the yellow pages, the uneven writing with a few corrections and careless inkspots, is faded — "Dear Mama, I am writing this in the nursery. Ghermosha, Tolya Mammontov, Vera and Volodya are playing cards beside me. They are laughing, shouting — my ears are ringing. Mama, Osa is very bad to us. The large pot of jam you left especially for us, she herself has finished. She gave us only little spoonfuls and ate saucerfuls herself and when we asked for more called us gluttons. It is unjust. We have hardly any stockings left, as she will not darn even the smallest hole, but drops the stockings in the toilet. Babushka caught her and was very angry. They say at school that we are going to be taught English, in which case I should get nothing less than 'fives'. Ghermosha and I are planning to give everyone presents for Christmas with the money we have saved. There isn't very much to buy. In your drawer I have found a new box of pretty handkerchiefs and that should help us. We will give Marga, Marina and Tyotya Peeka two each. I hope Grandma is well. Give Grandpa and Grandma our love. Mama, please find an icebreaker and come back soon. — Your loving daughter, Ena (Jenya)."

No icebreaker brought Mother for Christmas and it was impossible for her to come through Finland on account of the troubles. Children are known to be resilient. Swallowing our disappointment, we found consolation in a special scheme of our own. This year, for once, all those who would arrive on Christmas Eve would receive a gift from us. The fact that shops had ceased functioning did not deter us. There was still one we knew which sold stationery and a few small items.

A few weeks before Christmas, during the short hours of daylight, we embarked for the centre of the town, dragging our sledge. To take a tramcar of course would have been easier, but we imagined, it being the Christmas season, the sledge was more appropriate. We spent long hours in the shop, carefully working out our money to the few useless articles for sale. A shop-soiled book on flowers was bought for Babushka — it was more than we could afford, but Babushka was worth it. Three prints were eagerly snatched up before anyone else could buy them. Two were identical, depicting a dead Japanese soldier on the field of battle, and one the fall of Port Arthur. The identical prints did not bother us unduly; they could always be hung in different rooms we reasoned. They were meant for Dedushka, Seryozha and Yura. Why we should have thought that they would be delighted to be reminded of the disastrous Japanese war is difficult to imagine. There were pens and pencils, little coloured boxes and notebooks and finally a roll of crimson crinkled paper for wrapping up the presents, paid for with our last kopecks.

The moon was high when we turned homewards, trailing the sledge between the sparkling snowdrifts. We hid the sledge under the bed. The following day we spent exciting hours wrapping up the parcels and arranging them inside the sledge, now decorated with cottonwool and tinsel.

On Christmas Eve the yearly gathering took place.

After dinner, when everyone gathered in the ballroom, Ghermosha and I dragged our sledge up to the Christmas tree. Everyone appeared to be delighted with our gifts, although the pictures of the dead Japanese were never seen hanging in any room. This Christmas, one of the last, offered all the hospitality and joy Babushka could muster, but it was like a fire bursting into a bright flame before dying away.

5

1918

"Great and terrible was the year that followed the second revolution. It abounded with sunshine in the summer months, with snow in winter. Two stars brighter than all others shone from the heavens — the shepherd's star — the evening Venus and the red vibrant Mars."

These are the opening words of the great and almost forgotten novel of the Russian civil war, *Byelaya Gvardiya (The White Guards)* by Mikhail Bulgakov. Many accounts, novels, have been written about the civil war, some competent, others biased and inaccurate, but even out of the best of them, written after patient research, it is difficult for the average person to grasp the whole aspect of a civil war, the like of which the world has never known before.

From all that I have read and what I heard, and from my own youthful experience of over sixty years ago, I only see this civil war as a special creation devised by Satan himself. Here we have people of the same culture, speaking the same language and the same religious beliefs, ingrained from childhood, busily engaged in destroying their own land. In every corner of this great expanse battles are raging, the frontiers are fluid, horses are galloping forward and rushing back, men are attacking and retreating, towns, villages taken and retaken, savage reprisals, flames, smoke darkening the skies and helpless women and children trailing through blackened villages, dying on the dusty roads under the blazing heat of summer or below the winter snows of the frozen steppes.

All of that came later. In the beginning, after the taking of the Winter Palace and Petrograd had fallen, Lenin, having decided to take over the whole of Russia, sent instructions to that effect to all the provinces. They were backed by an army of experienced leaders, commissars and agitators. The takeover of Archangel, in December 1917, could be described as a bloodless affair and by January 1918 the Bolsheviks were in complete control. After the town was taken, many of our supplies, brought over by the Allies, were sent on to the south so that life for the inhabitants became more difficult. The atmosphere was uneasy. Some people were arrested and rumours floated around that all industries would be nationalised, and private property confiscated with no redress. It was also noticed that people who had previously been friendly and even servile now became insolent.

One day Vassily came to the house to complain that Vakhonin, still living in the lodge, was conducting a little private business of his own by stealing the precious firewood and selling it to someone in the adjoining courtyard by the simple device of breaking a plank in the woodshed and pushing the logs through the hole. Babushka, highly indignant, went to the lodge to investigate the matter. Vakhonin made no attempt even to deny the charge. "You bloodsucking bourgeois have had it good too long," he said and, shutting the door in her face, added the old proverb, "There is going to be a holiday in our street." What could Babushka do but retreat? From that day Irisha stopped coming to the house to help with the laundry and when meeting any of us face to face would turn away. Irisha was obviously ashamed but at the same time frightened of her Bolshevik husband. There were a few more similar incidents that had to be suffered in silence, but all of these, as the Russian saying goes, "Were as yet only the little flowers, the berries were still to come."

Meanwhile, although there was grave concern over Russia abandoning the war, which enabled Germany to transfer her forces to fight on the Western front, relations between the Allies and the Bolsheviks were maintained in the hope that an alliance could be formed to continue the war on the Eastern front. Military assistance was offered by the Allies, but was categorically refused. Lenin's trump card was "Peace" — peace at any cost, and he had no intention of resuming hostilities and endangering his own cause.

During this period, when Russia and Germany were conducting their peace negotiations, ships of the Royal Navy, which had been previously engaged in escorting the supply ships to Archangel and Murmansk, were now stationed in Murmansk. Due to the proximity of the Gulf Stream the port remained open, unlike Archangel which was frozen.

In February, Germany, tired of Russia's procrastinations over the signing of the peace treaty, unexpectedly launched an attack which forced the surprised Bolshevik leaders to resume their approaches. Germany promptly responded and in early March the treaty was concluded in Brest Litovsk. To describe this treaty as shameful is a rich understatement. Russia was reduced to the size she was three centuries earlier and in handing this vast territory on a plate to the Germans, one-third of the population went with it.

To the Allies this disaster left only one option, and the only hope for the war to be continued by the Russians. They simply had to join the forces who opposed the Bolsheviks and get rid of them. They were in a position to do so.

During that eventful year, our family life continued much the same. One evening as we sat as usual around the samovar, Marga announced that she was leaving the hospital to accept a post offered to her in the gymnasium as a class mistress in the junior department. Marga had nursed the sick and wounded from the beginning of the war, but recently seemed tired and despondent. Two years earlier she had met a young officer, Viktor Telyatin. They fell in love and planned to marry, but Viktor was called away to the front and during the first revolution a letter came saying Viktor was missing, presumed killed. From the time Marga joined our school she and I set off together every morning. Gradually, perhaps on account of being back in the cheerful throng of young people, she returned to her old self. Now that I was older, we often got together on some ploy. Once, both of us being hungry and searching the house for something we could eat, we came across some corn. Deciding to experiment, we roasted it and ground it, added milk and drank it. We were delighted with the result, as it proved to be very satisfying and we imagined tasted just as good as coffee. We were easily pleased during these hungry days.

We talked a lot about the activities in the school. The school held a special attraction for me now. It was not, of course, the lessons: a play was being produced. One of my friends in the class, Shura Rubtsova, and I were chosen for the two main parts. I could neither speak nor think about anything else. It was called *The Magic Mirror* and was about a princess who is cruel and wicked until she sees her true reflection in the magic mirror and realises what she is. The dresses to be worn had to portray the ancient period of Russia. Babushka, with her usual resourcefulness, made mine from an old satin dress of a heavenly blue, complete with a high traditional headdress trimmed with imitation pearls and precious stones.

Shura was to me something special. She was everything I wasn't. From the time when she was five years old, she had been taught music and now, at the tender age of twelve, played the piano, balalaika and the guitar with the ease of an accomplished adult. She was unusually talented, danced and sang in a fine contralto voice to her own accompaniments. Lessons came easily to her — she held her own against the cleverest pupil in the class. The large grey eyes, the calm expression were particularly attractive and became more so as she grew older.

The only child of her parents, she was bereft of her father when he was killed at the beginning of the war. Her widowed mother, undaunted, decided to let the top flat of their house while she, Shura, the old nanny and a cook moved down to the ground floor. The flat above them was usually let to groups connected with the theatre who used to come from Moscow and Petrograd.

I loved to visit the house. The warm comfortable rooms, low ceilings, and small square windows draped in flowered chintz, combined together to offer a cosy intimacy. Shura's own room with the patchworked cover on the bed, prints of Russian fairytales hanging on the walls, shelves filled with our favourite books, the cat sitting on the chair beside the little table where she worked, the balalaika thrown carelessly across the bed — drew me like a magnet.

At times the players would come down and join us in the living-room. They talked of plays, the parts they played in them. I heard such names as *The Seagull, Uncle Vanya, Trilby*, and was transported to the enchanting world of the theatre. One day, Shura and I were invited to play the parts of two children in Ibsen's play *The Doll's House*. Although the parts were merely confined to sitting at a table supping out of empty bowls, with no words to be spoken, we were enthralled with the idea of appearing on the professional stage. Later we were offered the parts of two children in the play *The Bells*.

A few days before the opening night Shura developed a chill and was forced to cancel her appearance. After much persuasion and bribery, Ghermosha stepped into the breach. All members of the family decided to support us, even including Dedushka.

We were meant to represent two ghostly children. Dressed in white gowns, Ghermosha with a yellow wig sitting askew, we had to make our entrance from the back and walk slowly to the front carrying between us a large two-handled urn. We are approached by a man who, overcome by our appearance, enquires in trembling tones, "Who are you?" I had to answer, "We are your children." Turning to my brother, he asks, "What are you carrying?" and he had to reply in soulful tones, "Our mother's tears." This little piece of acting was rehearsed until we were word perfect, except that at times my young brother had the disconcerting habit of repeating exactly what I said.

At last came the dramatic moment when we made our entrance. "Who are you?" asked the tall handsome man. "We are your children," I replied, in that emotional drawn-out voice that I had often heard used on the stage. From immediately beside me came the echo in a loud assertive voice, "We are your children." There was a moment's hesitation and a fleeting smile from our supposed father. "What are you carrying?" he continued. "Our mother's tears," came again the loud-voiced answer, leaving no doubt whose children we were and whose tears were in the urn. This remarkably talented presentation, lasting a mere few seconds, was followed by deafening applause from the box occupied by our supporters to the astonishment of the rest of the audience. Behind the scenes there was a heated argument — little brother had stolen my thunder and hadn't expressed the sensitivity I had.

At the end of April, the river, which only recently was a mass of swirling ice and water, threatening destruction to anyone who crossed her path, now reverted to her old sweet self, flowing serenely between her banks with scarcely a ripple to be seen.

The bridge was thrown across to Solombala, the rails relaid on the wooden surface. The packed tramcars resumed their journeys, if only for the next few months. The old activity returned to the reconstructed pier. Small craft kept sailing to and fro, women brought their laundry, men stood in groups having long discussions, and once more the steady hum of voices was heard drifting over the water.

To the north of the pier, close to the river's edge, the boulders, heated by the sun, became a meeting place for the children in our street. Vera and Volodya came and brought their little brother, Shurick. There was no orderly now to take care of them. Their father, the general, had gone away — no one knew why or where. That summer we were joined by newcomers from the Ukraine, named Pento. The two elder children, Elena and Boris, were our own age, the

other two, Zina and Grisha, were much younger. All spoke in a strong
Ukrainian accent; all, without exception, like their musical parents,
played balalaikas and guitars and had splendid voices. They
approached us a little timidly at first and had to suffer being teased on
account of their strange accent, but later, when accepted, became
members of our gang. We spent long hours beside the river, jumping
in the warm water,coming out to sit on the boulders, only to go in
again when others joined us.

To Father our activities by the river were always a source of worry,
especially when the timber rafts arrived and the boys played the
dangerous game of diving in the deep water between them, taking the
terrible risk of being trapped below. Periodically the young maid,
Katinka, would arrive and call down to us from the river front,
"Gherman Aleksandrovich says you must leave the river and play in
the garden." The garden, of course, was a fine place in which to play
such games as "Cossacks and Robbers", when we scattered all over the
grounds, hiding in the old banya, summerhouses, behind trees and
bushes. Vassily, who imagined that he owned the garden, would on
occasions chase us with his broom, but that just added to the
excitement of hiding, only to appear in a little while to begin our
interrupted play. Most of the time we went hungry but that didn't
trouble us unduly. Children can make a world of their own and,
looking back, I believe we were quite happy.

One evening in late June, Petya Emelyanoff, our singer friend, called
to say goodbye. He was leaving for Petrograd to join a group of
operatic singers. Disquieting reports were circulating of open anarchy
on the streets of Petrograd, of innocent people being arrested and
executed. Petya was undaunted — this was to be the first rung of the
ladder to success, a chance he couldn't disregard.

We were joined by Yura's closest friend, Dmitri Danilov.
Everybody knew that Mitya was more than interested in Marga,
calling at the house on the slightest pretext, but Marga was
indifferent. When teased, she merely shrugged her shoulders saying,
"He's only just a boy." Although a year or two junior to Marga, Mitya
was not just an ordinary boy, but a mature and handsome flaxen-
haired giant of prodigious strength. I remember how overawed we all
were when once, during a playful display of strength between Yura
and his friends, Mitya laughingly bent down and gripping the leg of a
heavy chair by one hand only, raised it high above his head. He
belonged to a wealthy family of peasant origin who owned several
houses in the town.

After tea, we all adjourned to the ballroom. For the last time we sat listening to Petya singing. The doors leading to the balcony were left open and when the last note died away, loud applause was heard coming from a group of passers-by standing below our window.

Later, we all went out on to the balcony and for a while watched the crimson disc of the sun gliding on the horizon. The white nights had returned with their tender, melancholy stillness. From a distance came the faint sound of music from a band playing in the summer garden.

We never saw our "Northern Nightingale" again. Through his sister we heard he had arrived safely, but soon the civil war broke out in earnest in our parts and we became cut off from Petrograd. After eighteen months contact was resumed, but he had disappeared.

One morning, during breakfast, I suggested to Ghermosha that we should search the garden for some mushrooms. The previous year, in July, mushrooms had been found, after rain, near the fairy summer-house. Through the night there had been a heavy thunderstorm and I imagined that we might be just as lucky this year.

The sweet scent of lilac met us as we entered the garden. The sphere-like bushes guarding the gates were once again covered by deep purple blossoms. After the downpour the morning was unusually bright. Each rain-washed flower was opening its petals to the sun. A silver mist was spreading over the lawn. Raindrops like tiny diamonds sparkled on the lacey twigs of the birches and beyond, beside the pond, the storm-ridden willows hung limply over the water.

We found no mushrooms, but while searching around the trees we were surprised to hear a strange grunting. We stopped to listen. The sound came clearly from the bushes growing close to the summerhouse. Forgetting all about the mushrooms, we dived into the undergrowth and there to our amazement were suddenly confronted by the rosy snout of a little pig, peeping apprehensively through the leafy twigs. There ensued a frantic tussle, accompanied by the shrill squealing of the pig and our own, "Catch it — hold it," the despairing "You fool, you've lost it." "Fool yourself." "Grab its legs." "Sit on it." And finally, "I've got it."

We emerged covered in scratches, mud and leaves. The pig was dragged into the summerhouse, the door bolted and the next plan of action discussed. I was all for keeping the pig. "A pig can have two dozen piglets every year," I lied shamelessly. "You need two pigs for that," rejoined my brother, no longer green. "Well," I agreed, "but Yura or Mitka Shalai could perhaps find a boy-pig in some village?" "How do you know what we've got?" I didn't and that was that. The pig was to be taken to the house.

The going was hard. Although not big, the pig was heavy. All my strength was being expended clutching it in my arms with Ghermosha supporting its plump behind, which dangled down my side. The pig's earsplitting, agonising squealing continued throughout this epic struggle until step by step we reached the kitchen, passed the astounded servants, climbed the back stair and entered the nursery.

Uncle Sanya was sitting talking to my father. "You must return the pig to its owners," Father advised us, after listening to our account. "You'll be accused of stealing if you don't." I was indignant. "The pig came by itself — we never stole it and do not even know to whom it might belong. Anyone could claim it, if once we started asking." I was full of bright suggestions. "The pig could be housed where the ewes were — we could breed them and never go hungry again." At this point Uncle Sanya intervened. "The pig," he assured me, "didn't fall like manna from the heavens." It belonged to someone. Vakhonin would be the first to report the matter to the authorities. We would then all land in serious trouble. Uncle Sanya and Father spoke in soothing tones. "Just leave the pig with us and everything will be alright," they said and promised they would not give it away. In the end, feeling apprehensive, we decided to part with our little pig.

Father and Uncle Sanya kept their promise. Some days later the pig returned in the shape of tender chops, succulent hind quarters and various tasty bits. Vassily, who had a good idea where the pig came from, took part in some of the more unpleasant operations.

We had a feast such as we hadn't enjoyed for a considerable time. Uncle Sanya and his family all participated. Every morsel was eaten up and not a trace of our little pig was left. The following day a young man called at the back door. He came from the adjoining land, where an important commissar had arrived and foisted himself on a family living in one of the houses. He had brought a pig with him from the country and was feeding it up so that he could eat it later. He was rather more than grieved when he discovered that the pig had vanished. The young man was sent to discover who might be responsible. Everybody pleaded ignorance. A few days later two stern-faced men from the militia appeared. Ghermosha and I were swimming in the river and so escaped all the questioning, which was perhaps just as well as we might have been frightened into giving the show away. The men demanded to examine the garden. They found no trace, as it had been raining and in any case found it irksome going over every corner of the garden. Just the same we were warned they would return and if proof was found that the pig was stolen by us, the consequences would be serious.

Providence sometimes works in a mysterious way. We were now approaching the end of July. Events of greater importance were looming ahead. The commissar suddenly left and we were spared all further enquiries. The file on the pig was closed.

On the first day of August I awoke with a delightful sense of well-being as if something good was in the offing.

The day before rumours had been spreading that the Allied Fleet was sailing across the White Sea on its way to Archangel. An air of eager anticipation hung over the town. Yet, exciting as it was, my own concern was directed to a totally different matter — a leg of mutton.

During the previous evening, Uncle Sanya, whilst sitting with his cronies over a glass or more of vodka, was introduced to a man who happened to be a cook on one of the steamers plying up and down the river. He turned out to be a friendly soul, who, as he sat, lending a sympathetic ear to Uncle Sanya's tales of hardship, generously offered him a leg of mutton, an offer my uncle gratefully accepted. It was arranged that the following morning Uncle Sanya would collect the leg of mutton from the ship. As Uncle Sanya no longer kept a horse, and to carry such a rarity as a leg of mutton on a tramcar was to invite unwanted notice, he decided to borrow our old horse. Harnessing him to the trap he set off to the docks. At the last minute, he invited Ghermosha to keep him company. Ghermosha, needless to say, was delighted.

They arrived at the landing stage and boarded the steamer. The cook, faithful to his promise, produced the mutton and invited them to join him in the saloon. There, seated round a little table, they proceeded to hold an amiable conversation. Some light refreshments appeared, along with a bottle of vodka. While they were thus pleasantly engaged, a young member of the crew suddenly rushed in, in a state of great excitement. "The steamer's leaving," he shouted. "You'll have to jump for it." Uncle Sanya, grabbing the leg of mutton with one hand and Ghermosha with the other, made for the deck. The paddles were already churning and the steamer was swiftly moving from the landing stage. Not hesitating for a second, Uncle Sanya threw Ghermosha on to the pier, with the leg of mutton after him, and leaped across the widening gap.

The river was an extraordinary sight. All the paddle-steamers, every type of craft the Bolsheviks could lay their hands on, were hurrying up the river to the south. The Bolsheviks were fleeing. Uncle Sanya and my brother had barely escaped being carried away with them.

Thankfully they scrambled into their trap and turned homewards, but when they reached the main street they found themselves between two firing lines. Behind them the Reds were still defending the south end of the street; facing them were the attacking Whites. At this point, Uncle Sanya decided on the only possible course. Handing over the reins to Ghermosha and telling him to hold them as tightly as he could, he raised the knout and lashed the horse, which took off at full speed and galloped through the crossfire. He continued flying like the wind until he reached the familiar gates.

The sound of firing from the south went on throughout the afternoon but, by the evening, the town was in the hands of a strong underground force. The old national flag was once again fluttering over the town hall.

That evening we celebrated the victory by a feast of roasted mutton followed by platefuls of "moroshka", now ripening in the woods. The following morning more rumours began to circulate. The Allied flotilla was now supposed to be approaching the Dvina Delta. Throughout the day people gathered on the river front and by evening a great crowd had collected. They were standing on the pier, sitting on boulders close to the water, on the banks and, higher still, closely packed against the railing of the boulevard. As from our balcony there was a perfect view of the river, many friends called and sat with us, waiting to see the first ship appear. Ghermosha and I, wishing to be with the crowd, sat perched on the railings. Yura and Marina were beside us. The tension was increasing with every moment. Of course, even as we waited, people were saying that the ship sunk by the Bolsheviks, to block the passage, would take a week and more to remove. But they were mistaken. All obstructions had already been cleared with comparative ease.

I remember how clear and warm the night was, with just a gentle touch of autumn. A young schoolboy succeeded in climbing up a telegraph pole and called down to the crowd that he had seen a mast moving behind the island of Solombala. All eyes were now fixed on the island. The boy was not mistaken. As if entering the stage from the wings of a theatre, the first ship of the flotilla came into view. The others followed. They were all there — Russian, British, French, American. They sailed serenely, majestically, one after the other, in perfect formation, against the pink glow of the setting sun. There was a breathless hush followed by tremendous cheering, growing louder as each ship passed before our eyes. The sound of our voices echoed across the water and reached the men crowding on the decks. They in turn cheered back to us and waved their caps. Never before had the banks of our river seen such a glorious armada. I have never forgotten that stirring sight nor yet the old lady beside me, tears streaming

down her face, crossing herself and repeating over and over again,
"Slava Tyebye Gospodi" . . . "The Lord be praised."

The Allied Intervention had begun.

Long after the last ship vanished out of sight people remained talking
on the balcony. Now and again the silence was broken by the sudden
spurt of the engine of a motor-boat scurrying up the river intent on
some urgent business.

Lights moving on the road towards us from the direction of the
town caught our attention. They were coming from a motor vehicle —
a strange sight in our parts — which appeared to be in some kind of
trouble as after puffing and steaming, it halted in front of our balcony.
Two men got out and, speaking English in an accent which sounded
different to my mother's, held an anxious discussion. Father, on
hearing them, leaned over the railing and enquired if he could be of
any assistance. "It is good to hear you, sir, we sure are in trouble,"
came the answer. It transpired this was the advance party of the
cookhouse for the American contingent to be housed in the second
girls' gymnasium. The water in the radiator of their lorry had
evaporated and although they were close to the river they had no
means of carrying the water to refill it. We immediately offered them
all the water they required and extended an invitation to come into the
house. The men, hot and bothered and uncertain of the road, gladly
accepted our hospitality. The samovar arrived and all that we had was
offered.

This was our first acquaintanceship with Americans. Memory has
retained their names — Sergeant Boverley, a tall broad-shouldered
man, and Sergeant Grey, smaller with a round face and humorous
expression. Both came from Detroit and both, from that night for the
whole of their sojourn in Archangel, became our friends and called
constantly at the house. On seeing the poverty of our table, Sergeant
Grey immediately hurried to his lorry and returned carrying tins of
biscuits, jam and cheese. A happy gathering followed at the end of
which, escorted by Yura to show the way, our new friends left.

The following day the lorry drove through our gates. The boys
returned, bringing a sack of flour, sugar, bacon, lard and butter. All of
us were too thankful and delighted to enquire how they were able to
conjure up such goodies.

During the next two months more troops were disembarked. Five
thousand Americans landed in September and in early October,
before the river froze, General Edmund Ironside arrived,
accompanied by French, British and Canadian troops. General
Ironside, an imposing figure, was placed in command of all the Allied

forces and billetted in a fine residence in Troitsky Prospect. The house belonged to a family named Desfontaines, who were wealthy timber merchants and related to us by marriage — the wife of my godfather and my father's uncle were Desfontaines.

The town became crowded to bursting point. On the jostling pavements were now heard all the different voices of foreign soldiers — British, French, American and even Serbian.

In August, filtered through from Siberia, came the news of the slaughter of the Royal family by the sadistic thugs of the Bolshevik party. Horror and revulsion touched every decent thinking citizen in the town. To execute the weak Tsar and his neurotic wife in this barbaric fashion was bad enough, but to butcher the four young girls and the helpless boy was the work of mindless criminals. In churches people went down on their knees and openly wept as they prayed for the souls of the Tsar and his family.

Recently, the martyred family have been sanctified. "People will pray to them instead of praying for their souls," it was being said. I cannot but think how much better it might have been had they been spared this martyrdom. At the time of the Tsar's abdication Britain offered him and his family protection which the Tsar gratefully accepted only to have the offer cancelled by the Government of Lloyd George, and the cancellation endorsed by George V. France likewise refused to suffer their presence. Conveniently forgotten was the fact that when they had all begged him for his help, the Tsar responded by transferring his armies to save the Western front at the cost of sacrificing the flower of Russia's sons, his country and himself.

At the end of August, the weather rapidly deteriorated. Torrential rain poured down from leaden skies and a cold east wind blew from Siberia. Up the river, battles were being fought in woods and villages in the worst possible conditions, for as usual in the late autumn, the whole surrounding countryside became a vast quagmire, making the maintenance of supplies well-nigh impossible. This is the time of year when even our own hardy peasants try to avoid crossing the sodden wastes and prefer to wait until the frosts bind the earth together. Yet the ding-dong battles continued with soldiers struggling knee-deep in mud, fighting and dying in this foreign land.

We children, when the weather permitted, still gathered beside the river. By now, white horses were galloping across the Dvina and the water was too cold for swimming. Instead we gathered large quantities of driftwood, lit enormous bonfires between the boulders and sat around baking potatoes in the glowing embers, having endless discussions, arguments and, on occasions, joining in some rowdy singing to the amusement of the passers-by above us.

One day, sitting by the river, we saw a large barge floating to the north. Usually barges were accompanied by two or more men, but this one, rolling on the waves, appeared to be deserted. It vanished round the island out of sight and we soon forgot about it, but the following day it appeared again, this time sailing up the river. It continued floating up and down with the tide, sometimes vanishing from view only to appear once more. Gradually it drifted a little closer to the shore, and so didn't interfere with the traffic in midstream. By now our curiosity was aroused. There was something mysterious, something ghostly about this barge that made us wish we could inspect it closer, but it was still far out of reach and we had no means by which we could approach it. There was nothing we could do but hope that in becoming ice-bound it might present an opportunity to board it.

One day, peering through the frosted window panes, I saw in the distance the dark shadow of the barge firmly wedged in the river. Snowstorms and intense frost prevented any attempts to go near it, but one bright Sunday morning, Tolya Mammontov called at the house. Tolya had seen the barge and was rounding us all up. Donning our skis, we all set off down the incline to the river.

The day was perfect — the sun and frost, and the river dazzling white. In great excitement, laughing, shouting, we skimmed towards the black mass of the barge. The sides proved to be too high for us to climb over with any ease. After a long struggle of climbing, falling back, rolling in the snow and refusing to recognise defeat, we eventually reached the top and fell inside, landing on something soft. Lying below the snow we discovered large hessian-covered bales. Impatiently tearing the covers apart, we found to our astonishment the skins of precious furs — mink, sable and ermine. The barge was packed with these bales. We had stumbled on a treasure of great worth — or so we thought. But as each bale was opened and anxiously scanned, it became obvious that someone had been there before. The best of the skins had been removed, leaving those on the outside which, exposed to the weather, had rotted away. We were too late.

The puzzle of the barge remained. Where did it come from, who were the owners, and what forced them to abandon their precious cargo and allow it to drift away, perhaps for hundreds of miles? No one ever discovered. Many strange things were happening in those turbulent days.

As to the mystery of who had forestalled us, that was solved in the early spring. In our street there lived a family, named Duletov, of six daughters and three sons. On Easter Sunday all the girls arrived in

church wearing stoles, muffs and hats of mink and ermine. Their
mother, Madame Duletova, excelled them all, appearing in a
handsome sable jacket with muff and hat to match.

In November the long wished-for news arrived from Scotland. Mama
was coming back on an ice-breaker, and was hoping to be with us in
time for Christmas.

For some months past, Father had been preparing to welcome
Mother with a special gift which he knew would please her. It was
impossible to find anything in the few shops still functioning, but
peasants trading in furs often called at our house offering the skins of
animals trapped in the woods. Father decided to order a mink stole for
mother's arrival. The skins had to be carefully chosen and out of each
bundle that the men brought only a few were picked. The shades
likewise had to be matched and required careful scrutiny. In doing
this, Father often appealed to me, which puzzled me a bit as I, of
course, was not the expert he was. His eyes, he explained, troubled
him at times. In the end enough skins were collected to be made up
into a handsome stole by our local furrier. It was carefully put away
for mother's arrival.

The icebreaker on which mother was travelling was called *Canada*. It
was considered to be the most modern and strongest of all the ice-
breakers in the group. On the day Mother was expected, Uncle Adya
phoned from the mill to tell us that the *Canada* had now entered the
middle channel and was travelling past the long row of the timber
mills.

In the early afternoon the usual gloomy darkness took over, but in
the evening the moon rose high, flooding the whole river with brightness. Ghermosha and I, hardly able to contain our excitement, kept
staring out the windows and were rewarded in the end when we saw
the dark shadow of the ice-breaker gliding past our house, its light
flashing. We, in turn, signalled back, by turning on and off the lights in
the ballroom. Babushka, accompanied by Seryozha, immediately set
off to meet Mother. That evening there was a joyful reunion followed
by one of our old happy gatherings, with Sashenka as usual sitting at
the samovar pouring out the tea, Osa still with us, and everybody
talking at once, laughing, asking quesions.

Christmas was happy that year, with the touch of the old
Christmases gone by. Mother had brought presents for everyone and
now that there was no scarcity of sugar, Babushka had prepared
homemade sweets and passed them round in attractive little boxes on
which she painted colourful designs of flowers. There was food on the
table and candles on the tree.

It was the last Christmas party to be held in this house.

6

1919

The new year was met with glowing optimism. The Bolsheviks were on the run — it was only a question of a month or two for the final rout, so they said. Yet those who fought knew they were up against a determined enemy, who had the advantage over his adversary of having been born to stand up to the rigours of the Arctic weather.

The war continued with the troops fighting in sub-zero temperatures. At times the thermometer dropped to —40°C. The coffee in their mugs froze, their eyelids stuck, and any wounded left lying survived only for a short time.

Life, on the whole, was good that winter. British, Americans and a sprinkling of French flocked to our house. In return there were invitations to receptions, parties and other functions. Mother and Marga usually attended them. It was at one of these parties that Marga met a young American officer who became a frequent visitor to the house and was obviously attracted by her. Frank was congenial, danced well, and had a certain panache which appealed to Marga.

In the heart of the city, the Canadian troops built an ice mountain, the like of which had never been seen before in our part of the country. From the top the tobogganist raced the whole length of the street, down the steep bank and finished up on the river. Steps led up to the high platform and the mountain and the slide were bordered by small conifers, embedded in the ice, which were decorated with colourful lights presenting a wonderful display in the early darkness.

This construction was built for adults only. On account of its being considered dangerous, all children were banned. A soldier, standing at the foot of the steps, kept a steady watch. Yet it drew us like a magnet and often, succeeding in distracting the guard's attention, we dodged past him and, racing down, were followed by a volley of strange words which we later learned described us all as being born out of wedlock.

On one occasion Mother volunteered to accompany us and have a word or two with the guard on our behalf. The solder, agreeably surprised to meet a nice-looking lady who talked in pleasant tones in his own language, allowed us to go up. We immediately bounded up the steps with our toboggans while Mother remained talking to the soldier. As we continued blissfully racing up and down, the frost hardened and Mother, waiting patiently, was overcome by the intense cold and began to shiver. The shivering persisted at home and the following morning she went down with a chill which developed into double pneumonia. Only Dedushka's constant attention, assisted by a Royal Navy doctor, saved her life.

Soon after, Scotka went missing. In the past he had been known to go off on some amorous adventure and occasionally, when walking home from school, I used to meet him. He, after halting long enough to bestow on me a gracious nod and a friendly wag of his tail, would hurry on to his assignation. This was something different. His old friend the watchman, after missing Scotka's faithful presence, likewise became anxious and searched for him through the various courtyards while doing his rounds.

One day during my music lesson, with Madame Susanova keeping time while standing with her back to the double doors, I noticed one of the doors quietly opening and the figure of my brother crawling under the grand piano. He was pushing on the floor towards me a piece of paper which appeared to have something written on it. When it reached my feet I looked down at the brief message, "Scotka has died." To Madame Susanova's astonishment, who had no reason that day to smack my fingers, I burst into loud wailing and rushed out of the room.

It so happened that a week earlier Vassily had occasion to do some work inside an old disused stable, utilised for storing garden tools and such like. On finishing his chores, he walked away and closed the door behind him. Going back a week later, he found Scotka lying dead behind the door. It will never be known if Scotka had accidentally been locked in or if, seeing the door ajar, as it often was, he had gone in there perhaps to die. None was more saddened than the old watchman. "Scotka was my friend — my only friend," he wept.

It was impossible to bury Scotka in the frost-bound earth. He was placed in a small box and kept in the same place where he was found. In the early spring Vassily dug a little grave beside the summerhouse and planted a young birch on top of it.

In the spring the watchman died too. The ancient custom of keeping a watchman walking up and down the street in the dead of night was abolished. The small stone hut was removed, leaving a bare patch of earth as a reminder that it was here that the old Russian peasant and his Scottish friend used to shelter.

Soon after the arrival of the Allied Intervention, a lively bartering grew up between a few of the more enterprising troops and the inhabitants. The forests of our countryside, rich in furs, offered an opportunity for any soldier to take back a handsome souvenir. As contacts were usually made through private houses, my father, being a fluent English speaker, frequently acted as a middle-man.

Peasants, arriving at our house with their precious bundles, invariably preferred to barter for such scarce commodities as sugar, tea, flour and even soap rather than cash. As time went on, the old nursery, which in the past had witnessed many scenes, became a trading station with Father presiding in his chair, surrounded by great heaps of valuable furs. Our two American friends, Sergeants Boverley and Grey, were the main source of supply of goods. No one questioned how this was achieved — we had been too hungry for too long. We only knew there was no better sight than the lorries laden with sacks of sugar, flour, tins of tea, coffee and whatever, rolling through the gates.

Easter was as joyful as the Christmas before it had been and held the same bright hopes for the future.

Our British and American friends were invited to attend with us the midnight service and later came to the house for the Easter celebrations. It was decided that we would go to the Cathedral in the centre of the city, so that our friends would see the fine interior, hear the service presented by the Archbishop himself, and listen to the voices of the choir.

The Cathedral with its white walls, five golden domes and below them the unique frescoes depicting biblical scenes in glowing colour, was the pride of the town. It was destroyed a few years later by the vandals of the godless society. On that dreadful day, the citizens foregathered and stood watching helplessly. Men bared their heads and both men and women, going down on their knees, wept as the explosion shook the ground and the ancient church, treasured for generations, was reduced to a mass of rubble.

But the monstrous crime which destroyed the Cathedral and planted in its place a theatre was as yet hidden by a curtain of dark, distant years. Meanwhile, inside the church, all was light and gladness. The ancient ritual of the procession, the triumphant Easter message, the glorious voices of the choir, were there to be remembered.

We walked back to the house with our lighted candles, through a sea of twinkling lights to the joyful ringing of the bells from every church in town. Everyone gathered round the table which, if not as lavish as in the days gone by, was still sufficient to please our guests. Protocol was abolished. The American sergeants, officers, the Royal Marines all mingled together with our relatives. It was a memorable party which lasted well into the morning.

At times I used to ask myself, where are they now, these boys who like birds of passage came from distant climes, lingered a while and all too soon vanished out of our lives? There was one exception. Some time during the 'twenties Sergeant Boverley returned and after some difficulty in finding where my grandmother lived, called on her. He was a member of a mission permitted by the Bolshevik government to take back to America the bodies of the men who died during the time of the Allied Intervention. Knowing the prevailing scarcities, he brought a generous gift of food, just as he did on that distant autumn evening when we first made his and Grey's acquaintance.

The early days of spring went by and we were into summer when all schools closed, allowing us to roam at will. The sun was again slowly circling overhead, setting and rising almost in the same place. In the garden the warm scent of the young grass mingled with the fresh sharpness of the wild cherry racemes. The old poplar was shedding its crimson catkins.

In the parks the bands played well into the night. Couples strolled below the leafy trees, holding hands. The strange beauty of these nights, silent, with a hint of sadness, held their own magic. There were tender romances, a few weddings and many lighthearted affairs, the results of which are perhaps living in our parts still.

Other activities, with less romance and a more down to earth approach, blossomed out. In the other end of the town there was a house known as "the house with the green roof". For some reason, which to me was mysterious, soldiers flocked there. Travelling in packed tramcars, the men, like homing pigeons, knew exactly where to go. At times I used to see young ladies in flamboyant dresses sitting in the tramcar coming from the direction of that mysterious house. Their painted cheeks, khol-rimmed eyes and fuzzed-up fringes never failed to fascinate me.

In those days people travelling in tramcars were allowed to stand beside the driver. I remember one hot day, enjoying the cool breeze, standing there, leaning against the railing. Close beside me was one of those fascinating ladies, all dressed up in an eye-catching confection. A lorry, full of American soldiers, was travelling alongside. Suddenly my companion became strangely animated and, rudely pushing me aside, began to make beckoning gestures, wink and point in the direction of the house. This was much appreciated by the soldiers who obviously got the message. I thought she was ill-mannered. On arriving home I related the incident, but this for some reason only aroused amusement. Although I had some knowledge of the facts of life, I didn't know the purpose of that house and imagined it was some kind of club where there was dancing and perhaps a special entertainment. Enlightment as to how entertaining it was came some time later.

A long chain of events followed that summer. There was the day of the great parade. All the troops assembled in the Cathedral Square where a short service took place, along with the traditional ceremony of welcome with the bread and salt. The various contingents then proceeded to march along the main street.

They were all there. Our own White Russian Guards with the old three-coloured badges on their caps, the British contingents, including the Green Howards, the Royal Scots and the Royal Marines in their white helmets. The French passed by. The Americans followed along with their marines. Then the sunburned Serbians in grey uniforms and a small group of Italians in picturesque plumed hats. The bands played stirring marches, dying away and starting up again. It was one of these hot sultry days with the sun beating down on the marchers, winding their way along the cobbled roadway between the wooden pavements lined with watching crowds. I have a memory of myself dancing alongside a stout drum-major who was draped in a leopard skin. Ignoring the exhausting heat, his face drenched in sweat, he kept on stoically beating his drum, no doubt longing for the moment when it would all be over.

Another innovation launched by the British was the formation of the first group of Girl Guides and Boy Scouts in Russia. This was enthusiastically welcomed. I, along with other girls, hurried to be enrolled.

We were divided into patrols with the senior girls chosen as our leaders. Each patrol was named after some wild animal, the name and coloured tab of which were sewn on the shoulders of our tunics. Our patrol was named "Beaver". We had to wear khaki tunics over navy skirts. The uniforms we somehow managed to achieve, but the flat hats proved to be difficult until the Canadians came to our rescue by providing us with their hats, which we wore with the leather straps under our chins. We all had to have a small flag, representing the old three colours, stitched on front of our tunics. They were fashioned out of ribbons, but in my case I wore instead a brooch depicting the old Russian flag done in coloured enamel on gold, given to Mother by my father when they became engaged. Under the guidance of an English

lady, dressed in the navy blue uniform of the British Girl Guides, we
received the usual training, drilling, doing good deeds and such like.

There was even a jamboree, inspected by General Ironside. His tall,
imposing, if slightly arrogant, figure passed the long row of girls and
boys standing to attention. He stopped to say a word or two to some of
us in his broken Russian. Beside him was our Russian General Miller,
quiet and dignified, dwarfed by his tall companion.

There were bonfires, baked beans and sausages and some kind of
pancakes, tasting all the better for being burned. Tents were erected
as well as a large screen, which projected a Western film all about Red
Indians chasing a stagecoach and scalping the unfortunate occupants.
The film, drawing crowds, held for me a morbid fascination combined
with the naive thought as to how lucky we were to be so far away from
America.

The jamboree continued well into the night. Mother, Marga and
Frank, along with Yura and Marina, came in the early evening to
watch the fun. At the end the tents were folded, the bonfires put out
and the tired scouts and guides, after a happy day, returned to their
respective homes.

The summer was unusually hot that year. In the garden not a leaf
stirred; no cooling breeze disturbed the still surface of the pond and
the Dvina herself lay like a burnished sheet of steel with barely a ripple
to be seen.

We children spent many hours by the river. The water was cool and
soft as silk. Women came and brought their babies, who shrieked with
excitement and delight when gently lowered into the water. It was to
our quiet part of the town that the bathers flocked. There were no
facilities for bathing higher up the river amongst busy wharfs and
constant traffic of large ships.

In the south of Russia, no doubt, there were fashionable bathing
resorts and people wore bathing suits. Here, no such thing was ever
seen. As in the villages the women came to the part reserved for them,
where they undressed, waded into the water, swam for a little while,
came out, sat drying themselves, gossiped with their neighbours and
eventually walked away. Needless to say my mother and Babushka
didn't indulge in such pastimes, although Marina on occasions joined
us and Marga liked to join us in the early hours of the morning when
no one was about.

This custom, as old as the town itself, was repeated every year,
drawing no attention. Men walking on the boulevard never gave a
passing glance. Now foreign soldiers appeared from nowhere, jostled,
pushed to reach the railings so as to have a better view, and made no

pretence of hiding their delight at seeing so many ladies bathing in the nude. At first the women suffered this intrusion into their privacy with patience, but as more and more men arrived, they became resentful.

One scorching day when I was bathing with the others under the gaze of numerous spectators whose remarks could be well imagined, the women became incensed. With threatening gestures, they began to hurl abuse at the onlookers, except for one sturdy lass, more tolerant than her companions. "What are you going on about?" she asked. "These poor souls are far from home, their wives and sweethearts — what do you have to lose if it gives them pleasure?" With these words, she turned to face the soldiers spreading wide her arms. "Have a good look, my darlings — gaze to your heart's content if it makes you happy!" The appreciative cheering, shrill whistling and applause only served to infuriate the women further and after hurling the offender into the river, they marched off to the authorities.

The following day a sentry appeared on the scene. His orders were to remain on duty, standing with his back to the river. Any optimistic passerby showing signs of loitering was smartly ordered to continue walking.

Shortly after this incident, Mother was sitting on the balcony with her close friend Lidochka, Uncle Vanya's daughter. While they were happily chatting about this and that, they saw two riders cantering in their direction. These turned out to be two dapper British officers, who dismounted, tied their reins round a lamp-post, and walked towards the railings. "Let's have a look at these Russian bathing beauties," Mother overheard one saying. Whereupon she stood up and called out loud and clear in English, "Don't go far out, Ena!" The effect of this acted like magic. "My God, Freddie, there's an English-woman here," and with this they hurriedly mounted their horses and galloped out of sight.

Of course there was a more serious side to the Intervention. Shortly after the troops landed, many were struck down by Spanish influenza. For some strange reason it particularly affected the American boys. In spite of the strict policy from Washington for the troops to be deployed only for garrison duty, guarding the port and stores and not for any active service in the interior, many of the American soldiers did fight and were killed in action. Yet it was known that those who perished from influenza far exceeded the number who died fighting.

Daily, throughout the whole summer, the funeral processions were seen winding along the Troitsky Prospekt on their way to the cemetery. We got to know the sad refrain of the funeral march, the solemn beat of the drum. At times, while playing, we would hear the approach of the procession and, dropping everything, would run to the top of the street to watch the cortège pass by. With the callous indifference of children we were at the same time always curious to know which flag covered the coffin. Was it the Union Jack, our own Imperial flag, the tricolour French one, or the Stars and Stripes? There were always more of the latter. The boys usually followed the cortège for the sole pupose of collecting the spent cartridge cases after the final salute had been fired.

One afternoon Sergeant Grey called. He was a young man of a cheerful disposition, always ready to laugh and joke. I have a happy memory of him bringing all the ingredients and demonstrating the best method of producing the famous American doughnuts. Now he was neither laughing nor joking, but instead was grieving over the loss of a close buddy who had caught the 'flu and died a few days later.

On hearing this, Babushka hurried down to the garden and brought back an armful of flowers from which she fashioned a beautiful wreath. From that day there was a steady stream of soldiers requesting flowers. No one was ever turned away. There was not a day that Babushka wasn't seen, surrounded by cut flowers in the dining-room, busily engaged in making wreaths, crosses and sprays. She refused to be paid for them but accepted small tokens of gratitude in the shape of a tin of fruit, sweets, tea or coffee. The garden, usually a riot of colour, was emptied of all flowers, but there was many a wreath placed on the coffins and graves of soldiers.

One sunny morning, Marga announced that she and Frank had decided to become engaged. After breakfast Frank called for Marga and they set off to our local church for the ritual of a betrothal. When they returned, they were wearing each other's future wedding rings according to the old Russian custom.

Although in the American forces there were a few cases when permission was granted to get married, Frank wasn't one of the lucky ones. It was then arranged that once Frank was back in America and discharged from the army, Marga would join him. The plans included a wedding in a Russian church followed by Marga settling down to a married life in America. Meanwhile a small family celebration took place.

My grandparents' reaction to these arrangements was one of mixed feelings. Marga was happy, but America seemed so far away, the times were uncertain and they knew very little of Frank's background.

Added to this was anxiety for Aunt Olga and her family in Finland. After the revolution, Uncle Oscar had to report to Kerensky's

Government in Petrograd to receive instructions about his position. He took with him two of his daughters, Ariadna and Zlata. While they were there, the Bolsheviks took over and Kerensky fled. Uncle Oscar and his daughters found themselves stranded in Petrograd with no position of any kind and nothing to sustain them.

In Finland, Aunt Olga, left with the younger daughters and little son Igor, was existing by selling her precious antiques. Beyond this worrying news, written by my aunt almost a year earlier, and with Petrograd now being cut off, no one knew what was happening to the family.

At the beginning of July, the school authorities decided that the children should have an educational trip up the river, lasting for a week. No one discovered which of the learned fathers conceived the idea of an expedition with such a lighthearted disregard of any constructive planning, but needless to say all the schoolchildren flocked to have their names placed on the list. As the Bolsheviks had removed most of the paddle-steamers and the remaining few were utilised by the army, only a small steamer was available, which could carry no more than fifty passengers. The first names on the list were picked, and included our little company of Vera, Volodya, Elena and Boris, Ghermosha and me.

Our parents were informed that although there were no cabins, mattresses would be provided. It would be no hardship, sleeping on deck during our lovely summer nights. We had to bring our own towels, soap, toothbrushes, mugs, plates, forks and spoons and a change of underwear. Simple food would be supplied from the various villages on our way, including health-giving milk straight from the cows. The villagers, we discovered later, had other ideas.

On the appointed day we duly arrived, carrying our little bundles. Although not instructed to do so, our fond parents prepared a few pirozhkis, cookies and cakes. At the last minute I pushed into my bag the little pillow known as "Dumka", without which I have never travelled anywhere throughout my life.

At first everything went smoothly. It was pleasant meandering between wooded banks, villages, with their isbas and nestling churches, but as the day wore on and the merciless rays of the sun beat down upon the crowded deck, we passengers began to feel the heat. The large barrel of tepid kvas was soon emptied, the pirozhkis and cookies eaten. We were luckier than most in finding a small corner where we were able to fashion out of our towels a kind of tent, which offered us some shade.

We sat there longing for the glad moment when we would go ashore to that hospitable village where we were promised simple food and health-giving milk. No such thing happened. The villagers were aghast at such an invasion and totally unprepared to feed a multitude of children and their teachers. In the end they gave us what they could. Some ate boiled potatoes, others buckwheat kasha, but there was not enough milk to go round.

After we had strolled around the village and talked to the children, the trip continued. The promised mattresses never materialised. During the night a chilly wind sprung up from the river. We took down our little tent and rolling ourselves in the towels, slept the best we could on the bare deck. I was thankful to have my "Dumka".

In the early evening of the next day we arrived at an old monastery. Unexpectedly, the monks were prepared for our arrival and had several horses and carts awaiting us on the landing stage. The evening was cool and peaceful. The long line of carts moved through fields of ripening corn, grassy verges, the sweet-smelling pink clover. Someone in front began to sing a well-known folksong, the rest all joined in. The countryside with its numerous lakes, tall ancient cedars, dark against the white trunks of the birches, the dignified geese ambling beside the lake left an impression of a scene depicting ancient Russia. That night we were accommodated in the large airy bedrooms of the guest house. The mattresses on the floor were clean and comfortable, the pillows and sheets spotless.

The following morning we were meant to go further up the river to another monastery, but after sailing for a few hours, we ran aground and in spite of all the efforts of the crew there we remained stuck fast in the blazing heat. After what seemed a long time, during which the anxiety of the crew and teachers began to transfer to us and we all became frightened, rescue came from an unexpected quarter. It was no less than the British Navy which saved us. A destroyer sailing down the river observed our plight. Lowering their lifeboats, the crew took us all aboard. This proved to be the most exciting part of the whole expedition.

The sailors were delighted to have us in their midst and couldn't do enough. We were fêted and given what was, to us, wonderful food — sausage and beans, tinned peaches and cocoa. We spent the night aboard, in hammocks rigged up by the sailors, which was, of course, a great novelty for all of us. As the ship was on its way to town, we arrived there the following morning in great style.

On returning home we were greeted with the news that the detestable Vakhonin had at long last vacated the lodge. There had been a few more unpleasant incidents, culminating in Vakhonin being told to leave. We no longer were under a Bolshevik government which might have sprung to his defence so that, as the old saying goes, the holiday was now in our street. Irisha had been with the family many years and was a good woman, well liked by us, but being married to Vakhonin she, naturally, went with him. We never saw them again.

A few days later another family arrived to settle in the lodge. They were refugees from the south of Russia. The man had been an overseer on an estate belonging to some princess who, after the revolution, fled to France. The estate was plundered and destroyed. The overseer, finding himself destitute and his life threatened, decided to seek refuge in the north. There were many more like him. Between the foreign troops and refugees the town was bursting at the seams. Whole families were living in garrets and in single rooms, suffering great privation.

Yura's friend, Mitya Danilov, called one day. He was now going off to fight the Bolsheviks. The British officer's uniform, issued to the recruits, sat well on his massive shoulders. A few days later Yura joined up too, and returned wearing the same uniform, complete with "Sam Browne" belt. Most of the boys, having finished their schooling, joined the White Army. All were young, all had high hopes for their future. Many had planned, like Yura, to enrol at the universities of Petrograd or Moscow. All these aspirations were now discarded for the joint effort to defeat the Bolshevik menace which threatened to engulf not only Russia but the whole of the world.

As the summer wore on, rumours began to spread. It was said that our allies were not always of one mind. Mutinies and desertions were taking place, with British and Russian officers being murdered. In our local barracks, after the men refused to obey the order to proceed to the front, thirteen of the ringleaders were rounded up. General Ironside signed the death warrant for their execution.

Worrying as these rumours were, they were overshadowed by our own personal tragedy. For some time I had noticed Mother laboriously reading the newspapers to Father and imagined she was practising her Russian until I saw Seryozha or some other person doing likewise. I was reminded of how Father had asked me to match the skins for mother's cape, which for an expert such as he was seemed a strange thing to do. Father was obviously requiring glasses.

One afternoon Dedushka arrived with another gentleman who, I discovered later, was an eye specialist. Both, with Mother and Babushka, vanished into Father's bedroom, while I remained, hovering anxiously, in the hall.

When Babushka came out, put her arms around me and told me

Father was losing his eyesight — I did not cry. I simply couldn't take it in. That Father, deprived of the use of his legs, was now condemned to lie in darkness, never again to see the brightness of the sun, the faces of his friends, his children, was beyond my understanding.

Realisation came later. Pain stabbed each time I saw his eyes, blue and perfectly clear, looking beyond me, or when his slender hand searched for some small article on the bedside table. There was one small consolation. Father was never alone. He at all times was surrounded by loyal and loving friends. He himself, perhaps given some inner strength, remained cheerful, always ready to joke, to laugh and at times quietly to hum one of his favourite songs.

He was 38 and I thirteen when he lost his eyesight. From that time I formed my own philosophy. Not understanding why the all-powerful, all-loving God should have allowed this to happen, I came to the conclusion that He could only be one or the other. I have never had, since then, any reason to change my mind.

Our American and British friends continued calling. They often gathered round the piano with Mother playing the popular war songs. At other times, with Frank and Marga joining in, there was waltzing. The garden was also a great attraction with its summerhouses, shady walks, romantic setting, the scent of fading flowers. But over all there hung a sense of foreboding. Sooner or later, we all knew the Allied forces would be returning to their own lands. What would happen then? Those who knew the answer remained silent. The civil war was now in its second year and still there was no sign of any definite defeat of the Bolshevik forces.

Only Marga was full of happy optimism. She was gathering together all her belongings and packing them inside a trunk brought down from the garret. Marga, like a little squirrel, liked to collect things, especially those connected with our Van Brienen ancestors. She was friendly with two old ladies who were the last of the Van Brienen family. After visiting them, Marga never returned empty handed. There was the old ivory fan, a miniature, a snuffbox or a precious piece of porcelain. Marga treasured them all. Her best acquisition was a half-length portrait of one of our female ancestors, painted by a Dutch Master about the end of the seventeenth century. The portrait was hung on the wall of Marga's bedroom, which she shared with me. It depicted a fine-featured, faintly smiling face framed in dark ringlets in the style of that century. The bare shoulders are draped in lace and crimson velvet. Now the portrait was carefully being crated in readiness for its journey to that wonderful new world — America. Some members of the family resented this, especially

Seryozha who said he did not mind which one of us possessed it, as long as it didn't leave Archangel. Marga, however, refused to entertain any ideas except her own and wasn't slow to point out that the portrait was hers and hers alone.

Her plans were carefully prepared. When she got a letter from Frank after his return home, she was to set off for Britain and from there cross over to America. It all sounded simple and somehow not quite real.

What was rumoured, what was feared, had happened. Our allies were preparing to abandon us. One by one friends called to bid goodbye. The marines, like happy schoolboys going on holiday, were leaving with the first batch. Almost a year had passed since the war with Germany had ended. There was peace in the West. Yet they had continued doggedly fighting on this foreign soil, plagued by mosquitos in the swamps, tormented by the heat of summer and the terrible frosts of an arctic winter. Britain had done her stint. Of the three main allies it was the British who had the largest contingents in the north, did most of the fighting and suffered the most casualties. Their graves scattered in woods and marshes have left no mark and are long forgotten.

One morning a chain of ships, half-hidden by the early mist, slowly stole past our shores and vanished behind the island on its way to the White Sea. Only a year earlier these ships had been met with great rejoicing and now they were slinking away in silence. We watched them from our windows. Only Seryozha passed a bitter comment. "Why did they come at all? We shall pay a heavy price for this."

The Allied Intervention was over. There was no hope of any reinforcements or supplies. The decision for the evacuation of all British and non-Russian forces was kept secret and the departure of the troops had to be accomplished in a manner so as not to attract the attention of the White Russians.

Everyone knew, of course, the main reason for the Intervention. The Bolsheviks had to be defeated so that Russia would continue fighting Germany and in this way save the seriously threatened Western front. The other reason for the Allied presence in Murmansk was to prevent the Germans attacking Russia through Finland and gaining control of the sea. Once Germany was defeated, there was another reason, but only in the minds of those who fondly imagined that the Allies did not wish to see a communist régime in Russia. In reality the Allies did not care what government took over Russia.

No one appeared to realise that Lenin and Trotsky were not ordinary revolutionaries bent on freeing Russia, but men passionately intent on imposing their doctrine over the whole world. The Allied Intervention has been described as an unmitigated disaster; a disaster paid for by the needless loss of Allied soldiers and savage reprisals against millions of White Russians.

A civil war differs from all others in that people of the same nation are locked in bitter conflict over an opposing ideology, and when one side is supported by a foreign power, the trump card is automatically handed over to the opponent. To Lenin's slogan of "Peace and land" was added the clarion call, "Down with the foreign invader".

After the Bolshevik revolution the White Army remained loyal to her allies, determined to fight the Germans to the bitter end. To achieve this aim help was required to defeat the Bolshevik menace and when it came in the shape of the Allied Intervention, they were duly grateful. But this support should have had a more diplomatic approach, a little more of an equal partnership. Instead, the Russians found themselves completely under the control of the British in the north, and the French in Siberia. General Miller, a man of great integrity, loved by his officers and men, was subordinate, along with every Russian, to General Ironside, and Admiral Kolchak, the Supreme Commander, subordinate to the French General Janin, who in the end did nothing to save Kolchak from being murdered by the Bolsheviks.

This was perhaps only one factor amongst more important others, but is there any wonder that there were mutinies and wholesale desertions of even able officers to the Bolsheviks?

Uncle Adya called one evening. He was now running the family timber business, which was causing grave anxiety. There had been a fire in the mill and valuable timber, lying in readiness for export, went up in flames. Sabotage was suspected, but difficult to prove. We saw the crimson glow splashed across the skies, while men continued fighting and finally succeeded in averting a disaster of an appalling magnitude had the blaze spread to the long line of neighbouring mills.

Uncertain of the situation in the town, Uncle Adya had decided to send his wife, Natasha, and baby son to England. His sister, Fanny, was likewise leaving with her small twin children. Uncle's other sister, Margunya, was accompanying her husband, Lieutenant-Colonel Dilakatorsky, to Murmansk where he was now in command of the forces fighting in that region.

The town was gradually emptying. So many of our friends and relatives were leaving for the safety of Europe. My patrol leader in the Girl Guides, a movement no longer functioning, was also sailing away. Her whole family, having sold their possessions, were emigrating to America.

I went to see her off. The landing stage was crowded with men, women and children. There were last-minute exchanges between them and the passengers, hanging over the railings, soon interrupted by the shrill sound of the siren and the ship slowly edging away from the pier. As the gap widened, there were the final desperate attempts to have some contact, messages that had no meaning, tears, the waving of arms, handkerchiefs and last farewells. Little did I realise that my parents had decided that Mother should take Ghermosha and me to Scotland.

When my young brother and I heard the news we became wild with excitement. To everyone we met, to all our playmates we kept proudly saying, "What do you know? We are going to Scotland."

One morning Mother and I set off to arrange our booking. From the shipping office a long queue stretched out on to the street. A young British officer was sitting at a desk. When at last our turn came he told Mother that the two classes on the ship, due to leave shortly, were completely booked. However, on hearing Mother speaking in English and discovering that like himself she was a Scot, he asked us to wait a moment while he made further enquiries. He returned and, smiling broadly, informed us that after all there was one available cabin left in the first class. The ship was due to leave on 11 September.

We had barely a week to get ready for the journey. Mother began to pack our trunks. She took with her some of the things she treasured, her china, a few small pieces of silver, the ornament presented to her by Aunt Olga in St Petersburg.

In the town, numerous sales were taking place inside the houses of the people who were leaving. Babushka and I attended one at which the owner was selling a valuable collection of books. Seryozha, now working as a librarian, accompanied us in the hope of purchasing a few on behalf of the town library. As a parting gift, Babushka presented me with a selection of our Russian classics, including the handsome crimson-bound works of Pushkin and Lermontov. On the fly-leaf of Pushkin's book she wrote: "To my beloved granddaughter Jenya who is leaving for Scotland on the 11th of September in this heavy year of 1919. With deep love from Babushka." After sixty years and more, the cover of the book is worn, the writing faded. It has traversed countless miles over continents and tropical seas, but has never left my side.

My brother also had something special to take with him, in the shape of a tiny carp which he had caught in the pond the previous summer and now flatly refused to leave behind. This little fish, fed on breadcrumbs, continued to survive, circling aimlessly around inside a large glass jar, and was now setting off for Scotland.

During the excitement of all the preparations, the running and calling here and there and perhaps with the lightheartedness of youth, the knowledge that Father was being left behind was pushed aside. There was, of course, the firm belief that the Bolsheviks would be defeated and this separation was only a temporary measure. The full impact of what it meant for Father came when everyone assembled in the old nursery before we left. According to the Russian custom, we all sat down for a few seconds of silence. I rose and knelt beside my father's bed. Silently he blessed me with a small ikon of the Mother and Child. I raised my head and saw his tears and utter desolation.

The *Videck* was packed with refugees: some going to England, others on to France, many hoping to reach the south of Russia where the White Army was achieving some successes. Our four-berth cabin was shared with an attractive young woman, Sonya, who had large brown expressive eyes and masses of curly hair. Sonya was engaged to a handsome American officer called Jack. Both were planning to go on to America where they were to be married.

Ghermosha and I slept on the top bunks. Sonya occupied the one below me. Sonya, not suffering from any inhibitions, used to perform her morning ablutions in a frank manner which fascinated me. Donning a fetching dressing-gown she would depart for the bathroom and on her return, after stripping herself to her waist, proceeded to sponge her body with eau-de-cologne and rose-water. This exercise aroused my young brother's curiosity who would hang over the side watching every movement until Mother ordered him to turn his face to the wall. Even more fascinating was the making up of her face and the tiny mole placed on her cheek which she kept in an equally tiny box. Her lovely black locks required the least attention. She merely gathered them together and fixed them with a Spanish comb.

Sonya and Jack were passionately in love and were not interested in anyone else. We only saw her in the late evening when she returned to the cabin. One day, however, when I was alone, dozing in my bunk, trying to ignore the seasickness to which I was inevitably prone, Sonya and Jack quietly entered and thinking I was asleep crawled into Sonya's bunk. Although I didn't see anything, I certainly heard plenty.

Late one evening, just as I had fallen asleep, there was a frightening crash. The ship shuddered. There was pitch darkness. After a second of dead stillness came the terrified screams of women and children. Of what happened in our immediate surroundings, memory has retained a rather disjointed picture. Of Mother calmly trying to find our clothing, helping to dress us. Ghermosha, having been thrown out of his bunk, crying with fright. Sonya hysterically rushing out of the cabin. The crew, carrying torches, going round the cabins telling the passengers to put on their lifebelts.

The lights coming on again calmed the situation and prevented any panic — at least in our part of the ship. We walked up the staircase to the deck, but no sooner did we reach it than we were told to go to the saloon and wait there for further instructions. After some time, it was announced that the Royal Navy was coming to our aid and we could return to our cabins. There was some difficulty in communications between the crew and passengers on account of the crew being English and the passengers Russian. Mother proved helpful as an interpreter.

It was thought at first that the *Videck* had struck a floating mine, but later it transpired the ship had gone aground and was holed in two places. All available men were commandeered to assist in pumping out the water from the flooded hold. Fortunately the crew succeeded in freeing the ship. The following morning in the brightest of sunshine and accompanied by the navy, we limped into the safety of the Wick harbour in Caithness. No sooner did we dock than two divers appeared to inspect the damage. Later, a member of the crew told me that although there were two holes, the largest was blocked by a piece of rock which minimised the flooding in the hold. During the morning a thanksgiving service for our safety was held in the saloon, at the end of which a special vote of thanks was extended to Mother for her assistance.

We were the first passengers to disembark. So, after an absence of eight years, Ghermosha and I stepped once again on to the shores of Scotland. Everything around was bathed in sunshine — the busy harbour, the fishing boats sailing out to sea, the silver-winged seagulls, with their piercing crying, darting over the clear waters.

The small station from where we had to catch the train to Inverness was an unusual sight to us — clean, orderly, laid out with lovely flower beds. The journey to Inverness was of absorbing interest. The passengers sharing our compartment were a bit amused hearing our peculiar mixture of Russian-English as we excitedly pointed out the various scenes and landmarks. "Look at all these sheeps. The reindeer on the mountain — he is so smaller than our own." All was strange, all was beautiful.

It was late evening when the Inverness train steamed into Dundee. A kindly taxi driver arranged our trunks. Thankfully we climbed inside. Ghermosha was still clinging to his fish, which had somehow survived its ordeal on the ship.

The taxi took us through the brightly lit streets of the town where people in groups were standing on the corners holding conversations with each other — a novel and curious sight for us. After a short and pleasant drive in the soft darkness of a warm autumn night we arrived, hungry and exhausted, on the steps of our grandparents' house.

Our grandparents, not expecting us to arrive that night, were just going off to their bedroom when we surprised them. In the morning they had read a brief notice in the paper saying that a ship carrying refugees from the north of Russia had gone aground, but somehow didn't connect us with it. We were warmly and emotionally welcomed. My youngest aunt, Vicky, came rushing out of her bedroom in her dressing-gown, followed by her sleepy six-year-old son, Charles. As my aunt's husband was with the army of occupation in Germany she was living with her parents.

In the morning I leaped out of bed and hurried to the window. The sun was up. The garden was ablaze with masses of roses and chrysanthemums. Blackbirds were cheerfully plundering the apple trees. Across the silver waters of the Tay, flowing serenely past the house, I saw again the green and brown hills of the shores of Fife.

Far back in Archangel there would be rain and cold winds blowing. The darkening river was preparing herself for the final battle against the relentless frost, a battle which she was doomed to lose. Here in this late September the sun continued to shine warmly and Jocky's cage was being carried out into the garden.

To us, arriving from a land of grim austerity, of shuttered doors and windows of the shops, empty shelves, of people wearing shabby clothing, Scotland presented a scene of unbelievable abundance.

What a delight it was to walk along the smooth pavements of Broughty Ferry and step inside the "sweetie shop". Our eyes were dazzled by the jewel brightness of the sweets in glass containers, chocolate bars laid out in tempting rows, coloured boxes tied with satin ribbons. Further along was a renowned baker's shop where the appetising smell of freshly baked bread, cream-filled cookies, biscuits and cakes met us at the entrance.

Fascinating too was the little shop, named "The Buttercup", which specialised in dairy products. There, rosy-cheeked girls in spotless aprons patted neat rounds of butter on a marble counter. Somehow the name, the great mounds of butter, milk and cream invariably conjured up visions of green meadows, buttercups galore, and plump docile cows bursting with goodness.

Exciting were the trips to town, by train or tramcar, when along with Mother we accompanied Granny for her weekly shopping. The shop I enjoyed visiting more than any other was the famous, fashionable "Draffens", where clothing of distinctive elegance was offered to discerning buyers. In the days of plenty, my father used to order articles of clothing, which were sent by cargo ships to our town and delivered to the house in perfect order. Now, to climb the luxuriously carpeted staircase and stroll from one department to another where ladies dressed in black, stylish dresses tempted us with frocks, coats, hats in the latest fashion, was a source of wonderment not seen since the early days in St Petersburg, now only a vague memory.

Owing to the uncertainty of our position, Mother could not indulge in a wholesale shopping spree, but she did buy me several dresses, shoes and stockings. Granny also added to my stock of clothing, which I welcomed. Mother herself could not resist a large picture hat, trimmed with osprey feathers. Sad to say, that same hat was fated to be lost in a way Mother could never have envisaged.

It was usual to finish off the day by visiting D. M. Brown's, another well-known shop, where on the top floor we listened to a small orchestra while demolishing platefuls of the renowned hot muffins, oozing with butter and jam. On seeing all the well-stocked shops, the cheerfulness of the people, their pleasant orderly way of life, one might have imagined that the war had never touched Scotland, but on looking closer one saw the deep scars of the heavy price paid by such a small country, where there was hardly a family that hadn't lost a son, a husband or a brother.

There was another dark cloud on the horizon, in the shape of unhappy news from India. During the war years Uncle Henry was an officer in the Auxiliary Forces known as the Calcutta Scottish. Towards the close of the war he contracted a virulent disease so often found in the torrid plains of India. He became seriously ill and had to be moved to a hospital in Calcutta. After prolonged treatment he partially recovered and wrote to my grandparents saying that he had decided to take the leave he was due earlier than usual. He hoped that a long holiday in Scotland would put him back on his feet. His cabin was already booked on a ship due to leave at the beginning of November. He looked forward to arriving home in time for Christmas. Granny hopefully began to prepare the best spare room.

Immediately on our arrival all the relatives came to the house to meet us. The Cameron family, in spite of the usual disagreements, were clannish. There was Mary, Mother's younger sister, who made a point of visiting her parents every week with her little son, Fraser. My two eldest cousins, Bertie and Mae, came also. Mae, now seventeen, was quite a young lady. Slim and perhaps on the small side, with bright auburn hair, she was vivacious, full of fun, always laughing. Although lacking in inches, she possessed all the confidence in the world and could be assertive when she liked. From the first day of our meeting we both were drawn to each other and in the years to come became as close as sisters. Our fates were strangely interwoven. We both married young men from Broughty Ferry, both went out to India. Our houses faced each other on the opposite shores of the Hooghly River, so that we were able to cross over and continue our contact with each other.

Long years after, when we were all old and retired, Mae, now widowed, went out one soft summer evening to trim her roses. The following morning the young milkman found her lying dead beside the flowers she loved so well.

To many of Granny's friends my brother and I appeared to provide a certain interest. We were constantly invited to afternoon tea parties by sweet old ladies who entertained us with delicious sandwiches, scones and cakes, but for which we had to pay by sitting quietly under the eagle eye of Granny as well as Mother, answering endless questions politely. On one occasion, having partaken of a lavish tea, we quietly slipped away to the delights of the Grassy Beach and Cousin Bertie's rowing boat, an escapade which didn't pass unnoticed.

We were, occasionally, when no one was about, given to exchanging our own private impressions. "Have you noticed," Ghermosha once remarked, "that Jessie, the washerwoman, wears a hat?" In Russia washerwomen didn't wear hats. In my brother's eyes the sight of Jessie in her hat was the essence of democracy. And there was also this obsession with the weather. Why did they talk so much about it? In every shop we entered they liked to tell us if it was sunny, cold or windy, and that if it rained today, tomorrow might be better. The capricious Scottish weather, of course, provided endless variations.

Strangest of all was this belief that all black cats were lucky. Wasn't there someone who could tell them that black cats were messengers of evil, friends of witches and an omen of bad luck if they crossed your path? Even worse was to receive from some misguided friends Christmas or birthday cards depicting green-eyed, black pussycats. The only way to deal with such a case was to destroy the card by committing it to the fire and to spit three times over your left shoulder to ward off the evil eye.

As October was drawing to a close, Ghermosha celebrated his twelfth birthday. That morning, Grandpa called Ghermosha to his bedroom where he cermoniously presented him with a silver watch and chain. In the afternoon our numerous cousins arrived and after presenting their gifts gathered round the table. All the girls wore their party dresses, the boys the Cameron tartan kilts. It was a noisy, joyful party, complete with sweets, trifles, a birthday cake and candles.

Meanwhile letters were arriving from Russia. After the last of the
Allied troops were evacuated, the White Army rallied and was now
advancing. There was a feeling of optimism prevailing in Archangel.
Victory was in sight and with it the end of the civil war. Once this was
accomplished, Father saw no reason for us to remain in Scotland. Our
education, he was anxiously pointing out, was of paramount
importance. He also mentioned that the ice-breaker *Canada* was due to
leave for England at the beginning of November.

Marga was hoping to join the ship, provided the letter from Frank
arrived in time. Frank had left shortly after our own departure, but
perhaps due to postal difficulties, the longed-for letter from him had
not yet arrived. Poor Marga was becoming more anxious with each
day. The letter never came.

This plausible young man with charm, his free and easy manner,
who had accepted the generous hospitality of people who fondly
imagined that he was possessed of the same sense of honour as
themselves, he who had become engaged to Marga and so captivated
her that she was prepared to follow him to the end of the earth, used
the simple expedient of sailing away — far enough to be out of reach
and never making any attempt to get in touch with her. Although he
had left his address, there were no replies to any letters.

About the beginning of November a telegram arrived from Uncle
Henry with the brief message saying that he was now aboard the
ship all set to sail for Scotland. Granny was elated. She began to
talk about having a Christmas party with all the family for once
getting together.

On Remembrance Day, 11 November, we all went out into the pale
winter sunshine and stood on the steps of the front entrance with
bowed heads, remembering the millions of dead soldiers. Two days
later, just before lunch, another telegram arrived. Uncle Henry had
died suddenly. When Granny read the message, she went deathly
white, and saying, "Leave me alone," went upstairs to her bedroom
and closed the door behind her.

Shortly afterwards, Grandpa arrived from his office and sat down
at the table. The telegram was handed over. I vividly remember him
covering his face with both hands and saying, "He was the youngest
and the best." He then asked, "Where is Mother?" and on being told
she was upstairs, went up to their bedroom.

Later it transpired that Uncle Henry had boarded the ship two days
before its sailing date. He suddenly became very ill and had to be taken
off the ship to the hospital where he died the following day.

Another letter arrived from Father. The icebreaker *Canada*, now lying in Newcastle, was leaving for Archangel on 2 December. Many wives and children were returning, including Uncle Adya's wife Natasha and their child. Father urged Mother to do likewise as the Bolsheviks were almost defeated. The White Sea was frozen. There was little chance of another ship until the summer, by which time we would have lost a year of schooling. After a great deal of thought and perhaps not wishing to be a burden to her parents, Mother decided to return to Russia.

Aboard the *Canada*, Mother and I were directed to our double-berth cabin. Ghermosha had to share a cabin with a Mr and Mrs Brown and their young son Vanya, who was a cripple. Mr Brown, as his name implies, was of English origin. He was returning with the hope of starting up his business again. Both he and his wife were pleasant people and kind to Ghermosha who wasn't happy at being separated from us in a cabin at the other end of the ship.

The little fish, still with us in its glass container, had to be tied securely to the handle of our porthole. It had miraculously survived the shock of having its water changed in Scotland and after at first floating lifelessly on the surface, recovered again. Now it was galloping around livelier than ever. Ghermosha had seriously assured it that, once the spring came round, he would give it back its freedom in the pond.

In the saloon we met the other passengers including Natasha, the wife of Uncle Adya, and their little son Shurick. Uncle Adya's sister, Fannie, who had left for England with her twin children in the autumn, had also toyed with the idea of returning, but in the end changed her mind. Many decades later Aunt Fannie and I met again. During our reminiscences she told me that when she was on the point of deciding to join her sister-in-law a telegram arrived from her husband. It contained a brief message. "Sit tight and do not move." Aunt Fannie didn't move and if only Natasha had done likewise, how different her life might have turned out.

We were introduced to the first officer, Billy Jordan, and his wife Maisie. Maisie came from Yorkshire. Twenty-two years of age with dark, silky hair framing a white forehead and large expressive eyes, Maisie was something special. She could dance, sing, was gay and friendly with all the passengers. Everyone liked Maisie. She and Mother, being the only two British women, were drawn to each other. Her husband Billy was of Latvian origin.

We were in dock for over a week — the sailing was postponed. During that time a small contingent of Russian officers and men joined the ship. They had all fought in the bitter struggle of the civil war and had been sent to England for training in the use of the tank.

Some of the tanks had already been sent to Archangel, others were in the hold of the ice-breaker. The officers were accommodated in the cabins while the men shared their quarters with members of the crew on the lower deck. In the adjoining cabin to us were two officers, Vladimir Alexsandrov and Kiril Yermolov. Both had known the horrors of the civil war, especially so Kiril. Kiril was the son of a well-known family of landowners. One day a band of drunk deserters and peasants arrived at their estate. They were sitting having a meal when the men barged into the room. One of the sons rose and asked the reason for this intrusion. In reply, the soldiers shot him. Another bandit grabbed his only sister and when their mother tried to protect her from being raped, both she and her daughter were bayonetted to death. Kiril, his father and young brother were tied up and taken to the nearby woods for execution. By some miraculous chance, Kiril succeeded in slipping away and hid in the deep undergrowth. He lay, hearing the shots of the executions, the footsteps of those searching for him. Hiding through the day and moving through the night, he eventually reached the line of the White Army. His whole being was now concentrated on avenging the destruction of his family.

Another passenger to join us was an Englishman who had fought in the civil war. His name was Osborne Grove. He obviously belonged to a wealthy family, for he had bought his own plane and was determined to continue the fight against the Bolsheviks. His co-pilot was a Russian Air Force officer, a daredevil called Kostya. The results of Kostya's previous exploits were seen on his scarred disfigured face.

The North Sea has an evil reputation. As the first night of the voyage wore on, the weather worsened. Soon we were in the teeth of one of its worst gales. At times the ship seemed to rise on end, shudder, fall back and roll over from one side to another. To the howling wind was added the sound of crashing crockery. The luggage, left outside the cabins, careered madly up and down the corridor. The articles above our hand-basin were swept on to the floor, including a small bottle of perfume which smashed to smithereens, soon filling the cabin with the sickly smell of violets. Mother, worrying over Ghermosha's fish, tried to reach the jar but was thrown back each time. I then struggled down and reached the shelf. The jar was still intact, but the water splashing around inside it had thrown the fish out. I could not see where it had landed and barely managed to clamber back to my bunk.

With the arrival of a grey dawn, the storm abated. My young brother, white-faced and ill, appeared on the scene and hurried to the jar. Seeing no sign of the fish he began a frantic search among the scattered debris. It was eventually found swept under a small rug.

Although it was tenderly placed back in the jar, there was no miracle. Ghermosha would not leave the jar and was found later lying on the floor of the cabin sound asleep beside it.

While the ship was still in dock many of the passengers, including us, went ashore to the shopping precinct of Newcastle. During that time I celebrated my fourteenth birthday. There were no presents, but Mother gave me money to spend whichever way I wished. I bought some little gifts — a string of white coral beads for Marina, knitting wool for Babushka. Something special had to be found for Marga. Remembering that I had once heard her express a wish to taste some exotic fruits, I decided on a bunch of bananas, so large that I could barely drag it up the gangway, and with difficulty found a corner in the cabin. Mother's warning that the bananas would never see Archangel fell upon deaf ears.

During a short break in Bergen some of the passengers, including mother, went ashore. She and Maisie came back bringing with them cheese, freshly baked bread and other items of food, as the cuisine on the *Canada* left a lot to be desired. Osborne Grove also went along to do some shopping and presented Ghermosha, Vanya and me with sweets, nuts, playing cards and a fine set of dominoes. He was a strange person, Osborne Grove, who never wasted any time in needless conversation, but would sit for hours at a time watching us playing or listening to our talk, barely uttering a word. Yet he was a generous man at heart, always ready to help anyone if need be.

As we moved further north, Christmas arrived. The saloon was gaily decorated. In the dining-room the cook, observing the festive season, for once opened his heart and cooked up a pleasant meal which included an English plum pudding and pancakes served with jam.

After dinner everyone assembled in the saloon. A party of soldiers came up from their quarters and sat together, looking a bit uneasy at first. Natasha, accompanying herself, sang in her fine contralto voice, with much expression, several of our renowned gypsy songs. Maisie stood up and, with Mother accompanying her, sang current popular songs. Maisie sang well and was heartily applauded. Best of all was the singing of the soldiers under their leader. Everyone joined in, singing in full voice our well-loved folksongs. It was an evening which has remained for ever clearly stamped on my memory.

A week went by. As the old year slipped away, celebrations broke out all over the ship. The officers got together in one cabin. The captain threw a party in his private quarters to which Mother was invited. I, considered too young to be included anywhere, was delighted when the young second officer invited me to his cabin to meet the New Year with him. There I drank a glass of wine and, when he offered me a cigarette, nonchalantly accepted it and smoked it in what I judged to be a sophisticated manner.

Back in my cabin, I was almost asleep when a crowd of officers burst in. They came with glasses in their hands to wish, as they explained, the youngest lady on the ship a Happy New Year. All were rather merry. Each one demanded that I should sip a little of the wine and allow myself to be kissed in the traditional manner, after which they cheerfully departed.

7

1920

On the second day of the new year, the ship reached the dismal port of Murmansk. My Aunt Margunya and her husband, Lieutenant-Colonel Dilakatorsky, in command of the Murmansk region, came aboard. There were glad reunions with relatives and friends. The same glowing optimism still prevailed. Everywhere was heard the Russian greeting: "New Year — New Happiness". A crowd of young cossacks had followed Dilakatorsky aboard the ship. One of them started to dance in the traditional manner, shooting out his long legs while gliding round the deck to the accompaniment of enthusiastic clapping.

Everything was going well, we were assured. The White Army was approaching the great fortress of Kronstadt outside Petrograd. It was only a question of days.

Two days later we were on our way to our final destination, cutting through the great frozen expanse of the White Sea. Anyone who travelled on an ice-breaker in those far-off days, perhaps can remember how difficult, how slow the progress was. The ship relentlessly forges ahead, cuts through the ice, then reverses and starts again. The awesome mass of ice, rising on either side and threatening to engulf the ship, falls back, showering the deck with sparkling crystals. The noise is deafening. In our wake, the narrow channel carved out of ice trails like a long dark ribbon, vanishing in the distance where the sky and sea blending together show no defining line between them.

One evening when I was standing on deck watching the playful magic of the aurora borealis, a member of the crew pointed out a polar bear lumbering across the ice. He was enormous, but intent on his own business, paid no attention to the ship.

Eventually we reached the outskirts of Archangel and docked in a small port called Ekonomiya, some twelve miles from the town. Uncle Sanya was waiting on the landing stage, but on being told that no one was to leave the ship until the following morning, he left, promising to return.

No sooner had Uncle Sanya gone than the passengers were told they could disembark if they desired to do so. Some wished to remain aboard the ship, others like the Browns and ourselves decided to go ashore.

From Ekonomiya a railway line ran into town. Assisted by members of the crew, we got our luggage aboard the train and settled down with the Browns. There was no sign of any driver. The cold was bitter. In the unheated carriages frost lay like thick white velvet on the window panes. In spite of Mr Brown's repeated enquiries, the driver could not be found. We sat huddled together, trying to keep warm, perhaps an hour, perhaps more, but just as we were making up our minds to return to the ship, the driver, yawning and stretching, appeared and started up the engine. After a few minutes the train halted beside a siding. For some unknown reason the engine was unable to take us any farther. There was no choice but for us to go on foot for the next few miles. Fortunate to find sledges in the adjoining shed, we got together and piled our trunks on top.

Seating Vanya on the luggage and harnessing himself to the sledge, Mr Brown, with Mrs Brown pushing behind him, set off on the snowy road for home. Mother also tied the rope around her waist and with her dragging and Ghermosha and I pushing the heavy load, we followed the sledge in front.

I remember the unusual brilliance of the moon, the high snowdrifts, the empty streets, the silence. There was something sad about this silence. We met no one and saw no sign of life in any of the darkened windows.

At the top of Olonetskaya Street we parted with the Browns, who had to go on further, and turned down towards the old familiar gates. The house was in complete darkness. At first no one heard our knocking, but eventually a sleepy Katinka opened the door and rushed upstairs to waken Babushka. Father was joyful. Babushka threw her arms around us and ordered a samovar to be brought to the nursery. But glad as she was to see us, I noticed while we sat talking that there was some anxiety in her manner which she seemed to try and hide from me. Although we did not know it, while we were travelling rumours were already reaching Archangel of reverses in Siberia.

No one had expected us to arrive in the middle of the night. Katinka hastily prepared beds for Mother and Ghermosha in the nursery, beside Father. Babushka took me into her room. We had all been almost frozen by the time we reached the house. Lying close to Babushka's warm body, I continued shivering for a long time. In the adjoining bed Dedushka was gently snoring, unaware of our arrival.

When I awoke in the late morning, the sun was streaming through the frosted panes. There was no one in the bedroom. Babushka and mother along with Marga and Marina were in the dining-room talking together beside the bubbling samovar. No one appeared to be unduly surprised at our return. Life resumed, just as if we had never left.

I duly presented my little gifts. Marina was delighted with the coral beads, Babushka with her wool. Needless to say the great bunch of bananas meant for Marga never reached her. To compensate her for the loss of her present, I succeeded in wheedling from Mother a jar of face-cream out of her precious store. Marga was most grateful, as all these little aids to beauty were now quite unobtainable.

A few days later Maisie Jordan, bored with life aboard a ship with no passengers, came to stay with us. Her visit coincided with Yura and Mitya Danilov arriving unexpectedly for a short leave from the front. Yura had been promoted to the rank of a captain as a reward for a daring feat when, regardless of his own safety, he had rushed down an embankment under a bridge and defused a bomb set to go off just as a troop train was due to leave. Both boys had changed and were no longer the callow youths who had so eagerly set off to fight the Bolsheviks.

It was now Epiphany, when young people play strange games by which they half-believe they are allowed to peep into their future.

Katinka, Marina and I ran out into the moonlit courtyard where we each removed a shoe and threw it high over our shoulders on to the snowdrifts. The toe of the shoe was supposed to point in the direction from where our future husband would arrive. Mine pointed north, which I thought was odd, but Katinka assured me that my fate could well be a Samoyed who would arrive from the polar regions with his sledge and reindeer.

Maisie, intrigued by all these ancient customs, decided to try the uncanny mirror game. We put her in Marina's room and sat her down between two mirrors — one in front and one behind her. We lit candles on each side, took down her hair and draped a sheet over her shoulders. We left her there and waited. After a little while she came rushing out, her face deathly pale.

Later in the evening, after a long session over the samovar, we adjourned to the ballroom and waltzed to the haunting melody of

"Autumn Dreams", played by Mother. Mitya approached Marga and she, brushing aside her unhappiness, cheerfully danced the whole night with him. Seryozha was rapturously waltzing with Maisie in his arms, while I was being whirled around by Yura. I enjoyed dancing with my young uncle and rather admired my reflection each time we glided past the mirrors. For a while, all fears and anxieties were forgotten.

This short interlude passed all too quickly. The boys left for the front in the early hours of the following morning.

Uncle Vanya came to see us. Although he had walked all over Russia, he had never travelled abroad. He asked many questions and displayed a great interest in all our impressions of Scotland. He left in the early evening to follow his usual route of taking the tramcar to the end of the line and walking across the river to his home. It was snowing and gradually the snowflakes fell faster and thicker. A blinding blizzard with a strong wind took over. Everyone became alarmed. It was hoped that Uncle Vanya might return to spend the night as he sometimes did if the weather was bad, but he didn't turn back. It was impossible to get in touch with Tanya as there was no telephone in her house. Babushka tried to console herself with the thought that her brother had crossed the river before the worst of the blizzard began.

Early in the morning, Tanya phoned from the station to enquire if her father was with us. Babushka, devastated, ordered the sledge to be harnessed and with Seryozha set off across the river. From the other side a party of friends, led by Tanya's husband, had already begun their search. They didn't have to look far. Uncle Vanya's body, lying under a thin blanket of snow, was found quite close to the shore and safety.

It seemed a mockery of fate that Uncle Vanya, who had walked the length and breadth of Russia, across the steppes in the heat of the summer, and Siberia in the terrible frosts of winter, in the end had to perish within reach of his home.

Meanwhile, as Ghermosha and I had lost a whole term, Father engaged a tutor to bring us up to date. When the question of payment was raised, the young tutor did not want money, but asked for salt instead. And so for two pounds of salt we successfully passed our exams. Such were the times.

PART IV

Change and Devastation

1

1920

IN February, the White Army on the northern front was falling back. A sense of impending doom, like a black cloud, hung over the city. To some, each Bolshevik victory brought open jubilation, to others only despair. In spite of bitter, desperate fighting for each village and town the communists kept on advancing. The old historic town of Kholmogor, lying some forty miles up the river, fell into their hands as did, a few days later, villages closer to our town.

The situation was fluid, abounding with rumours. There were people who said that the Bolshevik victory could not last and that help would arrive just as it did the last time. Some earnest souls also firmly believed the story that a group of children had seen the Mother of God appear in the heavens and with outstretched arms bless the suffering town. More real and frightening were the tales of innocent people and officers being summarily executed after capture. In our house there was deep anxiety for Yura and Mitya. No one knew where they were.

Before the town fell, a deputation from the local Duma called. They begged Dedushka to assist them to create some order in the chaos which followed after the flight of several of its members. Dedushka agreed — a mistake dearly paid for in the days to come.

The weather turned bitterly cold and windy, the skies darkened, heavy with snow clouds. The tramcars stopped running; schools emptied.

Kiril Yermolov with his fellow officers arrived one day. The tanks, on which so much depended, proved to be useless. Whoever thought of using them completely overlooked the danger of fuel and water freezing in the arctic temperature. Nor did they think of the unsuitable terrain of thick woods between villages. Forced to abandon the tanks, they had continued fighting but, in the end, surrounded and outnumbered, only a handful managed to get through and eventually reach the northern outskirts of the city. We gave them what we had, sitting with them in the nursery so as to be near Father, who wanted to hear everything.

There were only some six of them, but they were well armed with revolvers, rifles and grenades, which they calmly placed, to our alarm, on the table. They planned to try and reach the Murmansk region, if possible by train, if not, by walking, and to continue the fight from there. All this they knew was hopeless. The bravado was only to disguise the despair on their ravaged faces. When they left us, we watched the small group trudging through the snow until they vanished to the north. They didn't get far. All were caught and, for some reason, sent to Petrograd, where they were later executed.

The following morning, Babushka and Arsyeny set off together on the sledge to the market. The food situation was critical. Beyond buckwheat, barley and potatoes, there was nothing in the house. No meat, fish, butter or milk.

The whole town appeared to be deserted. The market-place was empty. Gone were the days when these same, now barren, tables used to be laden with a rich variety of food and when eager peasants tried to tempt Babushka by calling to her, "Barynya, Barynya, buy my fresh laid eggs — taste my curds, my smetana, my butter; I keep the best cows in the village." Shuttered were the little shops that specialised in such delicacies as smoked salmon, caviar, salted herring, and where the vendor, cutting a pink slice of salmon, would offer it on the edge of his knife to Babushka, and to me as well if I was hopefully tagging behind her. Babushka wandered sadly around these empty places, finding nothing, until by chance she met one of her old vendors who took her to his closed shop and produced a generous piece of salted cod out of his only barrel. Half of this lucky find was eaten in the evening, the rest reserved for the following day.

In the late evening, dark shadowy figures, fleeing to the north, passed our windows. Throughout the night, intermittent gunfire came from the south. The next day no one except Dedushka left the house. Dedushka, faithful to his patients, went to the hospital and later called at the Town Hall. After seeing there a lot of faces he did not know, he decided to return home.

Meanwhile, crouching with our eyes level with the window sill, we were watching the curious happenings on the river front. Groups of civilians, soldiers, officers, carrying rifles, were hurrying to the north. Mounted cossacks, lying low on their saddles and galloping madly, overtook them and vanished out of sight. In their wake, hot in pursuit, came the Bolsheviks. Soldiers, workmen, peasants. Some in tatters, feet wrapped in rags, some bareheaded and barefoot, heedless of the snow and frost, shouting slogans, running as if driven by some inner fire.

And now another drama was unfolding. From the town, moving down the river, sailed an ice-breaker followed by two ships packed with the last of the refugees. At the end of our street some men were hastily placing guns close to the shore. The ships were now directly opposite our street. Horrified, we watched, hoping for some miracle. A miracle did happen. The guns began to fire but instead of shattering the ships, the shells exploded harmlessly on the ice. While the frustrated and obviously inexperienced gunners were arguing with each other, the ice-breaker and its two followers were gliding on, to disappear behind the Solombala island.

Shortly after, we were astonished to see our old friend the *Canada* moving full speed ahead in the wake of the escaping ships. Why was she pursuing the poor refugees, and where was Maisie Jordan? Then to our further amazement, the *Canada* returned to town. What was the reason for this turnabout? The answer to these questions came from Maisie a few days later.

The ship's captain had been ordered, against his personal wishes, to chase and attack the ships. Guns and shells were placed on deck and a group of Bolsheviks came aboard. Maisie, in her stilted Russian, had succeeded in putting across her indignation. For this impertinence she was put inside her cabin. When she attempted to come out, the guard used the butt of his rifle to push her back. For the rest of this exploit, Maisie was confined to her cabin with the guard keeping watch outside the door.

As the *Canada* drew closer to the fleeing ships, the men prepared to man the guns. To their helpless fury they found that by some strange mistake the wrong ammunition had been brought aboard. The *Canada* had no option but to return.

Maisie by now had had enough of communism and was determined to get out of this unfortunate country and return to her beloved Yorkshire.

On that same day, Babushka prepared the cod according to a favourite recipe. Having had no food since early morning, we looked forward to that tasty dish, baked in the oven with potatoes and onions, and when Katinka brought it up, eagerly gathered round the table. No sooner had we sat down when we heard the stamp of heavy feet coming up the back stairway. Six men or more burst into the dining-room. Filthy, unkempt, some in black leather jackets and sailor's caps, they were all fully armed. "I see," one of them taunted us, "we are just in time."

It all seemed like a nightmare — these frightening men devouring our only meal, while we stood, shocked into silence, helplessly watching.

Marga, meanwhile, had slipped out to her bedroom, where she removed from the dressing-table drawer her treasured rings and other bits of jewellery and hid them under her pillow.

After these contemptuous creatures had cleared our table, they
scattered over the house examining each room, touching our curtains,
scrutinising each ornament, sometimes putting them into their
pockets and sometimes replacing them. They were not the usual run
of men who came later to search the house, but a band of hooligans,
one of the many, who taking advantage of the situation roamed about
the town, barging into houses, robbing and terrifying the citizens.

As soon as they eventually left, Marga ran to her bedroom and came
out weeping. All her precious rings were stolen. None of us knew how
to console her. if she had only left them in the dressing-table drawer
and turned the key, she might have still had them. For some reason
these men made no attempt to break any locks or open drawers.

Somehow even now, whenever I see that particular cod dish, which
on occasions I make myself, I am involuntarily reminded of that first
momentous day when the Dictatorship of the Proletariat was
established in our town.

In the ensuing days, a semblance of order was organised. Tramcars
resumed their running, children returned to school. Ration cards
were issued, and co-operatives established in various parts of the
town where the citizens queued for hours on end to receive their small
portion of bread, grain and a little sunflower oil. Our existence
depended largely on bartering with the peasants in the villages.

One day I was sent to a village across the river to fetch some milk
from a peasant who, in the days gone by, used to come to the house
with her dairy products. I donned my skis, took a silver spoon and,
carrying a "pologushka" — the wooden bucket with the fixed lid used
in our parts for holding milk — set off for the opposite side. Skiing as
fast as my legs could carry me I soon approached the middle of the
river and feeling breathless decided to lie down awhile. Around me
was the great expanse of the river sparkling silver white. I lay gazing
up at the lofty inaccessible sky, the rosy chain of fluffy clouds like pink
swans following each other on a turquoise lake. When I got up again, I
hurried on to the snowy banks of the opposite shore.

A woman with an indifferent expression opened the door of her
isba. After I told her what I wanted and showed her the silver spoon
she, half-smiling, asked me in. "I remember," she remarked, pouring
the milk into my pologushka, "working in the mill and how I had to
run during the short break to suckle my child — and he poor mite, only
days old, screaming with hunger. These were hard days for us — and
now here you are, Baryshnya, begging me for milk." She looked up
with a faint malicious smile. "It's fine to have a bit of silver," she
continued, softening a little. "If you want some more milk just come

back again and I'll see what I can do. Take this meanwhile," she added handing over a lump of butter, an unexpected bonus.

That night we all sat down to a good helping of buckwheat porridge with milk and butter, after which, exhausted by my expedition, I went to bed early and slept unusually soundly.

Next morning there was terrible news, with everybody plunged in deep despair. About midnight, four armed men had arrived and demanded to search the house. They turned out all drawers, wardrobes, presses. They examined every paper in Dedushka's writing desk, and emptied trunks and baskets in the garret.

Mother, describing the harrowing scenes, told me that when they entered Marga's bedroom where I was sleeping, and turned over her bed, they assured her that no harm would be done to her daughter. I was lifted and after ascertaining that nothing was hidden in my bed, they gently laid me down. Through all this I continued sleeping, quite unaware of what was going on. Ghermosha likewise never saw nor heard anything. As the early hours of the morning drew on, everyone was ordered to go into the dining-room. Their leader sat down and after scribbling something on a bit of paper, calmly said to Dedushka, "Go and get dressed, you are coming with us." Mother recalled how Dedushka's face turned deathly pale and then crimson.

At first these frightening words stunned everyone. No one spoke but when Dedushka began to put his coat on, Babushka, Marga and Marina burst into anguished tears. Most human beings have a reserve of dignity and Dedushka had more than most men. "Contain yourself, Yenya," he said in quiet tones to Babushka. "You know that I've done nothing wrong — everything will be all right." He then turned to the stone-faced man and with the same quiet dignity said, "I am ready — let us go."

It has been often said when anything such as this happens, people stay away for fear of being involved and later themselves arrested. That was not the case in our family. The few remaining friends and relatives gathered round to try and uphold our morale and to point out the more hopeful aspects. Tyotya Peeka came, the three nieces, and even Uncle "Mitka Shalai" arrived and offered to find out to which prison Dedushka had been taken. He was sure Dedushka would not be kept for long as there was a great shortage of doctors in the town and the Bolsheviks would need him.

Regardless of all hopeful assurances, a gloomy emptiness took over the house. There was still no news of Yura and now Dedushka, the backbone of the family, was suddenly removed from our midst.

My grandfather was confined in the grim buildings of the main prison. From the day we discovered where he was, Babushka, Marga and the others haunted the prison gates. Like all the women whose relatives were arrested, they gathered all the food they could and handed the parcels to a grim-faced warden. They were usually accepted but if they were returned with the short explanation that the prisoner was not there any longer, this was a way of conveying that the prisoner had been executed. Our parcels continued to be accepted.

A glimmer of light appeared when Sashenka was told by one of her pupils that his father, who had been in the same regiment as Yura, knew that Yura was alive. Soon after, Marga, walking along a back street, saw a group of pale-faced prisoners trudging with their guards to work somewhere. Among them she recognised Yura and rushed towards him. She was, of course, stopped by the guards but not before Yura managed to cry out, "For God's sake, bring me food!" It turned out that Yura was in the same prison as Dedushka. A terrible rumour was going around the town that all the imprisoned officers were due to be shot.

On finding in which commissar's hand lay the life and death of the prisoners, Marga went to see him. She went back and back again pleading, begging for the life of her young brother. She said later, "I was rolling on my knees in front of that man." In the end she must have kindled a spark of some compassion, for he told her that if she brought a recommendation, signed by not less than twenty soldiers, as to how Yura had behaved towards them, he, perhaps, would consider her case. Through the soldier Sashenka knew, Marga, running here and there, in town and villages, contacted the men and produced the necessary paper. The little light of hope burst into a flame.

Meanwhile the burden of finding food for our existence fell on Mother's shoulders. One morning, she and Madame Zaborchikova whose husband, the General, had been one of the first men to be executed, decided to cross the river to the same village where I had been previously. When they reached the middle, they found to their dismay that an ice-breaker had ploughed up the ice on its way to town. It was impossible to cross. There was no option but to follow the channel back to the point in town where it stopped and go round it. After the usual payment of a small piece of silver for the milk, carrying their heavy pologushkas they started on the return journey into town, where they hoped to get a tramcar which would bring them home.

Eventually, exhausted by these miles of trudging through the snow, they left the river and were making for the tramcar when a group of soldiers stopped them. "Up to your bourgeois tricks are you?" asked their leader. Unceremoniously they took the buckets and emptied the contents on the ground. Mother and Madame Zaborchikova were not alone — other women, carrying milk to their children, were subjected to the same treatment. Angry protests followed with some of the women, courageously, not mincing words. It made no difference. The whole exercise was meant to be a lesson to prevent the people from bartering with peasants.

A large pool of milk, together with broken eggs, formed on the frozen ground. From nowhere dogs appeared to lap up this unexpected bounty.

As Mother stood clutching her empty pologushka, one of the soldiers with cool insolence remarked to her, "What could be good for you is better for the dogs." Mother returned to the house in the last stages of exhaustion. She had always possessed great determination and courage, but now, was completely broken up.

The trouble was that as soon as our town fell, all the supplies the Bolsheviks could lay their hands on were sent off to the south. On the other hand, like a swarm of locusts, people arrived from the south in the false belief that the north was a land flowing with the proverbial milk and honey. The town became hopelessly overcrowded. A family with children took over the flat where Uncle Sanya once lived. A rather bold actress, her husband named Raisky, and their son arrived one day and, after producing a slip of paper, demanded accommodation. The rooms had to be changed over. Marina took my place in Marga's bedroom. Mother and I turned Dedushka's study into a bedroom and cunningly gave the couple Marina's smaller room. In this way we kept Dedushka's large desk, the press, and all his bits and pieces for the day when we hoped he would return.

In schools the old order was replaced by a new system. Prayers in the halls and classrooms were abolished. The priests, in their flowing black robes, who used to flit from one classroom to another imparting religious instruction to the young, were seen no more.

On account of the overcrowding in the city, the girls' school was requisitioned and its pupils moved to the boys' school. We girls commenced work at eight o'clock in the morning and after a short break, when we were provided with a small roll, continued until one p.m. The boys arrived fifteen minutes later and studied until six p.m. We were growing up now and this arrangement was a source of intriguing conversations, especially about the boys in the top form. We got to know the names of those we imagined were more outstanding than the others.

My attention was focused on a handsome, rather sophisticated boy in the top form named Alexei Anisyev, who was not even aware of my

existence nor yet of any of my classmates. At the same time I caught
the eye of a bear-like youth in the same top form called Sanka
Chekayevsky. Sanka excited only antipathy. The silly poetry and
notes left inside my desk, I found repulsive. Having once introduced
himself he continued to pursue me on the slightest pretext, trailing
alongside like a sad-eyed old St Bernard, but not so pleasing.

In normal times a literary evening used to take place each year in
March. Our headmistress, undaunted by the prevailing troubles,
decided to repeat the custom. The boys and girls gathered together in
the hall and sat divided by a centre passage. The evening commenced
with an ardent boy reciting the famous poem by Lermontov, *The Battle
of Borodino*. This he did with great style, accompanied by emotional
gestures, the rising and falling of his voice much appreciated by an
audience who already knew it all by heart. A senior girl climbed on to
the stage and sang a moving song all about love and white acacias. This
was followed by a short comedy presented by boys only.

When all the performances were over and the chairs cleared away,
the boys and girls, joining hands, started a Khorovod — the chanting
circle moving round a single figure. After a little while I was chosen by
some boy and stepped into the centre. As I danced, I noticed Alexei
Anisyev circling with the others. This was a chance I could not miss
and, as soon as the chanting stopped, I rushed up to my wonder boy
and kissed him on the cheek. He laughed and took my place. The
Khorovod began again but next time whom did he choose, but my best
friend Shura. After this I lost all interest in the Khorovod and
sauntered over to a long table where refreshments were being served.
In days gone by we used to be offered hot sweetened chocolate with
foaming cream, open sandwiches of various kinds, cookies full of
raisins and spices — now there was only watery cocoa to be had and a
single roll per head, which, being young and hungry, we still relished.

The moon was high when we were winding our way home. A fresh
fall of snow blanketed the sooty snowdrifts and lay thick on the
pavements, crunching pleasantly under our feet. In the group was my
faithful friend Valya, Nina Duletova and her father Duletov, the
headmaster of the boys' school, who were our close neighbours. Soon,
hurrying to join us, was Sanka, who lived in the street before ours. I
chose to ignore him and continued my conversation with Valya, who
unfortunately soon left us to turn into her own street. When we
arrived at the point where Sanka should have turned towards his own
home he, instead, continued with us down Olonetskaya Street. I
became apprehensive. At the entrance to their house the Duletovs
said their goodbyes and disappeared inside, leaving me alone with
Sanka. Between the Duletovs' gate and our own was the long length

of wall. For a few seconds we walked in silence, and then, deciding on the only course left for me, I took to my heels and ran. I had almost reached the gates when he caught me. There ensued a struggle during which we fell and landed in a snowdrift. The scuffling continued with Sanka determined to kiss me and I, like a wildcat, kicking, scratching, spitting, until suddenly out of the blue came a loud gruff voice saying, "What the devil are you playing at?" Standing above us, holding his rifle, was a soldier. Thankful for my deliverance I scrambled up. "I was only seeing her home," began Sanka. "And a fine way that was," the man interrupted. "Get," he added, pointing his rifle. The last I saw of my brave cavalier was him scurrying like a scalded cat to the top of the street.

"Where do you live?" The soldier turned to me and on being told, pointed to the gates saying, "They will allow you through." I looked up at the house. Every window was ablaze with lights. I realised that a search was taking place.

Soldiers guarding the gates and back entrance allowed me to pass. Upstairs in the hall were more men guarding the door leading to the nursery. I was ordered to go inside where all the members of the family were congregated as well as Katinka and Sashenka. Only Mother was missing. She, it transpired, was going round the house with the men, unlocking presses and drawers, and was now in the garret.

No one knew what the men wanted, but suspected they were looking for arms. Yura's gun, which he used for shooting game, was hidden somewhere, but only he knew where it was.

In a few minutes came the footsteps of the men stamping down the stairs from the garret. We were shepherded into the dining-room. The soldiers carried in a large wicker basket containing a bundle of flags. They were big flags which in days gone by were hung outside the gates during celebrations of royal birthdays. There were also flags of our allies which had been flown on special occasions during the war.

The basket was turned out, the flags spread on the table. The leader of the group, in his sheepskin jacket, sat down and after careful scrutiny of each flag laboriously marked something on a sheet of paper. We stood around wondering idly what was the strange purpose behind this confiscation. There they were. The old Imperial Russian flag, French, British, Belgian, Italian and finally one with the faded Lion Rampant. The man stared curiously at it.

Fifteen years ago on a bright winter's morning that flag had fluttered its welcome to a happy Scottish bride driving through the gates to begin a new life in a strange country. And now here it was again spread out before her. This royal flag of Scotland — her

Scotland.

She moved closer to the table. "This flag," she began, calmly placing her hand on it, "is the flag of Scotland. It is the flag of my country — you cannot have it." There was no reply. The man raised his head and stared. He saw no sign of fear in the eyes gazing serenely back — no trembling of the hand. In the oppressive silence, even his men were tensely watching.

He was the first to drop his eyes. Bursting into loud laughter he turned to his men. "Here's a wench for you, lads," he called, and, pushing the flag towards Mother, added in a tone that was insolent and yet admiring, "You can keep your flag." She did keep it. Many years later I found it amongst the few things she treasured.

The basket was carried down the staircase. I ran to the window and watched the soldiers in the moonlight dragging it through the snow on the river front.

Later, when we were sitting around the samovar, I heard Babushka say, "Nelly, you were foolish." And I who had always leant heavily on the Russian side, for once was on my Mother's. Foolish perhaps — but how magnificent!

The first signs of spring. Snow slipping off the rooftops, icicles shattering like glass on pavements, shrinking snowdrifts, slush under our feet, the sun shining longer. In the garden clumps of blue anemones are stretching their dainty heads to the sky through a blanket of snow. A warm wind is dancing through the trees. The firs shake and scatter the hoar-frost from their heavy laden branches. On such a day Yura returned.

After the final defeat, when many of his fellow officers were summarily executed, he, with the remaining handful, had been led away. Expecting to receive the same fate as the others, they were instead thrown into prison. Yura rarely referred to his ordeal there, but did mention that one of the more horrific tasks he and his fellow prisoners were ordered to do, after being escorted to the outskirts of the city, was to open the graves of the men executed during the time of the Allied Intervention and remove the remains for reburial in a small public garden where eventually a monument was erected.

Although rejoicing in his miraculous escape, we were dismayed to see him as he was. Unkempt, unshaven, hollow-eyed, reduced to skin and bone, he presented a pitiful shadow of his old self. His once smart English uniform, now in tatters, carried the stench of the prison walls. The old rocking bath was brought once more down from the garret and placed in Katinka's room. Yura and Seryozha vanished inside and when Yura emerged, shaven and his hair cropped close to his head, he bore some semblance to what he was before.

However, the relief of having Yura back was still overshadowed by the constant anxiety over Dedushka. As each day followed another, we still heard nothing.

On Palm Sunday the whole family went to church, carrying our decorated sprays of catkins. The church was packed, with people spilling out on to the parapet outside.

On Monday Babushka began to prepare for Easter the best way she could out of the small store of food saved for the holy day.

Early on Friday morning, just as Katinka brought up the samovar and we gathered for our spartan breakfast, Dedushka quietly walked into the dining-room.

Dedushka had been imprisoned in a cell packed with other civilians like himself. The well-to-do owners of mills and shops, priests, members of the local government. Night after night, deprived of sleep, Dedushka was questioned about his activities in the town council before the take-over. Dedushka stuck to the truth. He had never been mixed up in any politics and by the time he was approached for assistance to create some order in the chaos, it was too late for him to do anything at all.

The other prisoners in the crowded cell were questioned too. Gradually it was noticed that those called out in the early hours of the morning often didn't return. Later came the news that they had been executed. Gradually the numbers dwindled. Dedushka's turn came early one morning. He said goodbye to each remaining prisoner, and each in turn made the sign of the cross over him as was by now the custom. Calmly prepared for death, he followed the guards, but on reaching the room where he had been questioned for hours on end, he was told that he was free to go home, with the injunction that on no account was he to leave the town. Shocked by this sudden turnabout, Dedushka had walked along the empty streets with helpless tears streaming down his face.

No man can halt the ordained march of each successive season nor the lavish splendour of the sun melting the snow, warming the earth.

Again one heard the sweet murmur of little streams hurrying below the wooden pavements on their way down to the river. Once more people gathered to watch the awesome sight of swirling ice rushing out to sea. In our courtyard, the three remaining hens, jealously guarded by Vassily, are freed from their seclusion. They step uncertainly between the emerald blades of the drying green and blink their sleepy eyes in the dazzling sunlight. A plaintive note is heard in their usually contented clucking. They are, perhaps, missing the fond caresses of their golden-breasted defender — sacrificed for the Easter table — whose resonant salute to the rising sun is heard no more.

One day in May, when Babushka with Yura and Marina were planting out young seedlings, they saw Mitya Danilov strolling towards them. Mitya had been fighting up the river. We all anxiously wondered what could have happened to him. He had lost his parents in early childhood and lived with his aunt who worshipped him. Babushka had called on her, but the aunt, it seemed, knew nothing either.

Mitya, it transpired, finding himself surrounded, slipped through the net and succeeded in reaching the isolated cottage of his grandfather — a well-to-do peasant and a member of the sect known as "the old believers". The land and cottage, surrounded by deep forests, marshes, lakes, was a small oasis where the old man lived alone, grew his own corn, kept a pair of horses, cows, hens, dogs and cats and was generally self-supporting. He disliked the town and rarely went there. His only daughter, Mitya's aunt, attended to all the business transactions, the collecting of rents from the various properties he owned and had taken care of the orphaned boy. He remained with his grandfather until he thought it was safe enough to return. Mitya's luck held. No one searched for him or made any enquiries.

From that time, Mitya became a constant visitor to our house. The attraction, of course, was Marga.

Marga had erased from her mind the romance with her erstwhile American fiancé. Trunks had been unpacked, and the portrait of our distant ancestress, "Babushka Van Brienen" as we called her, was again seen hanging on the wall of Marga's bedroom.

Marga, back to her old self, went about the house singing soulful folksongs which seemed to signify that another romance was in the offing. In June they became engaged.

June was a month of many happenings. There was the day when Maisie Jordan called to tell us that after many applications to Moscow she had at last received permission to leave Russia. She planned to travel with a young couple. The maiden name of the wife was Mariya Ankirova — a name which was to figure prominently in our own lives. Mariya had gone through a civil marriage with a young Dane, a marriage recognised by the Bolshevik government, but not by the Tsar's, who only considered it valid if the couple had been married in church. By marrying the Dane, Mariya automatically became a Danish subject and as such was allowed to leave Russia. This strange arrangement was only a matter of convenience, generously offered by the friendly Dane, to enable Ankirova eventually to reach France where she would be met by her true fiancé and go through the proper marriage service of the Russian Orthodox Church.

Maisie called again, this time to say goodbye. She was leaving with her two friends the following day for Murmansk, where they were to board a ship for Norway. Once in Norway, the three companions planned to part and continue their separate journeys to their final destinations. Between Maisie and Billy was a secret arrangement. Billy also planned to escape and join Maisie in Britain.

Before leaving, Maisie called on several people offering to take letters — an offer which was eagerly accepted as no letters were coming through from Britain. She also made no secret of what she thought of the Bolsheviks and was determined to tell Britain all about them. Mother, fortunately, refused to give her any letters for our grandparents and warned Maisie that this was a dangerous activity — a warning Maisie chose to ignore.

Meanwhile we continued grappling with our problems, which were increasing with each passing day. The main worry was to find food in any form. Every day, from early morning we took turns to stand in long queues to receive our meagre rations. It seemed strange that in a large district previously rich in dairy produce none was now available, that a river and the sea nearby abounding with every variety of fish provided nothing for the people. One day it was rumoured that fish was being sold in one of the co-operatives. I was sent to fetch some and after a long wait returned with a piece which was only half salted and smelled to high heaven. We ate it just the same and somehow survived.

The savage reprisals continued. People we knew vanished from the face of the earth. Those living near the outskirts of the town saw, in the early hours of the morning, prisoners taken by back streets to the woods, and heard the sound of shots as they were summarily executed.

Searches of our house went on with a regularity to which we got accustomed. There was the day when the soldiers arrived following a report that we had hidden a hoard of silver. The whole house was turned out, pillows and cushions ripped. Not finding anything, they returned the next morning and this time transferred their activities to the frames and greenhouse which housed Babushka's plants. Seedlings of cucumbers planted in frames were dug out, the soil scattered on the ground. Frustrated once again, they had turned the flowerpots upside-down, smashed them with their heavy boots and trampled the rare, irreplaceable plants.

After that, Babushka lost heart and never attempted to grow them again.

Difficult to contain calmly, was the blatant insolence of those indulging in daylight robberies. One day some men arrived and produced a slip of paper which, they explained politely, gave them the right to confiscate our piano. They were the representatives of a group of workers who had formed a club where it was found necessary to have a piano. They had some difficulty in carrying our grand piano through the double doors of the front entrance and Seryozha had to assist them. The last we saw of our old piano, which had witnessed so many happy scenes, was it precariously shaking on a cart while being driven out the gates.

Some time later Madame Raiskaya and her family decided to leave our house for more spacious quarters. Before leaving she said how ideal Mother's three-mirror dressing-table would be for her as an actress and how in the past she had always admired this fine piece of furniture. Mother admired it also, but had to stand and watch in silence as it was carried out, with the little dressing-table stool thrown in for good measure.

Outrageous as all these acts were, there was no option but to accept them. The empty space left by the removal of the grand piano was occupied by Dedushka's writing desk. A small round table with a mirror replaced Mother's dressing-table.

June was wonderfully warm that year. The river resounded with the voices of children bathing, of men and women gathering on the pier. One of my favourite ploys was to go swimming in the late evening when the river was deserted and the water, heated by the sun thoughout the day, was warm and as soft as silk. One such evening when I returned to the house, everyone was sitting on the balcony watching the crimson disc of the sun gliding on the low horizon.

Dedushka looked tired. From the time he had returned from prison, he was kept busy in the hospital working late into the evening, and that day had not been different from the others. Now, enjoying the tranquillity of the surrounding scene, he was quietly talking to Babushka. Marga was engaged on some embroidery with happy concentration. I joined Seryozha and Marina leaning against the railings and stood with them watching the progress of a small boat rowing across the river.

The peace was suddenly shattered by the resonant ringing of the front-door bell. Marga, dropping her sewing, rushed through the ballroom to the hall and opened the door.

Two men, in plain clothes, but armed, entered the hall. They demanded to see Dedushka and when he came forward they explained to him in courteous tones that they had been ordered to take him to a nearby prison, from where he would be sent into exile. It would be necessary, they continued in dispassionate tones, for Dedushka to pack the clothing he required, but the packing had to be done quickly as they had no time to waste.

Stunned, unable to think clearly, we all ran around gathering together Dedushka's belongings. Throughout the stress and anguish, only Dedushka himself remained calm. He helped Babushka, who could not contain her tears, to pack the old Gladstone bag with his clothes, a small Bible, and the medical instruments he thought he would require.

In the hall where the men were waiting, he blessed and kissed Babushka and in the same way said his goodbyes to us all, at times even passing a little joke. He then went to the nursery to embrace Father, and finally, turning to the men, said, "I'm ready, friends — let us go."

Ghermosha and I ran to the nursery window. We saw the three of them walking in the middle of the road. Dedushka carrying his bag, striding firmly, towering above the men on either side of him.

That was my last glimpse of Dedushka. I never saw him again.

2

1920

Gradually with each passing day the structure of our way of life was crumbling. The daily routine, observed for years, was abandoned. Although the samovar was carried in each evening and some gathered round it, no table was set for lunch or dinner. The family split up and were eating any time, anyhow, whatever was available. Potatoes were the mainstay, with some cabbage, dressed in white sauce when milk and flour were available. Our three feathered friends, in spite of their own hardships, continued faithfully providing a few, much welcomed eggs.

One day someone remembered that there were carp in the pond. A long fishing net was found and stretched across. Seryozha and Yura, wading up to their waists, dragged the net the length of the pond. A great mass of struggling fish was scattered on the path. All the eager onlookers were delighted to receive a share of the catch.

We made the traditional fish soup with onions and potatoes, but in the end, hungry as we were, the revolting taste of stagnant water, combined with the knowledge that some neighbours used to drown the kittens in the pond, proved too much.

Mother became acquainted with a woman who was anxious to learn conversational English. Her husband was employed in the Customs Office. By some means, which Mother didn't question, she paid Mother for each lesson in kind — a little sugar, salt and some flour. Soap was one of the many commodities which were not available at any price. The few cakes of soap that Mother had brought from Scotland were treasured and used sparingly. The mother of the family who had taken over the flat once occupied by Uncle Sanya used to come to the kitchen to do her washing. "Oh, for a piece of soap," she would exclaim, as she scrubbed her children's clothing with the ashes from the kitchen grate. Once in some shed in the town we found a pile of string. The balls were eagerly bought up and slippers were crocheted from them. They proved to be useful during the summer and preserved our shoes and boots for the winter.

Yet, in this twilight world of chaos, starvation and accumulating horror, all was not tears and sorrow. Looking back over the long passage of years to that hungry summer, there still remains the bright memory of the companionship of the children in our street.

The meeting place was the boulders, lapped by the warm water of the river. There we spent long happy hours, darting in and out of the water, sitting in the sun having long discussions or making plans for embarking on some adventure. We named ourselves "The Olonetskaya Companiya", after the name of our street and we strongly resented any intruders into our own special circle. There were some nine of us. Our leader was Tolya Mammantov. The son of a local joiner, strong, resourceful, clever, with a natural ability for leadership, no one deserved this place more than him. In the years to come he became an important commissar, which was not surprising.

In the group were also the three children of the executed General Zaborchikov, Volodya, Vera and little six-year-old Shurik. The most popular member was a flaxen-haired boy, Petya Skroznikov, the son of the janitor of the adjoining Technical school. His good nature, lively, humorous remarks, endeared him to us all. There was also Nina Duletova, the serious young daughter of the headmaster of the boys' school. Finally there was Petya Karelsky, the son of the stoker of the Technical school. He was usually referred to as Petka to differentiate him from the other Petya.

Allowed more freedom than under normal circumstances, we

stayed out of the way of our elders and spent the time foraging for ourselves. On the lush banks where once roamed our blackfaced ewes, we found many edible plants — wild celery, the juicy stalks of angelica, the tiny pods of wild peas. We made excursions to the woods as in July the golden maroshka berry arrived again and mushrooms appeared below the birches. All these were gathered in pails and baskets and brought back to our delighted mothers. Mushrooms fried with potatoes and onions made a delicious and sustaining dish.

Once, while crossing a field on the way to the woods, we saw to our amazement a cow grazing. In our parts, in those times, this was a rare and wondrous sight. We came to the conclusion that it may have been delivered from a village to a commissar or some such important person. When we approached, the cow made no attempt to bolt away, but gazed serenely back with her large, docile eyes. White-breasted and golden-coated she was a handsome beast, but even more entrancing was the sight of her enormous udder, ready to burst and begging to be milked.

None of us were acquainted with the art of milking, but undaunted, if somewhat apprehensive, I knelt and placed the bucket in position. A trifle overawed by the close proximity of the great rotundity and four teats, I began to tug, squeeze and pull in all directions. Nothing happened. After a few more vain attempts and detecting signs of displeasure in the cow's manner, Vera took my place. Her little hands achieved success. The sound of milk spurting into the bucket brought shrieks of jubilation and further encouraging remarks of "Stick it Vera — you're pulling fine — there's more to come." But just as Vera was getting into her stride and the bucket was filling up, the cow, tired of our antics, gave a sudden swish of her tail and galloped off to the other side of the field. As we had no mugs or cups, the bucket was passed round for each one to sip a mouthful, all watching carefully that no one swallowed more than the other.

A few days later we spotted a goat on the river banks. No one knew where it came from, but like the cow she was also in need of milking. This time the operation was difficult. The goat, struggling and making loud protesting noises, had to be dragged from the banks to our stable, where, with me sitting astride, and firmly held by the others, Vera, by now an expert, milked her dry. When in the end we opened the stable door, the goat, still plaintively protesting, rushed back to the river.

The warm strong-flavoured milk, shared out in even cupfuls, was much enjoyed, but as the goat was never seen again that was the end of our free milk.

During the summer soup kitchens were opened in various parts of the town. By handing over our ration cards we were allowed to have a two-course meal each day. Our "companiya", with bowls and spoons, raced along the hot wooden pavements to the kitchen and hurried back to the river where we sat enjoying our meal. However, it was a poor affair, this meal, consisting of a kind of meatless stew and a bowl of kasha.

One day we took into our heads to have a picnic on Moisief island. This island, adjacent to the main island of Solombala, was planted out in trees during the time of Peter the Great and was a place where people liked to stroll, sit in the shade, and admire the river. Now, after two centuries of spring floods, it was reduced to a deserted narrow strip of silver sands. A few days earlier we had observed a rowing boat lying on the shore, complete with oars and a few old rusty tins. It was on this boat that we decided to embark for the island.

The day began hot and sultry with not a ripple on the burnished surface of the river. In the distance, the outline of the deserted island seemed to be beckoning. With our rations from the soup kitchen and a basketful of berries, seven of us piled into the boat and with Tolya rowing strongly were soon dragging it on to the sandy shores. There we had our picnic, gave full vent to imaginative games, built a bonfire from the splinters washed ashore, and swam in a delightful pool surrounded by stunted willows.

I can't recall who first noticed the dark cloud on the horizon drawing nearer. A sudden flash of lightning tore the sky apart, followed by a roll of thunder. Large drops of rain began to dance on the surface of the river. We hurried to the boat and made for the mainland. A solid wall of water poured down from the heavens on our ancient, overloaded boat. Lightning and thunder increased with every second. To the punishing storm was now added the horror that the seams of the boat were opening up. Desperately, with tins, bowls and with our hands, we began to bale. It was hopeless. The leaks increased, swamping the boat. Sitting waist deep, faced with the almost certainty of drowning, we turned to our only recourse of praying in loud voices to kind Jesus to save his little children from a watery grave. Only Tolya remained calm. Rowing for dear life, he kept on encouraging us, constantly repeating not to give up, but to keep on baling. We were almost there, he went on assuring us. Through a thick curtain of rain the familiar boulders were now seen to be drawing closer, but suddenly there was no boat. We found ourselves struggling in the water between oars, planks and baskets. Luckily we were all swimmers of different degrees and, although out of our depth, were not far from the shores. One by one we scrambled up the stones and sat there silent and dejected, yet at the same time thankful to be alive.

The skies cleared. Sunbeams broke through the mist. And we, like chirping sparrows pruning their feathers after a storm, became our usual cheerful selves.

When Ghermosha and I returned to the house, we found our parents talking earnestly together. Their expression was serious. At first, being as we were wet and bedraggled, I imagined we were in for a raging, but instead Mother had startling news. After a long discussion with Father, she told us, they had both decided that she with Ghermosha and me must try to return to Scotland. "What about Papa?" I asked. "I'll be all right," he cheerfully assured us. "If the worst came to the worst and the house was confiscated, as they say it might be, I would go and live with Uncle Sanya. Life is difficult just now, but once things settle down, you will, of course, return. Everything is bound to get better."

Somehow I knew that all that he was saying wasn't true and that he himself knew it, but I wanted to believe him. I wanted to be back in Scotland, away from all the searches, the fear, and this hungry existence.

My father had a lifelong friend whom we always knew as Aleksandr Aleksandrovich. He was a cultured man who spoke several languages including perfect English. It was he who always wrote my father's letters when he dictated in English, and it was he who wrote the application to the authorities in Petrograd for an exit visa. This application, however, had to go through the office of foreign affairs in Archangel. I had the job of haunting this office, where the waiting room was usually packed with people like myself waiting to be interviewed.

Eventually, after many visits and long hours of waiting, the commissar, a courteous young man, ushered me into his office and informed me that our request had been forwarded and was being considered.

Meanwhile there was Marga's wedding, planned to take place during July. Babushka, who from the time of Dedushka's second arrest had lost all interest in the running of the house and garden, now pulled herself together. Come what may, Marga had to have her day. All the linen, china and articles which were once going to America, were now carried downstairs and carefully arranged in the cart by Arsyeny. The Van Brienen portrait was once more removed from the wall. Everything was being transferred to Marga's future home with Mitya.

Mitya lived with his aunt in a pleasant two-storeyed house situated on the main street. The aunt decided that she would live in the ground floor flat and hand over the floor above to the young couple. This convenient arrangement, they hoped, would prevent other people from taking over any of the rooms.

As the date of the wedding drew nearer the bustle and the running between the two houses increased. Babushka was anxious that Marga should also receive her share of the silver. This silver, searched for by the Bolsheviks, was all the time hidden by Yura's mamka in her village. Babushka, forewarned by what went on all over Russia, was not so stupid as to allow the Bolsheviks to confiscate it and had made this arrangement with Yura's mamka, a faithful soul, who returned it later and thus allowed Babushka to exist by gradually bartering it away.

On the sunny day of Marga's wedding, she set off for our church with Babushka, with the rest of the family following behind. She was wearing a dress altered by our dressmaker, Nastenka. It was the dress of white chiffon which she wore on the evening of her graduation dance — the dance that I had watched so eagerly while hiding behind the ballroom door. Babushka, with her magic fingers, had created a wreath of white flowers and placed it on Marga's head over a gossamer veil, which Babushka herself had worn on her wedding day to my grandfather. Marga, tall, stately and radiantly happy looked beautiful.

Inside the vestry, Mitya was waiting. Both walked up together to the pink silk square placed in front of the lectern. Tradition has it that whoever steps first on the square will rule the roost. But when the time came I forgot to look at their feet, overcome by the sight of this unusually tall, good-looking couple and the great sanctity of the moment.

Yura and one of Mitya's friends were the two groomsmen who held the crowns over the bridal pair when the priest, holding the clasped hands of the couple, circled thrice round the lectern.

In the evening Marga and Mitya left the house where there had been a small reception. Arm in arm they set off to walk along the river front to begin their married life.

After Marga left, Babushka applied to the authorities for permission to join Dedushka in the depth of the country, where prison camps were springing up like mushrooms. During the rule of Lenin, as ruthless as it was, in certain cases wives were permitted to join their husbands. Perhaps Lenin remembered how he himself was allowed to have his wife beside him in Siberia, where together with their cronies they plotted the downfall of a reign which allowed this latitude.

After her petition had gone through endless channels, Babushka received the permission and from that moment began to look for ways and means by which she could embark on her journey.

One early morning in late July, while everyone was sleeping, Ghermosha and I crept out of the house and joined our friends waiting outside the gate. It had been arranged that we should take the road to a wood lying further away from the one we usually haunted and where, we had been told, grew masses of berries and mushrooms.

There had been several showers the previous day — a sign that mushrooms should be plentiful. It was better to pick them early before other people arrived.

Soon we were out of the town and following a dirt road flanked on one side by an open moor, on the other by barbed-wire fencing enclosing a young forest of aspens, conifers and slender birches. The fence led to a gate on which was a sign printed in large red letters, "Entry forbidden".

As we approached the gate we heard tramping behind us a small group of prisoners with their guards. As they drew nearer, we stood aside to allow them to pass. The prisoners, in civilian clothing, were carrying spades, their faces haggard, unshaven and deathly pale. Standing out among them was a boy with fair unkempt hair almost down to his shoulders. He was wearing a grey coat of the school uniform and might have been a pupil from our senior form. They walked past us without a glance in our direction and vanished inside the gate.

We continued walking towards the dark crescent of the wood and there scattered within hearing distance of each other. The little bushes were completely smothered by berries. A few yards from me Vera, humming to herself, was on her knees filling her basket. All around us was the sweet fragrance of the berries, moist earth, pines and birches.

Suddenly the sound of distant shots broke the silence. A flock of frightened birds flew overhead and vanished to the north. Puzzled, Vera and I looked up and listened, but hearing nothing more, continued gathering berries.

Some time later, with our full baskets, we were winding our way back past the rough fencing, the strange gate and on to the road to the town. We were again overtaken by the same soldiers, marching briskly back towards the prison. There were no prisoners in their midst, but flung over their shoulders were bundles of clothing, including the grey uniform of the young boy. Everything fell into place. The prisoners, the gate, the shots, the birds flying overhead, the grey school uniform.

We never again took the road which passed the gate with the threatening notice, nor went back to the area so close to that sinister wood.

As we continued on our way home and turned into Olonetskaya Street we saw Mother walking slowly in front of us. Ghermosha and I hurried after her, but when she turned to speak to us we noticed she looked upset and had been crying. During the morning she had met one of the officers from the ice-breaker *Canada* who told her that Maisie Jordan was dead. She had died, he went on to explain, from typhoid, in Petrograd. He also added that Billy Jordan was missing and was thought to be in England.

We could not understand this terrible story. Maisie, only twenty-three years old, beautiful, full of life — now dead; and dead in Petrograd. Why Petrograd? The officer had no further information. A week or two later, an elderly lady called at the house and introduced herself as Aleksandra Andreyevna Ankirova. Madame Ankirova was the mother of the girl who had married the obliging Dane. Everything had worked according to plan. After arriving in Norway, they parted company and Mariya went on to France where she was met by her fiancé, went through the proper orthodox marriage and was now happily settled down.

Madame Ankirova, anxious to join her daughter, was, like us, waiting for permission to leave Russia. The purpose of her visit was to suggest that we should try to travel together and in this way perhaps help each other if need be. Mother, of course, readily agreed.

Aleksandra Andreyevna belonged to a family who had at one time owned fishing trawlers and were in the profitable fishing business. Her brother, although not the owner any longer, was still employed by the new government. Through him Madame Ankirova received a letter from Murmansk in which he described what happened when the three travellers arrived to board a ship for Norway. On the day of their departure, they were first taken to a customs shed, guarded by soldiers, where they were thoroughly searched, their trunks emptied and every article examined. When it came to Maisie's turn, and her trunks were opened, they found the letters she was taking back to England. She was taken away for questioning, and arrested. All her explanations, the Dane's appeals, were of no avail. For some reason it was found necessary to take her to Petrograd.

The last the young couple saw of Maisie was her being led away, weeping bitterly, and calling back to them, "I know that I shall never see Yorkshire now."

Maisie was young, perhaps frivolous, but never a spy. There is something about the story of her death that does not ring quite true. Certainly all over Russia, torn asunder, every disease and especially typhoid was rampant. Maisie might well have caught some infection, but what was behind the purpose of taking her on a long journey to

Petrograd? And was it not a strange coincidence that on arrival she should develop typhoid and die?

Only those who took this young woman away know the answer.

At last a letter arrived from Finland. Aunt Olga had startling news to tell us.

Uncle Oscar with his two young daughters went to Petrograd to report to the Kerensky government for further instructions, but no sooner had he arrived than Lenin's hostile government took over. Faced with no prospects of any position, suffering great privations, unable to return to Finland and already in ill health, he became worse and died, leaving his two daughters completely destitute. Zlata, fourteen years of age, tried to cross the border to Finland but was caught and thrown into prison where she suffered degradation and iniquitous treatment, but in the end, after numerous appeals, was freed to return to Finland. Her sister Ariadna found work as a nurse on a train carrying wounded, but on two occasions narrowly escaped being executed when the train, halting in various stations, was taken over either by the Bolsheviks or White guards and in each case she was accused of spying for the other side. She too eventually reached the safety of her home in Finland.

Meanwhile Aunt Olga, now a widow, married General Hjalmar Walinquist, who had been a police official under the Tsar's government but being a Finn still retained the same position under the new government of Finland. The general was an old friend of the family. Aunt Olga in the fullness of time produced her ninth daughter whom she christened Nina. During that eventful period my attractive cousin Militza, Aunt Olga's eldest daughter, having divorced Volodya Pasternak, had also embarked on her second marriage.

All things considered, after reading this letter, the family arrived at the conclusion that Aunt Olga didn't do too badly.

It was unbelievable how fast everything was deteriorating and how incompetent were those who governed us. People were living on the borders of starvation, suffering from scurvy and malnutrition.

The rouble completely lost its value and could buy nothing. Savings, investments, insurances vanished, leaving those who had worked and saved nakedly poor. As it was considered a waste of time to pay for admittance to cinemas, tramcars and whatever, tickets became a thing of the past. People travelled free on overcrowded tramcars, which at times, depending on the whim of the driver, didn't appear at all. Neither was it necessary to buy postage stamps for letters. People posted letters and just hoped that they might eventually reach their destination.

Meanwhile autumn was drawing nearer and with it the dread of the coming winter with its grinding frosts and hardships. In this great timber land, the greatest in the whole of Russia, if not the world, where wood was used as fuel to heat houses, run trains and industries, those who used to sell it were for some strange reason not allowed to do so any longer. Yet, as in all past summers, the timber rafts were arriving in front of our house and moving slowly down the river on their way to the sawmills. After they left there was the usual residue of loose timber, broken free from the rafts, either thrown ashore or bobbing on the surface of the water. Due to the shortage of fuel, people were now gathering on the shores collecting all they could. In this arduous but profitable ploy the "Olonetskaya Companiya" joined wholeheartedly. At first it was comparatively simple to gather the small pieces on the banks, but later, having to wade out into the river and with the larger pieces slipping from our hands, we realised we had to find some ropes. Nearby in the garden of a house long since deserted, stood a maypole with ropes still attached to it. One morning the boys set off for the garden and while the solitary watchman was absent, scaled the maypole and returned with the necessary ropes. Logs were dragged out of the river, pulled up the stony shores, along the cobbled roadway and into our courtyard where they were sawn up in pieces and equally divided between us. But as the water became colder, the formidable task of swimming out for the timber, drifting further out each day, became more difficult.

Close by was the now abandoned Yacht Club, where inside a shed lay one or two scull-boats. By the simple expedient of "borrowing" a boat and rowing out to the drifting logs, we succeeded in towing some ashore. The hardest part of this activity was the dragging of water-logged timber into the yard, and the sawing itself, at the price of blistered hands and aching limbs. Looking back, I sometimes ask myself where we found the strength to do all that we did. We were young, thin, undernourished, deprived of the necessary proteins and vitamins one hears so much of nowadays. Yet with great enthusiasm, day after day, we went down to the now cold and darkening river, and in the end, when there was no more to be gathered, were rewarded by the sight of a considerable quantity of firewood stacked in the woodshed.

The hours we enjoyed best were in the falling dusk of the autumn evening when the river was deserted and we collected round a bonfire to roast potatoes filched from various gardens, some deserted and some not. Sitting in the warm glow of the fire, eating our scorched potatoes, we talked of many things, of our past and present exploits, of the mysterious disappearance of the Ukrainian family while the town was changing hands, of Boris and Lena who used to be always with us, but who had left unnoticed without any warning.

Politics meant nothing and were never mentioned. Perhaps there was an unconscious desire to avoid anything that could cause pain or trouble. No one ever questioned Vera or Volodya about their father.

The conversation usually revolved around the entrancing subject of food and particularly something sweet. "Tell us more about these sweetie shops in Scotland," they used to ask. "What is a sweetie?" enquired Shurick, who had never seen one. "We also had them long ago," remarked Volodya. "Perhaps they will come again," he added wistfully. "Of course they will," Tolya would confirm with unfailing optimism.

By now the summer was over. The river became unfriendly. Cold Siberian winds lashed the shores, throwing amber sparks and smoke into our faces. Some place offering more shelter was required. The choice fell on our garden. After all, Vassily didn't bother chasing us any longer. Now we decided that if we only had a boat it would add to our pleasure. Petka Karelsky, full of bright suggestions and unburdened by any scruples, suggested that we should remove a boat from the Yacht Club and transfer it to our pond. "But that would be stealing," Vera remonstrated. "Stealing nothing," Petka, who disliked being contradicted, rejoined. "How could it be stealing if there's no one to steal from?"

The boat was carried through the garden on to the pond. For a short while we derived a lot of amusement out of it. Circling around under the overhanging branches of the willows, the pond became the Mississippi, the Amazon with Indians hiding in the bushes ready to strike us down. At times it was our own mother Volga with the accompanying ballad of "Stenka Razin" and his cossacks, sung in ringing tones.

One evening Uncle Adya called. Uncle Adya, no longer his old debonair self, was bitterly regretting that he encouraged Natasha with their baby son to return on the *Canada*. Although his sisters and widowed mother were safely abroad, neither he nor Natasha were permitted to leave. The timber business, for generations in the Scholts family, was confiscated, as was the house of my late godfather. Adya was fortunate that he was not arrested and even executed, as some of the mill owners had been. But the future held nothing — nothing at all. As both he and Natasha were talented people, he planned to join a group of actors and in this way perhaps eke out some kind of living.

After talking for some time, he and Seryozha decided to take a stroll in the garden. On returning Uncle Adya remarked to father: "Do you know, Gherman, my boat is sitting on your pond tied to one of the white jetties?" Our parents were furious and both Ghermosha and I not only received a good dressing-down but had to apologise to Uncle Adya for stealing his boat. He, not caring much about anything, wanted us to keep it, but Father would not hear of it. And so in the end the boat had to be carried back to the Yacht Club, no doubt to be stolen eventually by someone else.

Meanwhile, during the rainy days of autumn, the two main cinemas in the town offering free admittance were as good a place as any to find shelter and amusement. Each cinema on alternate days presented two films. In the "Edison" in the heart of the city, we watched *Why America Declared War*. The next day there was a Russian film all about a brave young girl who, after being involved in revolutionary activities, is arrested and in despair hangs herself in her prison cell. It was called *Ogonky–Little Lights*, from the glowing lights in the eyes of the wolves chasing their victim when she tried to escape.

In our part of the town, in the "Cino-Art", we were shown the American classic *The Three Godfathers* and the mysterious *The Man in Grey*. The American films, souvenirs left by the forces, had captions printed in English which meant nothing to the Russian audience.

As these were the days of silent films, they had usually been accompanied by a pianist playing appropriate music, but now there was no such person to be found. At the beginning of each performance a disgruntled official would appeal to the audience for someone to come forward and fill the void. There was no shortage of enthusiastic amateurs, some of whom, with complete disregard to their lack of ability or the suitability of the music, would thump on the piano with all their might and main. The poor revolutionary hanging herself was often accompanied by the gay rippling of the *Cat's Polka*.

One might think that constant repetition would have killed all interest, but no, we savoured each well-known scene, each gesture, every tear, and when at times there were no volunteers to play the piano we replaced the music with our own vocal efforts.

The three outlaws shuffling through the hot sands of the desert with the baby were encouraged to go on by the earthy ditty sung by our soldiers on the march. The final dramatic scene, with the last surviving godfather stumbling into the church with the infant in his arms, was greeted by the rousing chorus of the "International" — "This was our last decisive battle — forward, forward, forward."

September. The mornings growing colder. With each passing day as darkness draws nearer the lamps have to be lit earlier in the evening.

Our annual visitors, the red-breasted bullfinches, are here again. With unbelievable speed and energy, accompanied by frenzied chirping, they dive into the elderberry bush and strip the crimson berries. The helpless bush sways and trembles under the onslaught of these tiny winged invaders, but in a day or more when there is nothing left to plunder they fly away. A peaceful silence descends upon the dying garden.

In the town, after six months of living under our new government, conditions remain chaotic. The minds of the authorities are too occupied with establishing their doctrine and persecuting those who happen to have opinions contrary to their own, to bother with less important matters such as clothing and feeding hungry citizens.

Meetings are held all over the town. Even children have to attend to be regaled with passionate rhetoric on the glories of communism and the ever-repetitive promise of a bright future. We are tired of hearing about this "bright future" and ask only for something better in the present — a little more food and clothing.

The bread queues grow longer every day and often, after standing for hours on end, there is nothing left. As usual there is an abundance of rumours, based on wishful thinking leading nowhere, of some rare commodities, from sugar and tea to felt boots and soap, due for distribution in various parts of the city. One such was of apples. Apples indeed — a rarity not seen for years.

Marina and I set off one morning to join the lengthy queue outside our local co-operative, behind the locked door of which were the promised apples. Someone had actually seen the boxes marked with the magic word "Apples" carried into the shop.

We waited an hour or two, whiling away the time studying some of the numerous posters plastered on the walls. One I recollect was of a giant black cat standing on its hind legs and dressed in a red shirt, with trousers tucked inside long boots. In its claws, dripping blood, were small birds wearing crowns. In the background was an overturned throne and the same crowned birds lying dead beside it. The rhyme, in large scarlet letters, read to the effect that the Tsar's birds were singing a different tune now that the worker's cat has caught them in her claws. There were more on the same theme, equally revolting, but they helped to pass away the tedious hours.

Eventually a plump woman appeared to unlock the door. "What are you waiting for?" she enquired. "Apples," was the hopeful answer. "Apples," she echoed, bursting into astonished laughter. "You'll find no apples here my friends — where do you think they would come from? Are you out of your minds? Away with you — take yourselves home." And that was what we sadly did.

That day of the apples was a momentous day, however, for that afternoon word arrived from the authorities giving permission for Mother and her children to leave for Scotland on a temporary visit to her parents. With this permission came the strict instructions to detail every article we were taking with us, and also to send all photographs, pictures and postcards for scrutiny by the authorities in Petrograd. In due course the list of our belongings was returned with the official stamp. The photographs and cards were likewise returned in a sealed envelope with further strict orders for the envelope not to be opened until we reached our destination. (When we finally did come to open the packet, all was in order — except that a photograph of Maisie was missing!)

The following day Madame Ankirova called. She had received her exit visa too. Now our joint efforts had to concentrate on finding a ship which would take us to Norway.

Meanwhile, Mother began to prepare for the journey. It was said that paper roubles bearing the head of Aleksandr III were still acceptable abroad. Although difficult to obtain, Mother succeeded in gathering together a substantial sum. This she hoped to exchange for foreign currency as soon as we landed in Norway. The money was put in a white cotton bag which Mother planned to tie round her waist. Most of our belongings had to be left behind. In any event we could not have taken them with us as they had to provide Father with some means of bartering for food and other necessities.

The search for a ship to take us direct to Norway turned out to be more difficult than we imagined. Week after week went by without any success. We were now approaching the end of September. In a matter of two or three weeks the river would freeze up and be closed to navigation.

Life continued to roll on. Friends and relatives called, usually in the evenings. Sashenka still presided at the tea-table at night when we drank an infusion of dried lime flowers gathered in the garden. It was not particularly pleasant, but kept us sitting and talking together round the table.

Other people came to live in the house. Marga's bedroom was now occupied by two young teachers. They were pleasant girls and occasionally joined us at the table. One of them, Masha, eventually married Seryozha.

One day, the lady who was taught English by mother, mentioned that she had heard of a ship called *Sever (North)* due to leave for Murmansk at the end of the month. Further enquiries confirmed this and Mother and Madame Ankirova decided to take it. It was our last chance. From Murmansk, it being an ice-free port, we optimistically thought it would be comparatively simple to cross over to Norway.

Meanwhile Babushka was now ready to join my step-grandfather in his place of exile in the depth of the country. On the evening before her departure, she asked me to spend the night with her in her room. The night was stormy, with wind and rain lashing the windows. I lay, curled up in bed, listening to the description of her journey to St Petersburg for an audience with Aleksandr II. In the morning the storm had abated. A pale autumn sun filtered through the windows.

I still remember her standing in the back hall. She was wearing an old travelling cloak and shawl tied over her head, peasant-style. Amongst the relatives who came to see her off was Aunt Peeka, now frail and sad — the only witness left of Babushka's departure for her momentous journey four decades earlier.

Final farewells, laden with grief and tears, are heavy to bear. I, wishing to lighten the moment and in some way show my grandmother how much she meant to me, ran out of the hall and, taking a cake of soap from the two in Mother's case, hurried back and pressed it in Babushka's hand. She threw her arms around me and held me to her breast. This was the last time I saw my beloved Babushka.

At the back door the old carriage was waiting. We all trooped out the back stair and stood watching Babushka settling down with her few belongings and Yura getting in beside her. Yura was to accompany her across the river and go on to stay for a while with his mamka in her village.

The carriage rolled through the gates and on to the cobbled street. Babushka turned and waved her hand in farewell.

After she left, the old nursery became the centre of our small world.

PART V

Farewell House and Farewell Home

1

1920

MOTHER went to finalise the date and time of our own departure. She returned with the news that the *Sever* was sailing on the last day of September at four o'clock in the afternoon. The luggage had to be brought aboard in the morning.

The whole of the previous day was spent, well into the evening, doing the last of the packing. Mother, exhausted, went off to bed. Ghermosha also fell sound asleep in his corner of the nursery. I, for some time, sat talking with Father. He spoke of his youth, of the happy days he spent in Scotland and how important it was that I should learn to read and write in English and make my way in life. A life, he warned me, that would not be easy. I had the sad impression that he was already somehow reconciled to the loss of his wife, children and everything.

I left him and crept into my bed in darkness. For a long time I lay wide awake tormented by unhappy thoughts. The broken home, of having to leave Father, and all those who meant so much.

In the morning our boxes were piled on the cart. Arsyeny set off for the docks. The ship was about two miles' walk away. We followed on foot, planning to see the luggage safely aboard and then to return to spend the last few hours with Father.

Madame Ankirova was already settled in. It was now midday. As we were leaving the ship the captain came over to have a word with Mother. There occurred one of these terrible mistakes that could alter the whole course of one's life. I distinctly heard the captain reminding Mother that the ship was leaving at the fourteenth hour. Mother, whose Russian was never perfect, misunderstood the time, taking it to mean four o'clock instead of two. "Mama," I pointed out anxiously, "the captain says the ship will leave at two o'clock, not four." "Nonsense." Mama brushed this aside and I, perhaps wishing to believe her, didn't argue. We still had time to return if we hurried.

At home everyone was gathered in the nursery. The samovar was lit. While it was heating, I ran out into the garden for my last goodbye to the trees, places I knew so well where I had played throughout my childhood. The scented poplar, a reminder of past springs and crimson catkins, now stood sadly drooping its naked branches. The fairy summerhouse was shabby and forlorn. I climbed up to the turret from where once long ago the gold and scarlet of the Lion Rampant fluttered its welcome to a Scottish bride. Before me lay the whole vista of our town. Houses, gardens with their stark denuded trees, wide cobbled roads, the golden domes of churches lit up by autumn sunlight, the Dvina, like a silver ribbon winding round her shores. I had to hurry. The samovar was already singing on the table when I sat down beside the others.

As we sat in silence, dreading the moment when we would have to say goodbyes, my father's friend Aleksandr Aleksandrovich rushed in, out of breath. He had planned to be with Father but called first at the ship to discover we weren't there and that the ship should have left an hour earlier. The infuriated captain was already preparing to throw our luggage on to the pier. Only our friend's pleading moved him to wait a little longer.

This startling announcement in some ways alleviated the pain of last farewells. I remember nothing beyond the poignant sight of my father clinging to Ghermosha.

We rushed out of the house. Outside the gates, waiting to see us off, was the "Olonetskaya Companiya". A quick decision was made that Mother and Aunt Shura should hurry to the main road in the hope of catching a tramcar, while we would go to the river front. Whoever reached the ship first would beg the captain to wait for the other party.

A race began. I have never known myself to run faster before or since. Far ahead, having overtaken us all, was lightfooted Petya Skroznikov, with Tolya and the rest of us stretched out behind him. He had now reached the ship and then I too rushed up the gangway. There was no sign of Mother. Infuriated by this, the captain immediately ordered the crew to unload our luggage.

At this point, in utter despair, I burst into tears, threw myself down on my knees and begged the captain to wait, assuring him that Mother was on her way. This touching scene appeared to move the hearts of the other passengers, who collected around us. A loud chorus of supplication to the captain broke out, with the demented man calling back, "They'll put me up against the wall, you fools — that's what they'll do to me for disobeying orders."

In the midst of this uproar Mother appeared, accompanied by my aunt, sauntering calmly and unhurriedly down the incline to the pier. There was not the slightest trace in her demeanour of anxiety or sense of urgency but only that of sweet complacency. It was too much. I bounded down the gangway to meet her with a volley of abuse such as she had never heard from me before and which I have since regretted.

Now, with everyone safely aboard, the ship began her journey down the river. Mother and Aleksandra Andreyevna went below to our cabin. I stayed on deck with Ghermosha. For a little while the "Olonetskaya Companiya" ran along the river front trying to keep up with the ship, but soon they were left behind. I stood leaning against the railing watching the familiar places slipping away one by one. The Naval College, the boulevard, the church, bringing back memories of Easter, midnight service, lighted candles — and now here was the house. Marina was waving from the balcony, but then the island came between us. And in that point of time I wished intensely with all my being that I could see it once again, if only for a moment. Did someone hear me? For in that split second, the ship rose on the breast of a wave above the island and I saw the house as I see it yet, all lit up by the crimson glow of the setting sun. Then it vanished for ever.

I look back with horror on that journey to Murmansk.

The *Sever* in happier days carried passengers, most of whom were pilgrims to such famous places as the Solovetsky Monastery and other beautiful little islands scattered on the White Sea. Then the ships were comfortable. Spotless cabins and plain good food were provided. All that was changed. Our cabins were indescribably filthy and alive with vermin. Throughout the whole of the journey, which lasted two or three weeks, we were devoured by day and night, helpless against the terrible onslaught of bugs crawling over walls and ceiling, and clinging like beads on to the seams of the bedding.

The ship carried two cargoes. One of them was grain being delivered to the outlying islands. The other, in the depths of the hold, consisted of political prisoners. Ghermosha and I used to look down on their pale upturned faces and smile to them. This appeared to give them pleasure for they in turn would wave back, ask us our names and try to talk to us. They were all pitifully thin and unkempt. As we approached the end of the journey, one day we noticed that the hold was empty. When and where the prisoners disembarked we never discovered.

The food brought aboard was finished within a few days. All hopes were centred on the islands, but when we went ashore to barter our belongings, the islanders, being fishermen and having nothing themselves, could only offer salmon. Big beautiful fish.

We went ashore on one of the small islands. With waterfalls, bridges, birches and pines surrounding a few cottages the village had the charm of a forgotten world. We knocked at the door of one of the isbas. A young blonde dressed in a sarafan asked us in and invited us to sit down on a form which, like the floor, was scrubbed white with silver sand. In the corner of the room was an ikon draped with a fine embroidered towel and close to it a large picture of the Royal family. Didn't she know that the unfortunate family were murdered two years earlier? One might have thought the war and revolutions had never touched this place.

She offered us some milk, which we gratefully supped from brown earthenware bowls while her three flaxen-haired children, with serious faces, sat watching us. Her husband, she explained, was fishing but was due back soon. We saw him later rowing ashore. The boat he beached was filled with salmon. All they could offer in exchange for clothing was still more salmon.

From island to island, for skirts and blouses, frilled knickers and petticoats there was more and more salmon. Large, silver-backed, thick, pink-fleshed handsome fish. Allowed the use of the galley, we ate it hot, and we ate it cold, we ate it boiled and we ate it baked. We ate it without bread, without potatoes, without salt.

Sometimes people take peculiar ideas and fancies into their heads, and perhaps the Russians are more prone to this than others. We don't know what possessed Madame Ankirova to come to the strange decision that the biggest and heaviest salmon was to be kept and taken to her darling daughter living in the south of France. Her Mariya would love nothing better than a salmon from her own distant north. The fact that there was nothing with which to preserve it was a mere detail. The salmon was sewn inside a pillow-slip, a rope was fixed to its tail, and my poor brother was condemned to carry this horrible bundle wherever he went.

Meanwhile our journey continued through the White Sea, and on to the Kola Peninsula skirting the bleak shores of the Barents Sea. The weather was surprisingly kind, but gradually it grew colder, with sudden gusts of fine snow peppering the decks. At long last, the forbidding snow-clad coast of the Murmansk region came into view.

We were back in the barren wastes of Murmansk where ten months before the *Canada* had called with us on board on her way to Archangel. Our captain, a kind man at heart, allowed us to remain aboard the ship until he received further orders. We were provided with tickets which allowed one meal a day in a communal kitchen. The meals consisted of a mysterious brew in which the heads of herrings figured prominently, a chunk of bread and a small bowl of boiled grain. After a concentrated diet of salmon it was a pleasant change.

Every day, from the time of our arrival, Mother with Madame Ankirova set off in search of a ship for Norway and every evening returned disappointed. Ghermosha and I used to spend the day playing cards in the deserted saloon or wandering around the dismal shores searching under the thin layer of snow for the crimson berry "klukva", a native of the arctic regions and a cousin of the cranberry, but bigger and extremely sour. We ate them greedily whenever we could find them.

At the end of the week and just as we were beginning to think that we might have to return to Archangel, Mother and Madame Ankirova brought the glad news that we were being allowed to travel on a trawler leaving for the island of Vardo the following day. The trawler was commissioned to take two important Bolsheviks, with a female secretary, on a secret mission to Norway, the purpose of which we were never to discover. It was only by chance, through the captain being a friend of Madame Ankirova's family, that the proposed journey to Norway came to light. With his assistance we obtained permission to travel on the ship, which in itself was nothing short of a miracle.

In the evening with eager anticipation we began preparing for the next stage of our journey.

The trawler's captain warned us that before we could board the ship an extensive search of all our luggage had to take place in the customs shed. At the same time he volunteered to take items for us, which he would return on arrival in Norway. We did not wish to take too much advantage of his generous offer, but we handed over a few articles. In Mother's case it was her precious bundle of roubles, one or two gold coins, and a few pounds left over from our last visit to Scotland. Madame Ankirova had a great deal of valuable jewellery, but there again, not wishing to overburden the captain, she only gave him a few pieces. We were now confronted with the problem of concealing on our persons what, if found, would not only be confiscated but get us into trouble.

Mother, who was wearing a black pleated dress, sewed inside it her rings and brooches. Madame Ankirova cunningly stitched a string of rare pearls and diamonds between the lining of the cuffs of her blouse, and another string inside her collar. A precious bundle of Norwegian currency was hidden in the soles of her stockings. This was an extremely dangerous thing to do as those attempting to smuggle foreign currency were severely punished. She also had a pair of aquamarine earrings which proved to be a problem. Large, ball-shaped, encircled by diamonds, they were beautiful but impossible to hide. It was then that I came out with the bright idea that Ghermosha and I could each hold one inside our mouths. Mother could not agree to such a stupid and dangerous suggestion, but in the end was overruled.

The following morning our boxes were piled on to a sledge and with the help of the crew dragged to the customs shed where the search was to take place. There we were at once surrounded by armed soldiers and officials who began to turn out the boxes, closely examine our belongings and lay aside the articles they intended to confiscate. At this point we produced the paper listing the items we were permitted to take with us. Knowing that the paper was signed by an important commissar in Petrograd and that timidity does not always pay, I argued heatedly, at times with angry tears, pointing to the form when they attempted to confiscate what was listed — especially a bracelet that was once given to me by Father. Mother, by now emotionally exhausted, was prepared to allow them to take anything they wished so I argued with her as well. Throughout all arguments and tears the precious earring remained nestling securely against my cheek. As the main purpose of the whole search was to find letters, jewellery and above all foreign currency, in which they were unsuccessful, they threw back most of the articles, content to justify the search by keeping some underwear and Mother's precious picture hat with the osprey feathers.

In the midst of the search we were suddenly made aware that my young brother had been taken away. There was a door opening into a narrow corridor from which a second door led into a small room. Both doors were guarded by armed soldiers. We heard Ghermosha crying and for one terrifying moment I thought the earring had been detected. Mother rushed to the door but was stopped by a soldier who explained that no harm was being done to my brother. He was only being searched. Ghermosha returned shortly afterwards, tear-stained and unhappy. He has been stripped naked. His silver watch, his most precious possession, given to him by his Scottish grandfather, a few pennies, and a silver shilling were taken from him. I was called next and stepped into a small closed room where, sitting at a table, was a young woman. Her expression was cold and distant. "Take off your clothes," she commanded curtly. I obeyed silently and while I stood naked, cold and shivering, she examined them and from my pockets removed a few shillings. These precious coins, sad reminders of our last visit to Scotland, she placed on the table. She then came over and ruffled my hair. Somehow it never occured to her to ask me to open my mouth. I was ordered to dress and allowed to leave. It was now Mother's turn. She likewise had to remove her clothing and to take down her hair. The pleated dress, lying over a chair was shaken and thrown back. After Mother dressed and stood pinning up her hair, the woman came up close to her and drew the flat of her hand down the front and back of Mother's dress. The pieces of jewellery inside the pleats were not detected.

The last person to be searched was Madame Ankirova. She and Mother met in the corridor. "Did they take off your stockings?" she whispered to Mother. "Yes," Mother replied. Madame Ankirova crossed herself. "I am finished," she said and entered the room. After undoing her hair and undressing she sat down on the small chair and began to roll down her stockings. It is difficult to say if at this moment a spark of compassion moved the young woman or perhaps the face of the naked old woman with the resigned expression reminded her of someone close to herself, but she suddenly stopped her: "Never mind, Matushka," she said. "Just leave your stockings on." Madame Ankirova was saved.

The search over, the boxes once again on the sledge, the two ladies and I pulling, Ghermosha trailing behind with the salmon dangling over his shoulder, and the armed soldiers marching on either side, we proceeded on our way to the trawler. Our luggage was dragged aboard by members of the crew. Soon the two commissars and their secretary, a fat, pasty-faced woman, arrived and were allotted the small cabin belonging to the captain. Ghermosha and I arranged ourselves on the bench round the crew's dining-table. Madame Ankirova and Mother settled on the floor of the tiny landing at the top of the stair.

Shortly before the trawler was due to sail one of the commissars came out of the cabin and sat down beside me. "So, young lady," he said, "we are all to be travelling companions." He sounded friendly. "Yes," I rejoined politely, looking up at his face. I was not sure what I saw there. After a short conversation on similar lines he casually, perhaps too casually, remarked: "It was a good thing they didn't find your letters." Somewhere inside me a little bell began to ring a warning. This friendly man with the warm voice was dangerous. "Oh, no," I replied in the same friendly tone, "we took no letters." "Nor money?" I shook my head. "What are you going to do in Norway if you have no money?" "We have relatives," I said truthfully. There was a little thoughtful silence. "Did they take anything from you?" he again enquired in a gentle tone. "Oh, yes," I rejoined, just as gently, nodding my head. "They took my mother's hat and knickers." He stood up, his manner changing abruptly. "My dear young lady," he said, in a voice full of venom. "You have been lucky. Some people not only lose their hats, they lose their heads." He vanished inside his cabin.

Any sailor who has had to travel round the coast of the Kola Peninsula knows how frightening these waters can be. Shortly after we left Murmansk a violent storm broke over our heads. Ghermosha and I lying head to head, were constantly thrown against the table. Yet it was our only safeguard against landing on the floor and being dashed against the walls. A poor sailor at the best of times, I became desperately ill, as was Ghermosha. We had not eaten that day and that made it worse. I dared not think as to what was happening on the small landing above. We could not see anything and only heard the terrifying screeching and howling of the wind like a lost soul in the wilderness. It was as if some fiend from hell itself was lifting this frail craft up to the heavens and casting it back into the depth of a mountainous sea. Yet it sailed on bravely, dipping in and out through the churning water, slowly, but surely making headway towards the safe shores of Norway. I do not know how long this journey lasted. Time lost all meaning. I did not think it was possible to survive such a storm and somehow reached the stage where I ceased to care. Suddenly there came a great silence. No wind, no pitching, no rolling. We had entered the sunlit harbour of Vardo. Mother and Aleksandra Andreyevna joined us. They had spent a terrible night rolling on the floor and praying to survive.

Two officials and a doctor boarded the trawler. The two communists and their secretary had their papers and a case stuffed with bank notes carefully scrutinised and apparently passed without any comments. It was now our turn. All the officials spoke in English and Russian. The doctor came over to where I was lying. "This girl," he said to Mother, glancing at me with compassion, "appears to be seriously ill. If it is something contagious she may not be allowed to go ashore." "Please, please believe me," Mother began to explain anxiously, "she is a very poor sailor. It is nothing but seasickness, and besides," she added humbly, "we have had nothing to eat for almost two days." The three men moved aside and conferred together. We became deeply alarmed that perhaps after all we would have to return to Murmansk. But with that, one of them turned to us. "Ladies," he said, a wide welcoming smile spreading over his face, "you and your children may go ashore. Norway waits to welcome you."

These wonderful words have for ever remained in my heart and mind. More than six decades have passed since the day when our feet first touched Norwegian shores, but I can never think of that wonderful country in any other way but with deep gratitude.

To the two commissars and their female companion our Norwegian friend used a different tone. "I regret," he said curtly in perfect Russian, "we cannot permit you to go ashore. Two of our ships will escort your trawler out of the harbour from where you can return to Russia. No one at all," he continued coldly, "will be permitted to leave this ship." And so in the end it was us, only us, the trawler took to Norway. It was all strange and some might say miraculous.

We left the trawler and walked slowly along the pier and up a steep incline to a small hotel on the corner of the street. It had been snowing and after the darkness inside the ship, the streets and the roofs of the houses appeared dazzling white. Little, rosy-faced children skimmed past us on their sledges. Groups of people stood silently watching this strange procession with the young boy carrying a large fish over his shoulder.

Inside the hotel in our room a peat fire burned cheerfully. The hot baths, clean sheets, and the food were wonderful and seemed something out of a world we had not known for a long time.

During a short stroll in the early dusk we saw the trawler, like a dark shadow, standing off-shore, guarded by the Norwegian navy. "Strange are the ways of our lives," Madame Ankirova remarked thoughtfully. "There it is, this trawler told to get back to Russia and guarded by nothing less than the Norwegian navy, and we, who were never meant to be on it in the first place, are safe in Norway."

Before we left the trawler, the captain had handed back the articles he had kept for us. Unfortunately, when Mother went to exchange the roubles she was told they were worthless. This was a bitter blow, for they had been gathered in exchange for objects dear to her which she would have been wiser to have kept. I still have the roubles, just as they were packed by Mother in little white cotton bags many years ago. Having relied on them to cover our expenses to Scotland, Mother was forced to cable her father for money, which he sent immediately.

On the morning following our arrival in Vardo, several people called at the hotel. There were reporters and refugees who were still living in Vardo anxious to have the latest news from Russia. One reporter translated an article from the local paper which read: "Yesterday a small group of refugees, consisting of two women, a young girl and a boy, reached our friendly shores. They told us they came from Russia, but we believe that they must have come from some other planet. Their faces had a strange unearthly look."

2

1920

Two days later we left the friendly island and boarded one of the lovely coastal ships for Bergen. The name of the ship translated into English was *Silver Waters*. Nothing in our eyes could have been more luxurious than this journey. Our two cabins, Madama Ankirova and Mother in one, Ghermosha and I in the other, were spacious studies in blue and silver.

The white damask tablecloths, silver, crystal, table decorations, excellent cuisine, served by immaculate stewards, all belonged to a world of a bygone age. The glorious moving panorama of the fiords, of sparkling waters, mountains, islands, revived memories of an early childhood when I used to imagine that the houses scattered on the hillsides were toys and the figures hurrying down the paths were the "little" people from some fairy world.

When we left Vardo, the island was under a blanket of snow and the children were skimming down on their sledges from the schoolhouse on top of the hill, but as we sailed on through the green and blue waters of the fiords, skirting the North Cape, on to Hammerfest, Narvik and down to the south, the weather grew warmer. At Bergen we saw roses and chrysanthemums growing in the gardens.

There we said goodbye to *Silver Waters* and set off to walk along the cobbled road to a hotel nearby. The salmon was still with us. When first sewn into a linen bag it had a pleasant tang of the sea, but now after prolonged wanderings it stank to high heaven. Ghermosha, a sensitive boy, found it wounding when approaching strangers turned aside clutching their noses. "Mama," he said despairingly, "I just can't carry this stinking fish any longer." Mama agreed that enough was enough.. "Aleksandra Andreyevna," she began in persuasive tones, "I don't think your dear Mariya would enjoy this salmon any more — and as for France, no self-respecting Frenchman would allow it across his borders." And to clinch her argument she added, "We shall be far from welcome in any hotel here." Madame Ankirova remained silent for a moment or two. "You are right," she said at last. "Just lay it on top of that barrel, dear," she said to Ghermosha. And that was exactly what Ghermosha did. No one said another word, but just continued walking.

As there were no barriers placed on our way, Mother being British, we sailed the next day for Newcastle.

Madame Ankirova, to our great disappointment, could not travel with us, as she had to wait for an entry permit from France. We had hoped to continue our journey together to the end, but that was not to be. She came to see us off. We all wept as she blessed and kissed each in turn.

It was another stormy crossing to Newcastle. There, a taxi took us to an hotel. We spent a restful night and the following morning boarded the train for Dundee. From the train we saw again the same orderly houses, neat gardens, fields with the solitary oaks, cows grazing, coppices in gold and crimson.

By the afternoon we were on the bridge, rumbling over the great expanses of the Tay. In the distance was the ancient castle and sweeping from it to the west the beaches of Broughty Ferry — our journey's end. The train was slowing down now. With screeching brakes it shuddered and stopped at the Tay Bridge station.

One short lap remained. We had to catch the train to West Ferry from the East station, lying at the other end of Dock Street. An obliging porter arranged our luggage on a barrow and set off along the cobbled street with us walking behind him.

After buying the tickets and tipping the porter, we boarded the train, sharing a compartment with a group of schoolgirls. Their smart clothing, lively chattering, attracted my attention, but we ourselves aroused curiosity too — I, in my heavy coat and fur hat, Ghermosha in his grey uniform with the black Persian lamb collar. Being too polite to stare openly, they stole sidelong glances, while continuing their cheerful gossiping — I, listening to their carefree voices, happy laughter, was overcome by a deep longing to be like them, to belong, to have both parents, my own home.

A few minutes later we drew up at the neat station of West Ferry. From all parts of the train children were spilling out and hurrying to the steps leading out of the station.

It was then we suddenly recognised the familiar figure of Grandfather in his navy suit, stetson hat and flower in buttonhole, walking sedately towards the exit. We had travelled on the same train unaware of each other's presence.

"Run," Mother called to me. "Hurry — catch Grandpa." Grandpa was almost at the top of the steps as I ran. Between us was this jostling crowd of children. Scrambling, pushing through them, I reached out and touched my grandfather's arm. "Grandpa," I said. He stopped and turned, amazement spreading over his face. "Grandpa," I repeated. "We've come back again — we are back."

EPILOGUE

We three who got away began our lives afresh in Scotland. I attended a small private school called St Margaret's where I was taught to read and write in English. My brother was enrolled at the Grove Academy in Broughty Ferry. On leaving school I joined Bruce's College in Dundee, where I received a business training, which enabled me to make my way in life.

On the death of my grandparents, Mother moved to a small flat in town. I later married and went to live in Calcutta and, like most wives in India, spent my life between my husband and our twin sons, who were educated first in Dundee and later in Edinburgh.

My brother, meanwhile, was forging ahead with the British-controlled oil company in Venezuela. While on leave in New York he met and later married an attractive American girl. As their children were also being educated in Edinburgh, both families settled there and were eventually joined by our mother who much enjoyed the company of her family and grandchildren. She died at the ripe age of eighty-two.

Up to the time of my father's death my mother kept up a steady correspondence with him and tried to ease his tragic existence in every possible way. The Bolsheviks allowed no parcels, but between the sheets of her lengthy letters she always enclosed a few Gillette razor blades. Blades of any kind were unobtainable in Russia and in this way my father was provided with a steady source of barter.

I need hardly add that we never returned to Archangel.

We were lucky. Of all the passengers who sailed on the ill-fated *Canada* I knew only one other who returned to Britain.

One day a young RAF officer called at Bay House. He was Osborne Grove. He accepted an invitation to spend the night and we sat up late discussing many things — the tragic death of his pilot Kostya when their plane crashed, the sad fate which overtook so many of our fellow passengers. He left the following morning. We never saw him again.

My father's cousin, Margunya, fled to Norway before the final debacle of the White Army. Her husband, Lieutenant-Colonel Dilakatorsky, continued fighting to the bitter end. When everything was lost and further action was futile he decided to join the remaining refugees on the last ship due to sail for Norway. On arriving at the landing stage he discovered that two of his young officers had not as yet arrived. Knowing the kind of fate which would await them if they were left behind and encouraged by the promise that the ship would be held back, he hurried off to fetch the stragglers. The three men returned to the docks only to find they were too late. The ship had sailed without them.

The only remaining escape route was to cross the border into Norway. The trek on skis in the worst arctic conditions demanded all their willpower and endurance, but they were almost there when, in the last stages of exhaustion, they were tempted by the sight of a cottage to beg for shelter. The peasant was friendly. Heating a samovar and offering some food he invited them to rest a while. There was no need for hurry he assured them — all were safe with him. While they sat, warm and refreshed, talking trustingly to their host, the cottage was suddenly surrounded. The peasant had betrayed them by sending out his son to inform the Bolsheviks. Dilakatorsky and his two officers were arrested. The intention was to take them back to Murmansk for interrogation. They did not go very far. Their guards decided to execute them there and then. After being tortured, their bodies were thrown into the sea. The body of Dilakatorsky was later washed ashore and identified by his loyal orderly, named Walenev. Peter Dilakatorsky was a gallant and able soldier who might have lived had he remained aboard the ship and joined his wife in Norway. Instead he chose to go back to save the lives of two young men and in attempting to do so lost his own.

What happened to the others left behind? One might well ask. Soon after our departure, the house was confiscated. Father, with his few belongings, moved to live with Uncle Sanya. Marina left for Finland. In time she married, led a contented life and had a son with whom I am still in touch, although my dear cousin has long since gone.

The authorities decided to turn the house into a hostel for students but, before this plan materialised, a fire broke out in the garret and spread throughout the house. Some said the house was set on fire for the purpose of appropriating certain articles during the confusion, others blamed the ancient wiring.

The family, arriving on the scene, fought the flames in a blinding blizzard, with the assistance of the occupants and strange "helpers" who came along to see what they could loot. In the end, with the arrival of the fire brigade, the blaze was quenched but not before the solid timbers had been badly scorched.

Undeterred by any aesthetic scruples, the authorities ordered planks to be hammered over the blackened walls. Both balconies were torn off and the final structure bore no resemblance to the imposing original. All the rooms were broken up and divided. When the vandalism was completed, students moved in.

Eight years went by. During this time, Babushka and my step-grandfather returned from exile. They were allotted a room and a half in a house where they shared the kitchen with other tenants whose homes had likewise been confiscated. The "half" was part of the entrance hall where Dedushka placed his desk and attended to his patients who still flocked to him in the evenings, paying in kind. Without this, the miserable pittance he received from the hospital where he continued to work as a surgeon, would not have been sufficient for their needs.

Seryozha, his wife and two children were now living in Petrograd, where he was fortunate to become a curator in one of the museums, work for which he was ideally suited.

Yura, now married, was engaged in breeding animals for their furs, which was a source of foreign exchange for the government. Although living with his wife and little son in a single room, they found life tolerable.

One day in January of 1928, on my way to visit a friend, I met a telegram boy as I came out of the gate. He handed me a telegram which brought the news of my father's death. A letter arrived two weeks later. "Do not shed your tears," Uncle Sanya wrote. "He is free from his suffering and longing. He sleeps beside our father."

My grandparents outlived him by four years. Both died within ten days of each other. They died in time.

We were now in the 'thirties and for some time there were a few letters from Yura and Marga — followed by a strange silence.

Ten years went by. There was a second World War and my sojourn in India. On returning to Scotland my further attempts to get in touch with my relatives were met with the same mysterious silence — and then through Finland and other sources I learned the truth. The reason was simple — they were all dead.

I was not aware, nor was anyone else to my knowledge, that the satanic activities of the all-consuming Kremlin monster had increased tenfold and had reached every corner of Russia, including Archangel.

The first to be executed on a trumped-up charge was Mitya Danilov. All Marga's possessions were removed. She with her three children were thrown out on to the street. In desperation she had run to Sashenka who sheltered her, but soon Marga herself was arrested and sent to one of the labour camps on the White Sea. Her two young sons perished — one killed, the other, aged fourteen, committed suicide. Marga, losing her reason, died and only the girl remained.

Yura, on learning that his contemporaries who fought against the

Bolsheviks during the time of the Allied Intervention were being executed, and realising he was doomed, forestalled his execution by taking his own life.

Never since the dawn of Russian history had there been such a time of fear, grief and horror — a time described by the poetess Akhmatova as "When only the dead could smile".

Seryozha and his family living in Leningrad were spared until the advent of the Second World War when he, his wife and their young son starved to death during the blockade of the town and were buried in the common grave in the Piskarevsky cemetery. A passing lorry saved their little girl, taking her across Lake Ladoga to safety.

Back in Archangel, the house on Olonetskaya Street, or what was left of it, still stands, but is doomed to be demolished — the lodge, coach-house, outhouses and fences are all gone, broken up for firewood.

In the garden the devastation is complete. All trees and bushes are cut down. There is no trace of the two summerhouses and jetties. The paths are overgrown and the golden flowering hedge has vanished. Only the pond remains, desolate and haunting. The whole landscape has reverted to the wasteland it was a century ago when a young woman took stock of it, planned, and in the end created a garden the like of which Archangel had never known before or since.

As for the town itself, it has advanced beyond belief. The population has increased tenfold. There are countless high rise buildings, like rows of cardboard boxes stretching to the skies. Bridges thrown across the river bear trains carrying passengers direct into the town. Imposing monuments, cinemas and theatres replace all churches. There is every convenience, hot and cold water — people do not go down to the river in the dead of winter to rinse their clothing or fetch water. The boulders on the shores where once the children in our street foregathered are there no more. A long stretch of golden sands has replaced them — a fine place for tourists if only they were allowed to go there. For Archangel is a closed city.